TAX POLITICS AND POLICY

Taxes are an inescapable part of life. They are perhaps the most economically consequential aspect of the relationship between individuals and their government. Understanding tax development and implementation, not to mention the political forces involved, is critical to fully appreciating and critiquing that relationship.

Tax Politics and Policy offers a comprehensive survey of taxation in the United States. It explores competing theories of taxation's role in civil society; investigates the evolution and impact of taxes on income, consumption, and assets; and highlights the role of interest groups in tax policy. This is the first book to include a separate look at "sin" taxes on tobacco, alcohol, marijuana, and sugar. The book concludes with a look at tax reform ideas, both old and new.

This book is written for a broad audience—from upper-level undergraduates to graduate students in public policy, public administration, political science, economics, and related fields—and anyone else that has ever paid taxes.

Michael Thom is an assistant professor at the University of Southern California's Price School of Public Policy, USA.

"Informed by a deep sense of history and philosophical scope, Thom brings a clarity to a subject too often relegated to a set of trite talking points on cable news. *Tax Politics and Policy* is a must read for anyone wanting to bring into view the full scope of what meaningful tax reform in America would have to look like."
—**Anthony Randazzo**, *Reason Foundation*

TAX POLITICS AND POLICY

Michael Thom

Routledge
Taylor & Francis Group

NEW YORK AND LONDON

First published 2017
by Routledge
711 Third Avenue, New York, NY 10017

and by Routledge
2 Park Square, Milton Park, Abingdon, Oxon OX14 4RN

Routledge is an imprint of the Taylor & Francis Group, an informa business

© 2017 Taylor & Francis

Library of Congress Cataloging-in-Publication Data
Names: Thom, Michael, 1982– author.
Title: Tax politics and policy / by Michael Thom.
Description: New York : Routledge, 2017. | Includes bibliographical
    references and index.
Identifiers: LCCN 2016037779 | ISBN 9781138183384 (hardback : alk.
    paper) | ISBN 9781138183391 (pbk. : alk. paper) | ISBN 9781315645889
    (ebook)
Subjects: LCSH: Fiscal policy—United States. | Taxation—United States.
Classification: LCC HJ257.3 .T46 2017 | DDC 336.200973—dc23
LC record available at https://lccn.loc.gov/2016037779

ISBN: 978-1-138-18338-4 (hbk)
ISBN: 978-1-138-18339-1 (pbk)
ISBN: 978-1-315-64588-9 (ebk)

Typeset in Bembo
by Apex CoVantage, LLC

ABOUT THE AUTHOR

Michael Thom is an assistant professor at the University of Southern California's Price School of Public Policy, USA. He holds a PhD in political science, with emphases on public policy and American politics, from Michigan State University, USA. Michael's research interests include public finance and government regulation. His work has appeared in *Public Administration Review*, *The American Review of Public Administration*, *American Politics Research*, *State and Local Government Review*, and *Research and Politics*.

CONTENTS

PART I
Theoretical Foundations

1

PHILOSOPHICAL AND CONSTITUTIONAL ORIGINS OF TAX POLICY IN THE UNITED STATES

The United States of America is the indisputable product of tax resistance.

Indeed, while motives have varied, the American people have repelled taxes—both domestic and foreign—longer than they have been called "Americans." A group of about three dozen residents of New Jersey refused to pay taxes in 1715 because the local tax assessor was Catholic. The War of the Regulation erupted in 1765 after citizens of the Carolina colonies grew incensed by corrupt officials and abusive tax collectors. And later, a succession of taxes imposed on the colonies by the British parliament, including the Plantation Duty Act (1673), the Sugar Act (1764), the Stamp Act (1765), the Townshend Acts (starting in 1767), and the Tea Act (1773), provoked distrust, boycotts, protests, the Boston Massacre, and ultimately the Revolutionary War.[1]

Little changed following American independence. In 1786, opposition to tax burdens in Massachusetts catalyzed Shays' Rebellion. A federal excise tax on alcohol enacted in 1791 incensed rural citizens and led to the infamous Whiskey Rebellion. Fries's Rebellion sprang from Pennsylvania farmers opposed to the Federal Direct Tax of 1798, a form of property tax that was also known as the "window pane tax." While the levy was unpopular to begin with, tensions boiled over when assessors went beyond land evaluation to also record the number of windows on each dwelling. Owners suspected that the government was secretly planning future taxes (Newman 2004).[2]

Tax resistance showed no signs of dissipating in the twentieth century. Following the end of World War I, some beverage consumers refused to pay the federal government's wartime soft drinks tax. The *New York Times* dutifully informed its readership on September 11, 1919, that this particular tax was still law, and the failure to pay could result in a fine of $10,000 or one year in prison.[3] In the mid-1920s, countless newly enfranchised Pennsylvania women refused to pay the taxes that, as voters, they owed the state government.[4] Decades later, hundreds vowed to fight a proposed Vietnam War tax. From the late 1970s forward, dozens of citizen-led tax limitations became law, including California Proposition 13 (1978), Massachusetts Proposition 2 ½ (1980), and Colorado's Taxpayer Bill of Rights (1992).[5]

And yet, from the period following the Civil War to the present day, American history is also marked by political movements in favor of taxation. As candidates and as presidents, progressive Democrats including Bill Clinton and Barack Obama are only two examples from a long record of elected officials that actively promoted "higher taxes on the rich." Launched in late 2011, the Occupy Wall Street movement and its myriad progeny decried inequality and proposed, among other reforms, higher taxes on anyone that did not "pay their fair share," especially high-income earners, the wealthy, and corporations. Fight for 15 Chicago, a group ostensibly formed to lobby for a higher minimum wage, entered the tax policy fray in May 2016 when, at a demonstration held outside the offices of asset management firm Citadel, protestors brandished signs that read "Millionaires, Pay Your Fair Share!"[6]

As interesting as these anecdotes may be, taxes are much more than the impetus behind conflicts that serve as guideposts to American political development. Taxation is an inescapable part of life in civil society. Taxation affects human behavior. Taxation makes government possible. And above all other considerations, taxes are coercive. "The messed up thing about taxes is you don't 'pay' taxes. The government takes them" said comedian Chris Rock. "You get your check and money is gone. It was not an option!"

Comprehensive study of taxation in the United States requires investigating its origins, especially the political theories that shaped founding thought and how the emphasis placed on those and other theories has evolved over the nation's history. Only within that context can the range of taxes levied on individuals and corporate entities, and all of the conflicts they inspire, be fully appreciated. This chapter addresses the relevant philosophical and historical developments.

Taxation in Political Context

Legal authority to impose taxes is vested in a decentralized system of state institutions.[7] At each level of the United States federal system, the executive branch, the legislative branch, and the bureaucracy wield significant influence over tax policy. Judicial branch involvement is tangential, emerging only to administer dispute resolution, but court decisions can and have had a decisive impact on taxes. Regardless of the level or branch from which policy originates, each individual citizen and corporate entity is expected to abide by what the state demands.

Simply stated, taxation exists at the nexus of the individual and the state. Proper study of taxation should thus commence *in principio* with a review of the theories that structure and direct that relationship. Two aspects are the most important: the first is a statement of the ultimate source and content of individual rights, and the second is a definition of the bounds of state coercion. While the Declaration of Independence and the Constitution address each aspect, mere examination of their text is inadequate. Deeper reflection on the higher law principles that serve as the foundation of each document is more important. Those principles are of great consequence to all areas of public policy, but especially to areas that involve state coercion, like taxes.

What are higher law principles? Corwin (1928) offered this description:

> Such principles were made by no human hands; indeed, if they did not antedate deity itself, they still so express its nature as to bind and control it. They are external to all Will as such and interpenetrate all Reason as such. They are eternal and immutable. In relation to such principles, human laws are, when entitled to obedience save as to matters indifferent, merely a record or transcript, and their enactment an act not of will or power but one of discovery and declaration.

The Declaration of Independence, the Constitution, and American founding thought broadly signal a recognition of one higher law principle, the theory of natural rights, and two applications thereof, classical liberalism and social contract theory. These philosophies have had an enduring influence on the individual's relationship to the state and its reflection in American civil society.

Over time, however, the emphasis placed on those higher law concepts in tax policy has been attenuated by progressivism, a political theory that conceives a much different function of the state in civil society. Divergence between the tenets of classical liberalism on one hand, and the tenets of progressivism on the other, can be observed in nearly every debate over taxation. Exploring the precepts of each theory is critical to understanding those debates, not only to appreciate and understand their formative role in tax policy, but also for their influence on political and economic life.

Natural Rights and Classical Liberalism: Individuals as the Foundation of Civil Society

Natural Law and Natural Rights

Philosophers for millennia have contemplated the proper order of civil society. Many of history's most influential political thinkers, including Plato, Aristotle, Cicero, Aquinas, and Montesquieu, believed in the existence of a higher, universal law of nature, or natural law, binding on all individuals.[8] They believed that, as rational beings, humans could deduce the contours of natural law through observation and reason. Natural law was, in other words, self-evident and axiomatic.

More importantly, the natural law that governed social objects was believed to be as much a part of the order of things as the laws that govern physical objects, such as the law of gravity and the law of conservation. Grounding civil society in any other foundation would therefore be irrational.[9]

What does nature reveal about natural law? At the most elemental level, human beings are directed by nature toward life. That each individual materializes and survives within a physical body is the result of natural, biological processes that the individual neither conceived nor can fully control. Humans are further endowed with the intellectual and physical abilities to perceive and obtain the necessities of survival. In defense of life, individuals harbor a powerful, instinctual survival impulse; we react strongly and often spontaneously to threats against our bodies. The collective implication of all of the above is that nature has endowed the individual with the mechanisms necessary to attain and preserve life. Correspondingly, the basis of natural law is a right of individual self-preservation.

The degree to which the concept of natural law influenced the structure of civil society has varied across time and place. Natural law was certainly embedded within the classical liberal philosophy that grew out of intellectual and political revolutions in seventeenth-century Europe. Classical liberalism and its greatest influencers, such as John Locke and Adam Smith, viewed the properly ordered civil society as one of extensive individual autonomy and minimal state interference. The ideal state was conceptualized as little more than an entity responsible for protecting individual rights.

The classical liberalism of American founding thought transcribed self-preservation into three explicit natural rights.[10] First, each individual has a right to their own life without harm from an external cause. An individual cannot, for instance, be coerced into sacrificing their life in the service of any other. Second, each individual has a right to liberty. An individual is free to make their own decisions, limited only by ability and effort, and provided that they do not infringe on the natural rights of another individual.[11]

Third and most significantly to tax policy, each individual has private property rights, i.e., the authority to acquire resources and exclude others from seizing those resources, provided that the acquisition does not infringe on another person's natural rights.[12] Private property rights are held by the individual, and are distinct in theory and in practice from public or community property rights. Private property rights further subsume a right of property disposition. If an individual possesses legally acquired resources, then that individual has sole discretion over whether the resources are used, transferred to another individual, exchanged via contract for a different resource, or retained for future consumption.[13]

The most explicit statement of natural rights appears in the Declaration of Independence, which unequivocally affirms that each individual is endowed by God with an inalienable right to "Life, Liberty, and the pursuit of Happiness," the latter indicative of private property rights.[14] This assembly of natural rights pervaded founding thought but was not original to the Declaration (Becker 1922). In 1772, Samuel Adams wrote in *The Rights of the Colonists*:

> Among the natural rights of the Colonists are these: First, a right to life; Secondly, to liberty; Thirdly, to property; together with the right to support and defend them in the best manner they can. These are evident branches of, rather than deductions from, the duty of self-preservation, commonly called the first law of nature.

George Mason went even further to include personal safety as a right. His 1776 Virginia Declaration of Rights affirmed the following:

> All men are created equally free and independent, and have certain inherent rights, of which they cannot, by any compact, deprive or divest their posterity; among which are the enjoyment of life and liberty, with the means of acquiring and possessing property, and pursuing the obtaining of happiness and safety.

Importantly, classical liberal thought held that natural rights superseded the state. All individuals possessed natural rights regardless of personal characteristics, time, or domicile. Those rights existed prior to and would outlast the state. Once again, natural rights were believed to be as much a part of human existence as the law of gravity.

The Defense of Private Property Rights

Private property rights are the heart of civil society. "The reason why men enter into society," wrote John Locke in his *Second Treatise of Government*, "is the preservation of their property." As the Supreme Court declared in 1795:

> the right of acquiring and possessing property, and having it protected, is one of the natural, inherent, and unalienable rights of man. Men have a sense of property: Property is necessary to their subsistence, and correspondent to their natural wants and desires; its security was one of the objects, that induced them to unite in society. No man would become a member of a community, in which he could not enjoy the fruits of his honest labour and industry. The preservation of property then is a primary object of the social compact.[15]

Private property rights are also the legal and economic substance of any market economy, and as a result are the most materially consequential of the tripartite natural rights. It thus comes as little surprise that property is also the most contested among those rights.[16] Life and liberty are easily experienced; they are biological defaults of the human condition and are more intuitively "natural." But acquiring resources does not occur by default; it requires mental and physical labor and is less "natural." Moreover, certain resources are scarce, and some individuals possess and have access to more resources than others do. The question of whether property is a natural right in the same vein of life and liberty is therefore a matter of philosophical dispute. But resolving that dispute is key to defining resource ownership and reconciling private property rights with coercive taxation.

Defenses of private property rights typically fall into three categories. The first appeals to basic fairness and justice. In a pure state of nature, an individual would acquire resources by applying intellect and physical labor to raw materials not owned by any other individual, perhaps by developing a plot of uncultivated land. Locke's labor theory of property held that blending labor with unrefined materials created a good of value. The right to benefit from that good in any way was therefore vested solely in the person who exerted labor and made the value possible. If an individual chooses not to exert labor, then that individual's condition relative to others is no one's fault but their own. It would be unjust to coerce the transfer of resources from an individual that did exert labor to an individual who did not, perhaps through taxation, thereby punishing toil and rewarding apathy. To violate property rights by redistributing resources in this way, Thomas Jefferson wrote in 1816, is to breach the "first principle of association—the guarantee to every one of a free exercise of his industry and the fruits acquired by it."[17] The labor theory of property also applies to contracts. If two parties agree to exchange resources and the exchange places no burden or harm on an uninvolved third party, then the transfer of resources is fair and just.

A second defense appeals to natural rights' consubstantiality. Herbert (1908) described the interconnectedness thusly:

> Destroy the rights of property, and you will also destroy both the material and the moral foundations of liberty. To all men and women, rich or poor, belong their own faculties, and as a consequence, equally belongs to them all that they can honestly gain in free and open competition, through the exercise of those faculties.

The association between life, liberty, and property rights is easily observed. It is evident that human life cannot exist apart from basic necessities such as food and water. But if individuals do not have private property rights, then they cannot truly secure those necessities; as a result, individuals have no reasonable expectation of a durable right to life. Acquisition of life-sustaining food and water is consequently theft, implying that some other individual or entity has property rights, or otherwise renders each individual beholden to the mercy of who or what controls those resources, which also implies the existence of property rights but not necessarily private property rights. In the absence of individual private property rights, resource owners—not nature—harbor ultimate control over the right to life. Owners could, hypothetically, withhold food and water and bring about the end of non-owners' lives. That is precisely what has occurred under political regimes that remove private property rights. Regarding life in communist Russia, Trotsky (1937) wrote:

> In a country where the sole employer is the State, opposition means death by slow starvation. The old principle: who does not work shall not eat, has been replaced by a new one: who does not obey shall not eat.

In sum, refusal to recognize private property rights as natural is inconsistent with a sacrosanct, natural right to life and liberty.[18]

A third defense is drawn from Darwinian liberalism, which links private property rights to human biology and evolution (Arnhart 2015; Fruehwald 2010). The biopolitical stance holds that private property rights are not a political or social convention but are instead embedded in human genetics, the evolutionary result of our ancestors' desire for stable survival strategies (Stake 2004). Hoffman (2004) states:

> The notion that things possessed by one individual cannot be taken by others may well be the most fundamental of all evolved behaviours, because survival is itself bound up with the use of things.

Because resource possession has evolutionary utility, property rights are observed across several species (Gintis 2007; Hare et al. 2016; Sherratt and Mesterton-Gibbons 2015). Knowledge of private property rights has also been documented in children unaware of political and social structures (Gintis 2007). Experimental evidence further indicates that humans link property rights to labor (Levene et al. 2015). Apart from theoretical justifications, the notion of private property rights appears to be, quite literally, very natural indeed.

These preceding defenses of private property rights are by no means exhaustive; others have been submitted. For example, having a property right in one's self—i.e., body and mind—is central to notions of bodily integrity and personal privacy.[19] Deny that right, and no individual has legal claim to their own flesh. Slavery and forced labor are therefore blatant violations of an individual's natural rights.

The Irreconcilability of Private Property Rights and Coercive Taxation

The relationship between private property rights and coercive taxes is deeply adversarial. Expending state power to force an individual to cede resources to the state via taxation violates that individual's natural private property rights. Nozick (1974) compared taxes to forced labor. Payment of taxes requires labor, and if an individual's ability to provide labor is a natural part of their body and mind (i.e., each individual has self-ownership), then the state's claim to any portion of an individual's labor is akin to a claim on that individual's body. By mandating taxes, the state claims a property right in its own citizenry.

Corruption of private property rights through taxation may have a ripple effect that endangers all rights, natural and otherwise. Chodorov (1954) criticized income and property taxes not only for their infringement on private property rights, but also for delivering revenues to the state that the state, in turn, uses to fashion itself rather than nature as the fundamental source of rights. Once rights are vested in state institutions, they can easily be expanded—or taken away—through direct democracy, popular voting, bureaucratic rule-making, and judicial decisions. This statist interpretation of rights is plainly orthogonal to the view of rights as sourced in nature.

The conflict between private property rights and coercive taxation leaves few options for ordering civil society, none of which are especially attractive. One option is to disavow property rights completely, both private and public, forming a society in which no individual, corporate entity, or state institution has a legal right to any resource. Such a society is prone to anarchy and a tragedy of the commons. Another option is to renounce private property rights. Yet this creates a society in which the state holds all resources, including all housing, natural resources, means of production, houses of worship, media outlets, arms, and creative expression, greatly reducing individual and corporate incentives toward productive ends. A third option is to establish state institutions but operate those institutions on the basis of noncoercive taxes or user fees. But this approach invites free-riders, may lead to a tragedy of the commons, and does not immediately solve the problem of allocating the cost of non-excludable public goods. Summing up the dilemma, Rousseau wrote in *The Social Contract*:

> voluntary contributions bring in nothing, and forced contributions are illegitimate. This cruel alternative of letting the State perish, or of violating the sacred right of property, which is its support, constitutes the great difficulty of just and prudent economy.

But if the state cannot exist without violating private property rights, what is the role of the state in civil society? Which functions, if any, justify infringement on private property rights? And how do taxes facilitate the transfer of resources from individuals to the state? Answers to these questions hinge on theories regarding what the state exists to provide.

Justifying the State: Social Contract Theory

Scholars have vigorously attempted to resolve the irreconcilability of private property rights with coercive taxation. Some modern academics resolve the dilemma by hand-waving. For example, Dworkin (1977) argued simply that natural rights do not exist. Others have asserted that rights are not sourced in nature, but rather a social construct informed by experience (Dershowitz 2005). For Murphy and Nagel (2001, 2002), private property rights are a legal convention that cannot be extricated from the state because the latter makes the former possible.

Earlier philosophers including Hobbes, Locke, Rawls, and Rousseau, as well as many other contributors to American founding thought, justified taxation by invoking the so-called social contract theory. This theory holds that individuals living in civil society tacitly agree to forgo some measure of their rights and freedoms to the state in exchange for state protection of those rights.[20] In other words, the basic social contract rationale for taxes invokes the necessity of a state to enforce individual rights and facilitate justice, Whereas natural rights—an abstract construct—supersede social institutions like the state, those institutions are needed to enforce the abstract's translation into policy. More practically, tax revenues are used by the state to compensate agents who provide labor to protect individual rights. Note that the state-forming social contract is not spontaneous or otherwise natural, but a reaction to perceptions of the human condition.

Across millennia, natural rights philosophers have hinted at social contract theory, acknowledging the necessity of institutions to protect life, liberty, and private property rights. Although Locke wrote in his *Second Treatise of Government* that private property rights compel individuals to enter society, he also wrote that the principal motivation for the state was so that

> there may be laws made, and rules set, as guards and fences to the properties of all the members of the society, to limit the power, and moderate the dominion, of every part and member of the society.

Without state enforcement, rights would be less secure. In *The Social Contract*, Rousseau wrote:

> the maintenance of the State and the government involves costs and outgoings; and as every one who agrees to the end must acquiesce in the means, it follows that the members of a society ought to contribute from their property to its support. Besides, it is difficult to secure the property of individuals on one side, without attacking it on another.

Recognition of private property rights further implies the need for a dispute resolution venue. Otherwise, there is no ordered method consistent with fairness and justice to resolve disagreements regarding resource ownership and disposition. In an 1829 speech, James Madison described the relationship as follows:

> persons and property are the two great subjects on which Governments are to act; and that the rights of persons, and the rights of property, are the objects, for the protection of which Government was instituted. These

rights cannot well be separated. The personal right to acquire property, which is a natural right, gives to property, when acquired, a right to protection, as a social right.

Correspondingly, Madison's 1792 "Property" essay stated:

> "Government is instituted to protect property of every sort; as well that which lies in the various rights of individuals, as that which the term particularly expresses. This being the end of government, that alone is a just government, which impartially secures to every man, whatever is his own."

As helpful as theoretical expositions are at foundation-setting, they don't offer a specific, optimal tax rate or specific guidelines on how to distribute the burden across individuals. Many classical liberal and social contract theorists argued, somewhat vaguely, that taxes should be minor. Montesquieu wrote in *Persian Letters* that a good government "moves towards its end with minimal expense." Others have contended that, in the interest of equality, each individual should pay the same tax (e.g., Schoenblum 1995). Indeed, classical liberal thought views graduated income tax rates with skepticism. Imposing higher taxes on one group of individuals compared to another, perhaps to facilitate economic justice, violates the higher-taxed individuals' equality before the law. The reasoning behind that system of taxes is also unbounded. "Unlike proportionality," Hayek (1960) wrote, "progression provides no principle which tells us what the relative burden of different persons ought to be." One way around that problem appears in Hobbes' *Leviathan*, where he argued that equality dictated taxing individuals based on their consumption:

> For the impositions that are laid on the people by the sovereign power are nothing else but the wages due them that hold the public sword to defend private men. . . . Seeing then that the benefit that every one receives thereby is the enjoyment of life, which is equally dear to poor and rich, the debt which a poor man owes them that defend his life is the same which a rich man owes for the defense of his. . . . Equality of imposition consists rather in the equality of that which is consumed than the riches of the persons that consume the same.

All things considered, the state, said President Thomas Jefferson in his 1801 inaugural address, should be minimal, working to protect citizens but otherwise leave them free to pursue their desires and reap the rewards:

> A wise and frugal Government, which shall restrain men from injuring one another, shall leave them otherwise free to regulate their own pursuits of industry and improvement, and shall not take from the mouth of labor the bread it has earned. This is the sum of good government.

Classical Liberalism, Social Contract Theory, and Taxation in the Constitution

Reconciliation of the property-taxation conflict was a subject of importance during the founding era. The earlier Articles of Confederation said only that state governments could, at their sole discretion, render voluntary contributions to the federal government. But the Confederation system did not create a strong federal government, nor did it establish a fiscal system that yielded enough revenue to finance the Revolutionary War. At the same time, residents of the colonies and some of the founders themselves had a well-established history of tax resistance. Colonists revolted against taxes, sometimes violently so. Balancing a desire for a more powerful federal government against a desire to minimize taxation—and hence tax resistance—was a key challenge for the nascent republic.

Against that backdrop, life, liberty, and private property rights as well as social contract theory emerged in both the Declaration of Independence and the Constitution. The Constitution established a central but minimal federal government funded through a nominal tax system. "Tax" occurs just six times across five separate clauses in the original Constitution. Those clauses stipulated the following:

> Representatives and direct Taxes shall be apportioned among the several States which may be included within this Union, according to their respective Numbers, which shall be determined by adding to the whole Number of free Persons, including those bound to Service for a Term of Years, and excluding Indians not taxed, three fifths of all other Persons.
>
> *(Article I, Section 2, Clause 3)*

> The Congress shall have Power To lay and collect Taxes, Duties, Imposts and Excises, to pay the Debts and provide for the common Defence and general Welfare of the United States; but all Duties, Imposts and Excises shall be uniform throughout the United States.
>
> *(Article I, Section 8, Clause 1)*

> The Migration or Importation of such Persons as any of the States now existing shall think proper to admit, shall not be prohibited by the Congress prior to the Year one thousand eight hundred and eight, but a Tax or duty may be imposed on such Importation, not exceeding ten dollars for each Person.
>
> *(Article I, Section 9, Clause 1)*

> No Capitation, or other direct, Tax shall be laid, unless in Proportion to the Census of Enumeration herein before directed to be taken.
>
> *(Article I, Section 9, Clause 4)*

No Tax or Duty shall be laid on Articles exported from any State.

(Article 1, Section 9, Clause 5)

Overall, the legislative branch was granted limited taxing authority. Congress could levy indirect taxes, including tariffs and excises. Congress could also tax imported persons (e.g., slaves or indentured servants). Some founders believed that this tax would discourage slave importation, thereby limiting the prevalence of slavery until Congress could pass an outright ban in 1808. But others resisted, reasoning that a levy on slaves reinforced the notion—one unambiguously inconsistent with natural rights—that slaves were a form of property that could be owned and traded like any other resource.[21]

The Constitution did not authorize Congress to levy direct taxes unless the proceeds were apportioned across the states by population. The Constitution contains no clear definition of "direct taxes," but the phrase most likely refers to the general property taxes that had already been used throughout the colonies (see Chapter 7). Resistance to a centralized property tax system was a reflection of the framers' desire to limit state intervention into private affairs (Brownlee 1996). But ambiguity over the meaning of direct taxes would eventually bring several tax law disputes to the Supreme Court.

The Constitution also codified a uniquely American take on social contract theory. The Constitution stipulates that tax revenues must be used to reduce the national debt, provide national defense, and serve the general welfare. Three policymaking institutions are mentioned: a bicameral legislative branch, an executive branch, and a Supreme Court. Members of each branch have constitutionally mandated compensation paid by the federal government. Certain policy functions are also itemized, each of which generates costs for the federal treasury: conducting a decennial census; operating a federal post office; maintaining an army, navy, and militia; establishing courts below the Supreme Court; and instituting a national currency. Several broader tasks are further identified, including the collection of taxes; maintenance of federally owned property; and regulation of commerce, foreign affairs, intellectual property, and bankruptcy.

Classical liberalism forged American founding thought and affected early federal tax policy. The nonintrusive state prescribed by classical liberalism and the American variant of social contract theory, as reflected in the Constitution, implied that federal taxes would be minimal. Protecting a limited array of rights is not an inherently expensive proposition, and subsequent ratification of the Bill of Rights did not significantly alter demands on the federal treasury. Moreover, the subsidiarity-driven federalism established by the Constitution decentralized most state functions below the federal level, and more than anything else, most functions were left to individuals.

As a result, the federal government could, and did, operate with the revenues collected from a small tax system, composed mostly of tariffs and excises on selected goods. State and local governments levied excise as well as property taxes, but tax burdens were minor. Outside of the Civil War period, there were no individual income taxes nor any corporate income taxes. There were no payroll taxes. The national debt, by contemporary standards, was nonexistent. Today, none of the above is any longer the case—far from it.

Progressivism: The State as the Foundation of Civil Society

The Roots of American Progressivism

Since the late nineteenth century, the state's role in civil society writ large and in individual affairs has expanded well beyond the original constitutional framework, both caused by and causing significant changes in federal, state, and local tax policy. That evolution occurred not only in the United States, but across the industrialized world. The expansionary state was and continues to be a product of progressivism, a political theory positioned against classical liberal thought as well as capitalism and laissez-faire economics. But state expansion was not only the result of progressivism; many of the movement's tenets, especially those governing taxation and private property rights, can be found in Karl Marx's *Communist Manifesto*.

American progressivism developed in part as a reaction to the United States' profound post-Civil War evolution: from an agrarian to an industrial economy, from rural to urban life, and from relative stability to greater economic disruption and displacement. The relatively unfamiliar harshness of capitalism and growing inequality motivated individual and collective action toward a new, seemingly more secure political and economic system that commanded a larger state.[22] Public sentiment was even reflected in popular culture. One of the best-selling science fiction books of the period, Edward Bellamy's *Looking Backward: 2000–1887*, described a future utopia in which all property was state-owned, economic competition was nonexistent, and all individuals subsisted on state-provided benefits both before and after retirement from mandatory labor at age 45. The text ultimately sold over 500,000 copies.

Progressivism was also a backlash against American founding thought. Indeed, unmooring the minimal state from its classical liberal foundation, en route to a larger institution responsible for economic and social control, necessitated a repudiation of its underlying political theories. Progressivism sought to achieve that end by pronouncing classical liberalism as ineffectual and outmoded. John C. Calhoun, a Democrat and former Vice President, Secretary of State, and Secretary of War, said in an 1848 speech before the Senate:[23]

> a proposition which originated in a hypothetical truism, but which, as now expressed and now understood, is the most false and dangerous of all political errors. The proposition to which I allude, has become an axiom in the

> minds of a vast majority on both sides of the Atlantic, and is repeated daily from tongue to tongue, as an established and incontrovertible truth; it is, that 'all men are born free and equal'.

Observed progressive political scientist Charles Merriam (1920):

> the idea that men possess inherent and inalienable rights of a political or quasi-political character which are independent of the state, has been generally given up. It is held that these natural rights can have no other than an ethical value, and have no proper place in politics.

Other well-known progressives, including John Dewey, viewed natural rights as outdated, undemocratic, and averse to social progress (Ceaser 2012). In a speech to the Jefferson Club of Los Angeles in 1911, Woodrow Wilson—who was elected president the following year—criticized the Declaration of Independence for focusing on "the issues of the year 1776." "If you want to understand the real Declaration of Independence," Wilson told the audience, "do not read the preface." Walter Weyl wrote that belief in natural rights retarded social progress: "Our hand is stayed by ancient political ideas which still cumber our modern brains; by political heirlooms of revered—but dead—ancestors" (Weyl 1913). To these countless and other progressive thought leaders, conceptualizing rights as outside the state was an old-fashioned notion—one that undermined any movement toward expanding the state's size and influence.

The diffusion of American progressivism was aided by social scientists in fields like political science and economics. Many economists trained in Germany, where social thought eschewed natural rights.[24] German faculty often promoted the state's warm embrace against the cold chill of industrial capitalism (Mehrota 2005). At that time, Bismarck's world-first social insurance programs were taking off. To German philosophers like Georg Hegel, civil society and the state were living organisms affected by history and experience. American social scientists functioned as westward vectors of such Germanic progressive thought and public policy ideas at a time when the American social climate was ripe for a paradigm shift. They believed humanity could observe its own successes and failures, learn from them, and advance toward utopia.

But progress was not believed to occur spontaneously. Societal progress (hence the term "progressive") would require coordination—state coordination. And it would require intervention—state intervention. For progressives, the state was the apex of civil society, the very conduit to utopia. Political scientist John Burgess (1902) declared:

> This is the universal human purpose of the state. We may call it the perfection of humanity; the civilization of the world; the perfect development of the human reason, and its attainment to universal command over

individualism; the apotheosis of man. This end is wholly spiritual; and it in mankind, as spirit, triumphs over all fleshy weakness, error and sin.

American progressive thought can be distilled into a limited number of basic tenets (Ely 2012; Kloppenberg 1986; Leonard 2016; Rogers 1982). Compared to classical liberalism, progressive principles stipulate a radically different relationship between the individual and the state, and with it, a very different view on the place of coercive taxation in civil society.

Rejection of Natural Rights, Especially Private Property Rights

The first tenet of progressivism and the theory's ultimate foundation is a disavowal of natural rights; one need look no further than progressives' well-documented but repeatedly ignored embrace of eugenics and other forms of social engineering (Leonard 2016). From the earliest days of American progressivism, private property rights have received the most derision and nearly all blame for economic and social ills. According to one progressive sociologist, property rights "violently thrust men apart" and drive society "farther and farther from the pristine equality that brings out the best in human nature" (Ross 1901). Smith (1907) and Beard (1913) reasoned that constitutional inclusion of private property rights was motivated by selfish interests among the founders, not a longing for an egalitarian society.

Private property rights were also a target of progressive Walter Rauschenbusch, a Baptist minister, theologian, and disciple of the social gospel.[25] Economic changes and population growth had "turned old rights into present wrongs," he wrote, and "property rights will have to be resocialized" (Rauschenbusch 1912). By "resocialize," Rauschenbusch meant

> that it [property] is made to serve the public good, either by the service its uses render to the public welfare, or by the income it brings to the public treasury. In point of fact, however, no important form of property can be entirely withdrawn from public service; human life is too social in its nature to allow it.

In 1910, between leaving office as a progressive Republican and his later run as a Progressive Party candidate, Theodore Roosevelt delivered his famous "New Nationalism" speech to an audience in Osawatomie, Kansas. Of private property rights and the state, Roosevelt said:

> We grudge no man a fortune which represents his own power and sagacity, when exercised with entire regard to the welfare of his fellows. . . . We grudge no man a fortune in civil life if it is honorably obtained and well used. It is not even enough that it should have been gained without doing damage to the community. We should permit it to be gained only so long as the gaining represents benefit to the community. This, I know, implies a policy of a far

more active governmental interference with social and economic conditions in this country than we have yet had, but I think we have got to face the fact that such an increase in governmental control is now necessary.

Roosevelt suggested a number of policy reforms, including a graduated tax on wealth, tariff reforms, new labor regulations, and social insurance programs similar to those in place in Germany.

Elevation of the State Above the Individual

The second tenant, one made possible by a denial of natural rights, is subjugation of the individual to the state. This reorientation necessitates both a dilution of the concept of the individual and a concomitant moral and legal elevation of the state over the individual. Progressive intellectuals advanced arguments to both ends. In his 1894 essay "The Significance of the Frontier in American History," Frederick Jackson Turner described the individualism and family reliance prevalent on the American frontier as "primitive" and "anti-social." Individualism, according to Turner, "produces antipathy to control, and particularly to any direct control. The tax-gatherer is viewed as a representative of oppression." Turner's anti-family comments echoed those from Marx.[26] Taking a pseudoscientific approach, Cooley (1902) claimed that hereditary traits and human sociability implied the existence of a common whole that rendered pure individuality impossible. An editorial in *The New Republic* (1915) excoriated natural rights as "unworkable" and said the following about the idea of a sovereign individual:

> Outside of society he has never existed and could not exist; his acquisitions, his capacities, his will, even his desires are all the creation of his time and of his people. What inalienable rights has he against the community that made him and supports him?

The following year, Frank Goodnow (1916), inaugural president of the American Political Science Association, wrote:

> We have come to the conclusion that man under modern conditions is primarily a member of society and that only as he recognizes his duties as a member of society can he secure the greatest opportunities as an individual.

Progressive thought held that personal fulfillment could not occur apart from the state, which indebted the individual to the state. According to progressive economist E.R.A. Seligman (1890),

> It is the individual who, from the very fact of his existence within the state, is under definite obligations towards the state, of which the very first is to

protect and support the state. For the state indeed can exist without the particular individual, but the individual cannot exist without the state. The individual must support the state, not because the state protects him, but because his life is possible only within the state.

Claiming that "the simple creed of individualism is no longer adequate," Seager (1910) argued that an emphasis on the "common welfare" instead of "individual success" was necessary and could be achieved through an "aggressive program of governmental control and regulation."[27] Ely (1888) summed up progressive sentiment the best, connecting individuals, taxation, and the state:

> Man, as a human being, owes services to his fellows, and one of the first of these is to support government, which makes civilization possible. Only an anarchist can take any other view.

Rule by Experts

The third tenet is a belief in expert-driven central planning and social engineering. Progressives believed that government administration should be divorced from politics or, as often described, that "scientific" lawmaking was more important than democratic lawmaking. Such scientific lawmaking would require instituting—and funding—new bureaucracies populated with teams of "experts" working to solve public problems. Emphasis on expert-driven policy resulted from the progressive belief that the path toward utopia would be encumbered until the educated dominated the ignorant (Ross 1907). This principle was not original to progressivism; Plato's *Republic* envisioned a caste society led by educated, reflective "guardians" that govern the masses.

Then as now, paternalism dominated progressive thought. Seligman wrote that experts were needed to "get people to feel their true needs and acquaint them with the means of their satisfaction" (Fink 1997). Ross (1901) held that "the state, when it becomes paternal and develops on the administrative side, is able in a measure to guide the society it professes to obey." Bureaucrats should, according to Woodrow Wilson (1887)—again, a future president—act in defiance of public opinion when dictated by their expertise. Economist Irving Fisher (1907) wrote that individuals need "enlightenment" to compensate for their ignorance and "restraint" to corral their lack of self-control. Once experts were in charge, he predicted, "we begin to see an almost boundless vista for possible human betterment."

Targeting Private Economic Concentrations

The fourth and final tenet is a distrust of concentrated private, but not public, economic resources.[28] Progressives accused corporations and the wealthy of having disproportionate political influence, which they viewed as both unfair and as having the potential to undermine their own cause. Not surprisingly, financial institutions, the wealthy, and Jews have historically been frequent recipients of progressives' blame for economic malaise.[29] As a result, taxes on corporations and the wealthy were one progressive policy toward social and economic justice. According to Weyl (1913),

> By progressive taxes on property, income, or inheritances . . . the state can do much towards preventing too insensate an accumulation of individual wealth. Theoretically there are no limits to taxation along these lines.

But taxes were not the only solution. The progressive era was also marked by a significant push to regulate monopolies (e.g., the Sherman Antitrust Act and Clayton Antitrust Act), commerce (e.g., formation of the federal Department of Commerce and Labor and the Interstate Commerce Commission), and the financial system (e.g., the Federal Reserve) with expert-led bureaucracies.

The progressive view of private property rights and taxation was regularly articulated under President Franklin Delano Roosevelt, a progressive Democrat. In his June 19, 1935, "Message to Congress on Tax Revision," Roosevelt remarked that "taxation according to income is the most effective instrument yet devised to obtain just contribution from those best able to bear it," calling the federal income tax enacted in 1913 "a wholesome guide for national policy." Denying the prospect of purely individual success, Roosevelt noted "the individual does not create the product of his industry with his own hands" and complained that existing tax policy, which by that time included income taxes, had "done little to prevent an unjust concentration of wealth and economic power." The solution, according to Roosevelt, was higher taxes. He would later propose a national income cap of $25,000 per year, the equivalent of about $368,000 in 2016 dollars, accomplished with a 100% tax on income above that threshold.

Overall, progressive thought regarded taxation as necessary to achieve two objectives. First, taxes were a direct tool of economic redistribution and control, serving as the instrument through which resources were coerced from those of high means and seemingly given to those of lower means. And second, taxes provided the revenue needed to operate state institutions from which expert-driven policies would flow to the masses as part of civil society's lurch toward utopia.

Tax Policy Development After the Constitution: Classical Liberalism Displaced by Progressivism

For most of the nineteenth century, tariffs and excise taxes provided nearly all federal revenue. By contemporary standards, the federal government was small, focused primarily on national defense and international affairs. State and municipal governments were minimal, with an emphasis on public safety, infrastructure, and, later, public education. Although a federal income tax was suggested as early as 1814 by Secretary of the Treasury Alexander J. Dallas, the plan never advanced (McMahon 2009). The idea of taxing individuals' income was relatively new, and given the Constitution's language about direct taxes, it was not clear if proceeds could be retained by the federal government or would have to be reapportioned to the states.[30]

Federal tax policy underwent an important change just months after the onset of the Civil War. Union combat expenses surpassed initial estimates, a situation exacerbated by Confederate secession, which lowered revenues. Making matters even worse, the Union's low credit rating made it difficult and costly to obtain credit. The Revenue Act of 1861 established the United States' first individual income tax, a flat rate of 3%. The Act also instituted a federal property tax and raised tariffs on several goods. Although some policymakers disputed the taxes as inconsistent with tradition and the Constitution, others countered that the measures were necessitated by circumstance, and apportionment concerns were muted by the enormity of the conflict.

Before the 1861 taxes were fully implemented, Congress passed the Revenue Act of 1862. The Act replaced the flat income tax rate with graduated rates— another first—and increased taxes on consumer goods including alcohol, feathers, billiard tables, certain medicines, and even newspaper advertisements (Smith 1914). The Act also created a new federal position, the Commissioner of Internal Revenue, better known today as the Internal Revenue Service (IRS) Commissioner.

To encourage full participation, all income tax returns were made public. Individuals could visit a local tax office to see how much their neighbors owed and whether taxes had been paid. Some newspapers published tax return information for all to see until the IRS banned the practice in 1870.[31] Civil War-era income taxes yielded modest revenues before expiring in 1872 (see Table 1.1).

TABLE 1.1 Federal Income Tax Revenue During the Civil War Era, 1863–1874

Year	Thousands of Nominal Dollars	Thousands of Constant 2014 Dollars
1863	2,742	51,736
1864	20,295	307,500
1865	60,979	883,754
1866	72,982	1,089,284
1867	66,014	1,047,841
1868	41,456	690,933
1869	34,792	610,386
1870	37,776	686,837
1871	19,163	368,519
1872	14,437	277,635
1873	5,062	99,255
1874	139	2,896

Source: Author's calculations based on data reported in the *Historical Statistics of the United States, 1789–1945*.

Following the Civil War, the American economy changed from agricultural to industrial dominance. The Gilded Age brought transformations to the ranks of the wealthy, which not only grew in size but whose wealth was increasingly tied to natural resources, raw materials, and finance. The "trusts" (oil, tobacco, and steel, among others) benefited from access to capital and disproportionate political influence. Wealthy individuals and business entities of that era paid state and local property taxes but relatively little to the federal treasury. Indeed, there were no federal income taxes, corporate taxes, or capital gains taxes. Some industries accrued further gains from protectionist federal policies (e.g., tariffs and import quotas).

As wealth grew more concentrated the ranks of the poor expanded, driven in part by growing immigration of low-skill labor. The influx of immigrants exerted downward pressure on wages in some industries, improving profit margins that benefited shareholders but reducing the income of employees, further widening the gulf between the "haves" and "have nots." Class divisions, previously unfamiliar to and now increasingly unpopular with the American public, raised interest in political and economic alternatives, especially the progressivism that had already gained currency in social scientific circles (Fraser 2015). The Socialist Labor Party, the Labor Reform Party, the People's Party, and the Democratic Party all demanded that the federal government adopt an interventionist, tax-and-spend policy orientation to reduce economic inequality. The People's Party's 1892 platform, known as the Omaha Platform, called for a graduated income tax with revenue used to diminish "the burden of taxation now levied upon the domestic industries of this country."

Calls for a federal income tax were not limited to progressives. State and local governments derived most of their own-source revenue from property taxes, and as their spending on social programs increased, property owners grew angry as their tax burdens also increased while non-property owners paid little or nothing. Many property owners demanded tax relief through a broader tax base, one that included new taxes on income, estates, and corporations—i.e., taxes on those who failed to pay their "fair share."

That overall environment increased the likelihood that the federal income tax would return. The elections in 1892 shifted power toward Democrats. Bank panics during the same timeframe created anxiety that heightened calls to redistribute wealth via the tax code. Progressive economists, including Henry Carter Adams, Richard T. Ely, and E.R.A Seligman, were outspoken in support of a federal income tax. Between 1874 and 1894, nearly 70 income tax bills were introduced to Congress, but none were reported out of committee (Pollack 2013).

Eventually, discontent with tariff policy facilitated the income tax's return. By the mid-1890s, members of Congress from both political parties believed that tariffs created a disproportionate burden on employees working in industries targeted by tariffs. Yet reducing tariffs would solve that problem but also create a new one—i.e., how to compensate for lower federal revenues.[32] Progressives continued to lobby for an income tax and ultimately achieved success with the Wilson–Gorman Tariff Act of 1894, which re-imposed a federal tax on individual and corporate income. The tax, a flat rate of 2%, carried an income exemption that meant the tax would only apply to a small number of high-income earners and corporations. Whereas progressives had raised the issue of fairness to resurrect the income tax, the law enacted represented a tradeoff between tariff revenue and income tax revenue. None of the "new" revenue was appropriated for redistribution programs. The Act merely recalibrated federal tax burdens; it did not redistribute income.

But the federal income tax did not last long. One year later, the Supreme Court overturned the law for not apportioning tax revenues according to state populations.[33] Undeterred, progressives continued to promote a tax on income and, in particular, a framework of graduated tax rates. The 1896 Democratic Party platform blamed the Supreme Court for causing the federal budget deficit. That year, Democrats became the first major political party in United States history to formally endorse a federal income tax.

Conditions were not immediately conducive to reviving the tax. Congress instead focused on other levies. To fund the Spanish-American War, Congress enacted the War Revenue Act of 1898, which included a graduated estate tax, a corporate income tax on sugar and oil companies, excise taxes on certain goods and services, and a telephone tax of one cent per call. The estate tax was challenged but upheld by the Supreme Court (see also Chapter 8).[34] The majority ruled that the estate tax was a levy on property transfer and not a levy on property itself, and was therefore not a direct tax that required apportionment.

Policymakers were also concerned about the boundaries of their authority to levy taxes. In a 1907 address to Congress, President Theodore Roosevelt, a progressive Republican, said:

> When our tax laws are revised the question of an income tax and an inheritance tax should receive the careful attention of our legislators. In my judgment both of these taxes should be part of our system of Federal taxation.

In the same address, Roosevelt also made the following remarks—and note the distinction between Roosevelt's comments in the second sentence and the classical liberal notions of private property rights and property disposition:

> The inheritance tax, however, is both a far better method of taxation, and far more important for the purpose of having the fortunes of the country bear in proportion to their increase in size a corresponding increase and burden of taxation. The Government has the absolute right to decide as to the terms upon which a man shall receive a bequest or devise from another, and this point in the devolution of property is especially appropriate for the imposition of a tax.

Attention turned, albeit temporarily, to taxing businesses. The Payne–Aldrich Tariff Act of 1909 implemented a flat 1% tax on net income earned by for-profit, shareholder-owned corporations. To circumvent constitutional challenges over the direct tax ambiguity, the Act defined the tax as "a special excise tax with respect to carrying on or doing business." Put another way, the corporate income tax wasn't legislated as an income tax. The law was challenged but, as discussed further in Chapter 4, was upheld by the Supreme Court.[35]

To garner congressional support for the corporate tax, Republican President William Taft agreed to back a constitutional amendment authorizing Congress to enact income taxes. Taft assumed ratification would be a slow process, delaying any real action on income taxes for the foreseeable future. If ratification succeeded, it would at least settle the question of the income tax's constitutionality once and for all. But if ratification ultimately failed, federal income taxes would remain a non-starter, perhaps indefinitely.

Taft's plan backfired. Congress's proposed Sixteenth Amendment passed on July 12, 1909, and was sent to state legislatures for ratification. The amendment read:

> The Congress shall have power to lay and collect taxes on incomes, from whatever source derived, without apportionment among the several states, and without regard to any census or enumeration.

Less than one month later, Alabama was the first state to ratify the amendment. The ratification threshold was satisfied in 1913. Ultimately, 42 out of 48 states approved the Sixteenth Amendment. Congress swiftly passed the Revenue Act of 1913, which reduced tariffs and reinstituted an individual income tax. Rates varied from a low of 1% to a high of 7%. President Woodrow Wilson, a progressive Democrat who had once recommended that government employees act in defiance of public will when they deemed it appropriate, signed the income tax bill into law on October 3, 1913.

The 1913 iteration of the income tax sustained subsequent legal challenges. The Supreme Court ruled in 1916 that the imposition of an income tax without either proportional or uniform apportionment was made constitutional by the Sixteenth Amendment.[36] The Court further ruled that taxation did not violate the Fifth Amendment's due process guarantee.

Tax rates were not fixed between 1% and 7% for long. Policymakers suspected, correctly, that American entry into World War I would burden the federal treasury and necessitate tax increases. Some were further concerned that industrial powers would profiteer from the war, behavior that could be blunted by tax increases on those industries. But progressives, who favored higher taxes regardless of the nation's war footing, hoped to leverage nationalist sentiment fostered by American participation in World War I into a much broader political movement for centralized, expert-driven social planning to influence other aspects of life (Leonard

2009). In "The Social Possibilities of War," progressive John Dewey praised the global conflict by writing:

> The immediate urgency has in a short time brought into existence agencies for executing the supremacy of the public and social interest over the private and possessive interest which might otherwise have taken a long time to construct. In this sense, no matter how many among the special agencies for public control decay with the disappearance of war stress, the movement will never go backward.

The Central Conflict of Tax Policy: Classical Liberalism Versus Progressivism

The American founding's classical liberalism and the progressivism that colonized political thought less than one century later presented fundamentally divergent views of the individual, the state, and taxation—a divergence that endures today. Conflicting worldviews regarding the proper order of civil society are a part of the human condition and have animated political life for thousands of years. But the locus of disagreement is always the same. As French social psychologist Gustave Le Bon (1899) wrote:

> The modern theories of social organisation, under all their apparent diversity, lead back to two different and opposing fundamental principles—Individualism and Collectivism. By Individualism man is abandoned to himself; his initiative is carried to a maximum, and that of the State to a minimum. By Collectivism a man's least actions are directed by the State, that is to say, by the aggregate; the individual possesses no initiative; all the acts of his life are mapped out. The two principles have always been more or less in conflict, and the development of modern civilisation has rendered this conflict more keen than ever.

Ponder the sharp contrasts between classical liberalism and progressivism in American political thought. Classical liberalism is rooted in absolutism; progressivism is rooted in relativism. Classical liberalism conceives of the individual as a sovereign being at the center of civil society; progressivism rejects that sentiment in deference to the importance of community. Classical liberalism holds individual rights as natural and inalienable; progressivism holds individual rights as social and subject to state discretion. Classical liberalism holds that rights are boundaries the state should enforce but not abridge; progressivism recognizes few such limitations. Classical liberalism emphasizes individual preservation; progressivism emphasizes state preservation. Classical liberalism requires a minimal state; progressivism demands an expansionary state. Classical liberalism embraces open markets; progressivism embraces state-regulated markets.[37]

The consequences for tax policy are clear. Classical liberalism's narrow conceptualization of rights as natural and its emphasis on individual autonomy require nothing more than a minimal tax regime, similar to that of the founding era and most of the nineteenth century. Progressivism's mandate for a large, expert-led, bureaucratic, and interventionist state commands a much broader system of taxation. For progressives, tax policy also serves as the principal mode of economic redistribution.

These points of difference are reflected in political parties. Classical liberalism is a component of conservatism and libertarianism, and is most consistently expressed within the Republican Party. Progressivism is a component of modern liberalism and socialist movements that are more or less in alignment with Democrats. There are shades of nuance today, especially over social issues, but in general terms, Republican-versus-Democrat tax policy disputes can be traced back to the conflict between classical liberalism and progressivism or, to borrow from Le Bon, individualism and collectivism.

Conclusion

With historical and political roots in tax resistance, the United States remains a nation of individuals skeptical of taxation and state interference in private affairs. The conflict came into focus during the decades following the Civil War, which witnessed the emergence of a political battle between classical liberalism and progressivism. That clash was initially one of theory but quickly became one of practice as the federal government, as well as many state governments, experimented with, and then made permanent, taxes on individual and corporate income in addition to other taxes and fees.[38] That period also illustrated the significance of tax policy entanglements, such as the tradeoff between tariffs and income taxes or between taxes on income or wealth, and the role of war in shaping tax policy decisions. The Civil and World Wars are long over with, but most of the taxes ordained to fund those conflicts stand. Our understanding of tax policy has grown, too, and with it our ability to analyze taxation and its effect on individuals and civil society as a whole. These subjects are explored in the forthcoming chapters.

Notes

1 In addition, trade restrictions imposed by the British Navigation Acts angered some colonists by raising the price of imported goods. The Navigation Act passed in 1663 specifically added an English tax to goods before shipment to the colonies.
2 Surveying window panes reminded some immigrants of the so-called hearth taxes they had hoped to leave behind in Europe, in which authorities charged property owners a tax based on the number of fireplaces on their property. But that mode of taxation had already diffused across the Atlantic; the New Netherland territory enacted a similar tax in 1657.
3 The 87-word article's cogent title was "Must Pay the Soft Drinks Tax." Responsibility for collecting and remitting the tax fell on store owners, who were put in a difficult position whenever customers refused to pay.

4 Motivations varied, but many women who refused to pay taxes had opposed female suffrage and did not believe it was fair to tax them based on the acquisition of a right they did not seek.

5 As noted in Chapter 7, property tax limitations were also common during the Great Depression.

6 Note an important contrast between the anti-tax and pro-tax movements outlined here. While anti-tax causes throughout American history have tended to spring from taxes that protesters believed were unfairly levied on them personally, pro-tax causes have tended to be motivated by protestors' belief that new taxes should be levied on other people. Unlike anti-tax groups, pro-tax groups rarely contest their own tax liabilities.

7 Throughout this and all following chapters, "state" is used to denote "government" without regard to level. The individual-state nexus and its policy implications are relevant within and across all levels of government.

8 For example, Montesquieu wrote in *The Spirit of the Laws* that "the government most in conformity with nature is that government whose particular disposition best relates to the disposition of the people for whom it is established."

9 The phrase "natural law" is used interchangeably in reference to two specific concepts: a natural *moral* law and a natural *legal* or *political* law. Philosophers have long debated the intersection of morality and law and its implications for the state and for civil society. Moreover, theories of a law of nature were not limited to Western philosophers. Different schools of Islamic philosophy (e.g., Ash'arism and Averroism) acknowledged a universal human law. Natural law concepts are also found in Chinese political philosophy (e.g., *T'ien-li*, the Confucian "principle of heaven"). In many traditions for which most or all laws are traced to a higher power outside nature, natural law is often known as "divine law."

10 As Zuckert (2005) notes, Lockean thought was a presence in the colonies well before the Constitution was drafted.

11 Philosophers differ on this question, but one view is that natural rights are bounded by the "good" of self-preservation—i.e., an individual cannot exercise their natural rights to the extent that it infringes on another individual's natural rights, and hence their self-preservation.

12 Definitions of "property" vary. For example, James Madison's 1792 essay "Property" defined the construct as "every thing to which a man may attach a value and have a right," including a person's opinion and bodily security.

13 Some philosophers held that property disposition was a natural right. In *A Treatise on Human Nature*, David Hume wrote of

> three fundamental laws of nature, that of the stability of possession, of its transference by consent, and of the performance of promises. It is on the strict observance of those three laws, that the peace and security of human society entirely depend; nor is there any possibility of establishing a good correspondence among men, where these are neglected.

14 The phrasing used in the Declaration mirrors that used by John Locke in *Two Treatises of Government* ("life, liberty, and estate"). "Property" also appears in the Fifth and Fourteenth Amendments to the Constitution.

15 *Vanhorne's Lessee v. Dorrance*, 2 U.S. (2 Dallas) 304 (1795).

16 Debate over the virtues of private property rights and the implications for civil society date at least to the divergent viewpoints of Plato and Aristotle. See Pipes (2000) for a comprehensive history.

17 Letter to Joseph Milligan, April 6, 1816.

18 Consider another illustration. Arguments in favor of a right to health care (however that term is defined) imply the existence of a right to life. Indeed, what good is a right to health care if one has no right to life in the first place? Yet this illustration presents

a new dilemma: how to square the implication that an individual's right to health care means that they therefore have a right to a medical professional's time, labor, and expertise—i.e., the professional's mental and physical self. In other words, does a right to health care imply a property right in medical professionals? Can the state compel individuals to train for and labor in the health care industry? The answer is well beyond this text, but worth considering.

19 See Radin (1982) and Russell (2010) for a more thorough exploration of the intersection of private property rights, the self, and personhood.

20 Relative to the others Rousseau was extreme, arguing that the social contract implied that any individual that refused to "obey the general will shall be forced to do so by the whole body."

21 While debating the tax at the Federal Convention in 1787, Roger Sherman argued that a slave tax demeaned slaves by treating them as mere property, thereby affirming the position of slave owners. The passage was almost dropped. But even then, founders knew that a strong central government was necessary if slavery was ever to be eradicated—and establishing that government would require uncomfortable, if temporary, moral and political compromises.

22 Scholars have noted that the United States had prior periods of growth in inequality; it was not unique to the post-Civil War period (Lindert and Williamson 2016).

23 See "Speech on the Oregon Bill," June 27, 1848.

24 Most progressive economists had one other trait in common: they never worked outside higher education or the government.

25 In his *Christianizing the Social Order*, Rauschenbusch described taxes as "a beneficent social institution; they buy more for us than any other money we spend."

26 Marx argued that the family unit existed solely for the acquisition of wealth and, to that end, parents would exploit their children; communism would halt that exploitation, and destruction of capitalism would also destroy the family. See Spargo (1910) and Weikart (1994).

27 Seager's book, *Social Insurance: A Program of Social Reform*, is available for free on the Social Security Administration's website.

28 Progressivism directs ire at wealthy individuals and corporations but not at government institutions, which enjoy budgets and assets, not to mention the coercive authority of taxation, that dwarf those of even the largest corporations. The largest corporation on the Fortune 500 in 2016, Walmart, collected $482 billion in revenues worldwide, a figure that represents just 13% of total federal revenue.

29 Many anti-Semitic stereotypes can be found throughout the writings of influential progressive and socialist thinkers. Karl Marx's *On the Jewish Question* described Jews as "money worshipers," Charles Fourier detested Jews for their role in trade and described them as "usurers," and Voltaire described Jews as "greedy." That these stereotypes diffused to the United States from Germany, where anti-Semitism was growing, along with Germanic progressive social thought, was no coincidence. Among countless other economic punishments, the Third Reich later banned Jews from working as tax consultants in 1933, instituted the Jewish Capital Levy (also known as an atonement fine or *Suhneleistung*) of 20% on Jewish-owned assets in 1938, and an escape tax (also known as the Reich Flight Tax or *Reichsfluchtsteuer*) of 25% on assets held by Jews emigrating from Germany.

30 Income taxes were administratively impossible until the advent of stable currencies and money-based economies. One of the first known income taxes was implemented under Wang Mang during the Xin Dynasty (9 AD–23 AD). England and France enacted a temporary income-style tax in 1188 called the "Saladin tithe," with proceeds ostensibly—but ultimately not—used to fight the Crusades. The first modern-era income tax in Britain went into effect in 1799. That tax ended in 1802 but was brought back from 1803–1816. While the founders borrowed many ideas from Britain, the income tax was not one of them.

31 At the state and local level, it is often still possible to determine a neighbor's property tax status by using public records search tools.
32 Proportionate spending cuts were, in the political climate of the time, not feasible.
33 *Pollock v. Farmers' Loan & Trust Company*, 157 U.S. 429 (1895).
34 *Knowlton v. Moore*, 178 U.S. 41 (1900).
35 *Flint v. Stone Tracy Co.*, 220 U.S. 107 (1911).
36 *Brushaber v. Union Pacific Railroad Company*, 240 U.S. 1 (1916).
37 Writing in Baltimore's *Evening Sun* newspaper in 1926, H.L. Mencken defined a progressive as "one who is in favor of more taxes instead of less, more bureaus and jobholders, more paternalism and meddling, more regulation of private affairs, and less liberty."
38 By design, the Sixteenth Amendment was never submitted to a direct vote of the people. It was written and ratified by elected representatives.

References

Arnhart, Larry. 2015. "The Evolution of Darwinian Liberalism." *Journal of Bioeconomics* 17(1): 3–15.

Beard, Charles A. 1913. *An Economic Interpretation of the Constitution of the United States*. New York: Macmillan.

Becker, Carl. 1922. *The Declaration of Independence: A Study on the History of Political Ideas*. New York: Harcourt, Brace and Company.

Brownlee, W. Elliot. 1996. *Federal Taxation in America: A Short History*. Cambridge, MA: University of Cambridge Press.

Burgess, John W. 1902. *Political Science and Comparative Constitutional Law, Volume I: Sovereignty and Liberty*. Boston: Ginn & Company.

Ceaser, James W. 2012. "Progressivism and the Doctrine of Natural Rights." *Social Philosophy and Policy* 29(2): 177–195.

Chodorov, Frank J. 1954. *The Income Tax: Root of All Evil*. New York: Devin-Adair Company.

Cooley, Charles Horton. 1902. *Human Nature and the Social Order*. New York: Charles Scribner's Sons.

Corwin, Edward S. 1928. "The 'Higher Law' Background of American Constitutional Law." *Harvard Law Review* 42(2): 149–185.

Dershowitz, Alan. 2005. *Rights from Wrongs: The Origins of Human Rights in the Experience of Injustice*. New York: Basic Books.

Dworkin, Ronald. 1977. *Taking Rights Seriously*. New York: Bloomsbury Publishing.

Ely, James W., Jr. 2012. "The Progressive Era Assault on Individualism and Property Rights." *Social Philosophy and Policy* 29(2): 255–282.

Ely, Richard T. 1888. *Taxation in American States and Cities*. Boston: Thomas Y. Crowell & Company.

Fink, Leon. 1997. *Progressive Intellectuals and the Dilemmas of Democratic Commitment*. Cambridge, MA: Harvard University Press.

Fisher, Irving. 1907. "Why Has the Doctrine of Laissez Faire Been Abandoned?" *Science* 25(627): 18–27.

Fraser, Steve. 2015. *The Age of Acquiescence: The Life and Death of American Resistance to Organized Wealth and Power*. New York: Little, Brown, and Company.

Fruehwald, Edwin. 2010. "A Biological Basis of Rights." *Southern California Interdisciplinary Law Journal* 19(2): 195–236.

Gintis, Herbert. 2007. "The Evolution of Private Property." *Journal of Economic Behavior and Organization* 64(1): 1–16.

Goodnow, Frank. 1916. *The American Conception of Liberty and Government*. Providence, RI: Standard Printing Company.

Hare, D., H. K. Reeve, and B. Blossey. 2016. "Evolutionary Routes to Stable Ownership." *Journal of Evolutionary Biology* 29(6): 1178–1188.

Hayek, Friedrich A. 1960. *The Constitution of Liberty*. Chicago: University of Chicago Press.

Herbert, Auberon. 1908. *The Voluntaryist Creed*. London: Oxford University Press.

Hoffman, Morris B. 2004. "The Neuroeconomic Path of the Law." *Philosophical Transactions of the Royal Society B: Biological Sciences* 359(1451): 1667–1676.

Kloppenberg, James T. 1986. *Uncertain Victory: Social Democracy and Progressivism in European and American Thought, 1870–1920*. New York: Oxford University Press.

Le Bon, Gustav. 1899. *The Psychology of Socialism*. New York: Macmillan.

Leonard, Thomas C. 2009. "American Economic Reform in the Progressive Era: Its Foundational Beliefs and Their Relation to Eugenics." *History of Political Economy* 41(1): 109–141.

Leonard, Thomas C. 2016. *Illiberal Reformers: Race, Eugenics & American Economics in the Progressive Era*. Princeton, NJ: Princeton University Press.

Levene, Merrick, Christina Starmans, and Ori Friedman. 2015. "Creation in Judgments about the Establishment of Ownership." *Journal of Experimental Social Psychology* 60: 103–109.

Lindert, Peter H., and Jeffrey G. Williamson. 2016. *Unequal Gains: American Growth and Inequality since 1700*. Princeton, NJ: Princeton University Press.

McMahon, Stephanie Hunter. 2009. "A Law with a Life of Its Own: The Development of the Federal Income Tax Statutes through World War I." *Pittsburgh Tax Review* 7(1): 1–41.

Mehrotra, Ajay K. 2005. "Envisioning the Modern American Fiscal State: Progressive-Era Economists and the Intellectual Foundations of the U.S. Income Tax." *UCLA Law Review* 52: 1793–1886.

Merriam, C. Edward. 1920. *A History of American Political Theories*. New York: Macmillan.

Murphy, Liam, and Thomas Nagel. 2001. "Taxes, Redistribution, and Public Provision." *Philosophy & Public Affairs* 30(1): 53–71.

Murphy, Liam, and Thomas Nagel. 2002. *The Myth of Ownership: Taxes and Justice*. New York: Oxford University Press.

The New Republic. 1915. "The Bill of Rights Again." April 17, pp. 272–273.

Newman, Paul Douglas. 2004. *Fries's Rebellion: The Enduring Struggle for the American Revolution*. Philadelphia: University of Pennsylvania Press.

Nozick, Robert. 1974. *Anarchy, State, and Utopia*. New York: Basic Books.

Pipes, Richard. 2000. *Property and Freedom*. New York: Vintage Books.

Pollack, Sheldon D. 2013. "Origins of the Modern Income Tax, 1894–1913." *The Tax Lawyer* 66(2): 295–330.

Radin, Margaret Jane. 1982. "Property and Personhood." *Stanford Law Review* 34(5): 957–1015.

Rauschenbusch, Walter. 1912. *Christianizing the Social Order*. New York: Macmillan.

Rodgers, Daniel T. 1982. "In Search of Progressivism." *Reviews in American History* 10(4): 113–132.

Ross, Edward Alsworth. 1901. *Social Control: A Survey of the Foundations of Order*. London: MacMillan.

Ross, Edward Alsworth. 1907. *Sin and Society: An Analysis of Latter-Day Iniquity*. New York: Houghton Mifflin.

Russell, Daniel C. 2010. "Embodiment and Self-Ownership." *Social Philosophy and Policy* 27(1): 135–167.

Schoenblum, Jeffrey A. 1995. "Tax Fairness or Unfairness? A Consideration of the Philosophical Bases for Unequal Taxation of Individuals." *American Journal of Tax Policy* 12: 221–271.

Seager, Henry. 1910. *Social Insurance: A Program for Reform*. New York: Macmillan.

Seligman, Edwin R.A. 1890. "The General Property Tax." *Political Science Quarterly* 5(1): 24–64.

Sherratt, T.N., and M. Mesterton-Gibbons. 2015. "The Evolution of Respect for Property." *Journal of Evolutionary Biology* 28(6): 1185–1201.

Smith, J. Allen. 1907. *The Spirit of American Government*. New York: Macmillan.

Smith, Harry Edwin. 1914. *The United States Federal Internal Tax History from 1861 to 1871*. Boston, MA: Houghton Mifflin.

Spargo, John. 1910. *Karl Marx: His Life and Work*. New York: B.W. Heubsch.

Stake, Jeffrey Evans. 2004. "The Property 'Instinct'." *Philosophical Transactions of the Royal Society B: Biological Sciences* 359(1451): 1763–1774.

Trotsky, Leon. 1937. *The Revolution Betrayed: What Is the Soviet Union and Where Is It Going?* Garden City, NJ: Doubleday, Doran & Company.

Weikart, Richard. 1994. "Marx, Engels, and the Abolition of the Family." *History of European Ideas* 18(5): 657–672.

Weyl, Walter E. 1913. *The New Democracy: An Essay on Certain Political and Economic Tendencies in the United States*. New York: Macmillan.

Wilson, Woodrow. 1887. "The Study of Administration." *Political Science Quarterly* 2(2): 197–222.

Zuckert, Michael. 2005. "Natural Rights and Imperial Constitutionalism: The American Revolution and the Development of the American Amalgam." *Social Philosophy and Policy* 22(1): 27–55.

2

SPIRIT, CONTENT, AND IMPACT

Principles of Tax Policy Structure and Evaluation

Irrespective of whether a tax policy is shaped by classical liberal, social contract, or progressive principles, additional choices must be made that specify the policy's structure. Many of those choices are centered on practical aspects of policymaking.

Normative considerations are inevitably made in advance of any policy change, chief among them decisions about how a tax will be molded according to different conceptions of equity and fairness. Both terms are popular in political debates and public policy more generally, but neither has objective meaning, generating substantial disagreement. Indeed, many debates don't revolve around whether the state should engage in taxation in the first place, but whether a specific tax is "fair" or "unfair."

Policymakers must also address administrative questions. Choices about policy structure, e.g., the tax rate or rates, the activities to which those rates will be applied, and how the tax will be collected, are key. More than any other part of the policy process, administrative choices reflect policymakers' beliefs about how to best translate abstract political theories and notions of equity and fairness into a concrete instrument of the state. Once decisions have been made and policy has been authorized, taxes become a real phenomenon that impacts real people.

Most importantly, tax policy has economic and budgetary consequences. All taxes influence behavior, and behavioral changes influence revenue collections. All taxes further generate unintended consequences. Attention to these matters often alters both the normative and administrative choices made during the policy process.

This chapter provides an overview of the mechanics of tax policymaking, from the initial matter of who should and should not pay a tax under consideration to the administrative issues that follow. The basic principles discussed here should serve as points of reflection when examining all forms of taxation.

The Spirit of Tax Policy: Who Should Pay—and Why Them?

The first and most important question to ask when a new tax is proposed, or when an increase or decrease to an existing levy is suggested, is why policymakers believe that particular course of action is necessary. That query may come from citizens, journalists, policy analysts, the groups upon which the tax burden will fall, or, preferably, all of the above. Policymakers may rejoin that revenues are needed to fund government operations or to fund a specific program. They may also invoke the necessity of raising or lowering taxes to achieve broader policy goals, including equity, fairness, maintaining competitiveness with other governments, or incentivizing economic growth. Whatever the justifications are, they may very well be accurate, honest assessments.

At the same time, it is reasonable and necessary to approach tax policy with a healthy degree of political and economic cynicism. Explanations offered to the public could very well be cover for ideologically motivated reasoning. What truly drives tax increases or cuts may be a desire to break the trajectory set by previous administrations, regardless of how revenues are spent or how cuts are distributed. Furthermore, policymakers at the state level often engage in strategic tax policy-making, whereby they seek to emulate policies in effect in other states regardless of those policies' necessity or effectiveness (e.g., Costa-Font et al. 2015; Leiser 2015; Sjoquist et al. 2007). Taxpayers can and should inquire as to whether that might be happening.

It is also fair for taxpayers and other citizens to demand whether a tax policy will achieve what its advocates claim. They should also question the nature and size of possible unintended consequences and investigate whether proposals have been sufficiently analyzed. Incidentally, these are also questions that policymakers should ask of themselves, their peers regardless of political affiliation, and bureaucrats.

As discussed in Chapter 1, tax policy decisions are made in accordance with policymakers' beliefs about private property rights and the role of the state in civil society. Regardless of those beliefs and other motives, tax development forces policymakers to make several normative economic choices. Chief among those choices is the question of who should pay the tax under consideration and the extent to which those parties should do so. When the matter at hand involves tax reductions or tax incentives, the question is just the opposite, i.e., who should receive the benefits and to what extent the benefits should be distributed.

Policymakers resolve these questions by integrating principles of equity and fairness with tax policy. Two principles are the most common: the ability-to-pay principle and the benefit principle. But given rising government debt, the growing cost of entitlement programs, and those programs' substantial long-term liabilities, it is increasingly recognized as important to also consider intergenerational equity.

The Ability-to-Pay Principle

According to the ability-to-pay (ATP) principle, the state should allocate tax burdens according to would-be taxpayers' financial capacity to pay the tax. Policy choices entrenched in the ATP principle reflect a belief that a taxpayer with a greater capacity to pay taxes—e.g., those with higher levels of income or assets—should sacrifice a greater share to the state relative to those with lower capacity. The ATP principle is based on assumptions by policymakers about what a group of taxpayers can, and should, afford.

But what is a taxpayer's ability or capacity to pay? Much like equity and fairness, "ability" is a nebulous concept, and attempts to objectively define the term fail. As de Jasay (1998) wrote:

> Both the economic and the political senses of the concept are shrouded in fog. No one has yet convincingly depicted the shape of the relation, nor did anyone measure its limits. Discussion of it is apt to degenerate into rhetoric.

One of the earliest attempts to define the ability to pay taxes appeared in Adam Smith's *Wealth of Nations*:

> The subjects of every state ought to contribute towards the support of the government, as nearly as possible, in proportion to their respective abilities; that is, in proportion to the revenue which they respectively enjoy under the protection of the state.

Following Smith's theory, many tax policies implicitly define ability as a taxpayer's revenue. For individuals, revenue is the earnings derived from wages and other sources of income. For corporations, revenue is typically some measure of net income or profit. Yet many methods of taxation are not based on a revenue-centric definition of ability. Certain forms of property tax are linked with the value of a parcel of land, often without regard to whether that land generates revenue with which to pay taxes, and often without regard to the owner's ability to pay them through other means. Consumption taxes are linked with the price of goods, not a consumer's income. Regardless of their ability, rich and poor alike pay the same retail sales tax on an insightful book about tax policy, for instance.

The ATP principle is commonly supported on the basis of efficiency. Beyond a certain point, the marginal utility of each additional dollar of income or assets declines; in theory, each additional dollar of income for an individual earning $1 million per year has little impact on their material well-being, but each additional dollar for an individual earning just $10,000 per year has a larger impact. Some economists thus contend that it is efficient to distribute higher tax burdens to those with lower marginal utilities, e.g., those with higher incomes or greater wealth.

Different views of equity also factor into the ATP principle and its translation into tax policy. Like ability, "equity" is an exceedingly popular but amorphous and relativistic concept defined by what an observer believes about fairness and justice, two more terms defined in the eye of the beholder. The equity concepts most common to tax policy are vertical and horizontal equity. Vertical equity refers to whether individuals with different abilities to pay actually have different tax liabilities. It is thus a direct manifestation of the ATP principle. Vertical equity is achievable with policies that institute graduated tax rates on higher levels of income, assets, or other measures of ability. Vertical equity might also be obtained by instituting taxes that take effect only after a taxpayer exceeds a specified ability threshold. Exempting lower abilities (e.g., lower incomes) from taxation lessens tax regressivity.

Horizontal equity refers to whether individuals with identical abilities to pay have identical tax burdens. More simply, horizontal equity demands that "equals are treated as equals." If that occurs, the tax policy is said to have horizontal equity. Advocates for horizontal equity note that adherence to the principle of vertical equity opens the door to differential treatment of taxpayers by the state and, furthermore, that taxes motivated by vertical equity disincentivize working toward higher levels of income, assets, and profit.

The weakness of both vertical and horizontal equity and the ATP principle as they appear in contemporary tax policy is their obliviousness to time. True ability to pay taxes—however defined—is not merely current revenue; it is the ease with which a taxpayer acquired revenue in the past, their current ability, their future ability, and their access to other resources. Those characteristics, in turn, are shaped by an individual's talents and abilities, physical attributes, location, occupation, amount of experience, and skillset compatibility with labor demand. For corporations, the ability to earn profits is shaped by cost structure, market positioning, regulatory burdens, and economic conditions. Likewise, horizontal and vertical equity judgments are often based on static snapshots of tax distribution at one point in time. But as discussed in Chapter 3, data on income dynamics in the United States suggest a high degree of lifecycle income mobility for individuals, and corporate profitability typically varies with the overall economy.

Yet income tax policies, for instance, simplistically levy tax burdens according to what a taxpayer earned in the preceding 12-month period. No allowance is made for long-term ability, or inability, to pay. Assets are ignored. Research shows that this short-term approach is a poor proxy for long-term ability (Auerbach et al. 2016). Moreover, although tax policy is often developed with allusions to the ATP principle, actual tax rates and the levels of income or assets to which they are applied is often a product of path dependency and inflationary adjustments, not quantitative analyses of what optimal tax policy should be. As a result, tax reform advocates suggest that future policy changes should incorporate more nuanced measures of ability and equity than the blunt instruments currently in effect, but there are substantial political and legal difficulties to doing so (see Chapter 9).

The Benefit Principle

The benefit principle holds that tax burdens should be distributed in proportion to how much a would-be taxpayer benefits, or gains, from public goods and services. This approach presumes a fundamentally different relationship between the individual and the state and how that relationship is reflected in tax policy. Whereas the ATP principle ascribes a proactive, interventionist state role, such as through judging ability to pay taxes and acting to reduce inequality, the benefit principle conceptualizes a market-based relationship in which the state provides goods and services that an individual may or may not choose to purchase.

The benefit principle is most easily applied to policies that govern charges for excludable public goods characterized by a market pricing mechanism. For example, the cost burden of toll roads, utilities, and some public recreational facilities can be assigned to those who utilize the goods the most by charging a simple fee for use. Fuel taxes paid by drivers are another way to transfer the cost of road construction and maintenance onto users. In many applications of the benefit principle, an individual's benefit is assumed to be proportional to their consumption. In each of the preceding examples, those who benefit from the good or service pay for it, and the more they benefit or consume, the more they pay. When a public good or service is priced purely in accordance with the benefit principle, those who do not utilize the good or service pay nothing.

The weakness of the benefit principle is not ignorance of time, but rather its bounded applicability. It is difficult, if not impossible, to apply the benefit principle to non-excludable, or "pure," public goods such as national defense and environmental protection. In theory, such goods could be financed through a user fee, but that would create a free-rider problem and a substantial administrative burden.

A Progressive Take on the Benefit Principle

A distinctly progressive variation of the benefit principle gained notice during 2011 and 2012. In August 2011, Elizabeth Warren, a progressive Democrat then contemplating running for senate, made the following remarks at a campaign event in Andover, Massachusetts:

> You built a factory out there? Good for you. But I want to be clear. You moved your goods to market on the roads the rest of us paid for. You hired workers the rest of us paid to educate. You were safe in your factory because of police forces and fire forces that the rest of us paid for. You didn't have to worry that marauding bands would come and seize everything at your factory and hire someone to protect against this because of the work the rest of us did. Now look, you built a factory and it turned into something terrific or a great idea? God bless. Keep a big hunk of it. But part of the

underlying social contract is, you take a hunk of that and pay forward for the next kid who comes along.

At a Roanoke, Virginia, campaign rally less than one year later, President Barack Obama, also a progressive Democrat, echoed Warren's remarks:

> If you were successful, somebody along the line gave you some help. There was a great teacher somewhere in your life. Somebody helped to create this unbelievable American system that we have that allowed you to thrive. Somebody invested in roads and bridges. If you've got a business, you didn't build that. Somebody else made that happen.

Both comments were made in the context of Republican charges that Democrats' advocacy for higher taxes on high-income earners amounted to "class warfare," but the sentiment was not limited to the 2012 election cycle. Speaking at an August 2016 Young African Leaders Initiative town hall meeting in Washington DC, Obama remarked:

> Our big problem here in this country is sometimes we forget how we became so wealthy in the first place. And you start hearing arguments about, "oh, we didn't want to pay taxes to fund the universities," or "we don't want to pay taxes to maintain our roads properly" because "why should I have to invest in society, I made it on my own?" And we forget that, well, the reason that you had this opportunity to go work at Google or to go work at General Motors or to go work at IBM had to do with a lot of investments that were made in science and research and roads and ports and all the infrastructure that helps preserve the ability of people who want to operate effectively in the marketplace to be able to make it.

Each of their respective remarks conveyed a tenant of American progressivism: that individual or corporate success cannot transpire apart from the state. Consequently, the progressive approach to taxes in general, and graduated taxes on higher income levels, does not reflect only the ATP principle but a combination of the ATP and benefit principles.

Critics pointed out that Warren and Obama were either lying to their audiences or ignorant of both tax policy and fiscal federalism. Both suggested that some individuals and corporations should pay higher *federal* taxes because they enjoyed disproportionate benefits from roads, schools, and public safety, but all three of those goods are predominantly funded by *state and local* governments. Moreover, neither Warren nor Obama seemed to consider that every individual or corporate entity that purchases fuel pays federal, state, and sometimes local taxes to fund road construction and maintenance, regardless of their income or profit level. Individuals and corporate entities alike also pay state and local income taxes, consumption taxes, and property taxes to fund schools and fire departments and to finance police departments that protect them from the "marauding forces" Warren cited. Why high-income earners or corporations should have an increased tax burden from the level of government that does not provide a majority of the funding for those goods was not asked of either candidate.

Regardless of their dubious face validity, both comments are a powerful reminder that crafting tax policy is just as politicized as theories about the proper role of the state in civil society. Principles of equity and fairness don't flow directly from classical liberalism or progressivism, yet there are undeniable affinities between the former and the latter, and conflicts about ability, equity, and benefits cannot be avoided. The ATP principle and vertical equity are more easily aligned with progressive thought, whereas the benefit principle and horizontal equity are more easily aligned with classical liberalism. It is not surprising that reforms suggested by progressives (i.e., contemporary liberals and/or Democrats) typically center on increasing tax burdens on high-income earners in accordance with the ATP principle, whereas reforms suggested by classical liberals (e.g., contemporary conservatives and/or Republicans) are more likely to advance lower or flatter taxes to fund a minimal state with wider use of user charges in accordance with the benefit principle.

Intergenerational Equity

Much of the deliberation regarding the ATP principle, the benefit principle, and horizontal and vertical equity views tax policy through a temporal lens. In other words, the debate often centers on how tax burdens are distributed now and in the immediate future. But given the size and scope of federal, state, and local debt, it is just as important to consider intergenerational equity, which refers to the distribution of tax burden across age cohorts.[1] Evaluating the degree to which one cohort has a higher or lower burden than another raises nuanced questions about equity and fairness. For example, is it fair that a grandparent paid less in taxes than their grandchild at the same age? What is one generation's duty to another? Whereas policymakers do not agree on how to address intergenerational equity, most concede that the issue requires more attention than it currently receives.

Consider the burden of federal payroll taxes, used for decades to fund Social Security and Medicare. The 2016 tax rate of 15.3%, divided equally between employees and their employer—at least in practice—is far higher than the rate instituted when Social Security was created, which was a relatively paltry 2%. Congress has increased payroll taxes multiple times, but the increases were never retroactive. Therefore, the payroll tax burden on an individual working in the 1950s was lower than the burden on an individual working in the 1970s, and anyone working in either of those two decades paid a lower rate than anyone employed today.

Table 2.1 illustrates the intergenerational disparity in the payroll tax burden. A 65-year old retiring in 2015 after 45 years in the workforce paid an average rate over their working life of about 14.1%. But the burden on a 65-year old retiring in 1985 after 45 years in the workforce was about half as much. Despite paying

TABLE 2.1 Intergenerational Inequity of the Federal Payroll Tax Burden

Working Years	Year of Retirement	Age at Retirement	Average Tax Rate
1940–1985	1985	65	7.1%
1955–2000	2000	65	11.3%
1970–2015	2015	65	14.1%

Source: Author's calculation based on statutory payroll tax rates in effect during periods specified.

higher payroll taxes, the 2015 retiree will not receive double the benefits of the 1985 retiree. Although cohorts entering the workforce today have a payroll tax burden of 15.3%, absent major reforms those cohorts will receive lower Social Security benefits than any previous generation.

The imbalance of Social Security tax burdens and benefits was a characteristic of the program from its inception. Social Security's first beneficiary, Ida May Fuller, retired at age 65 after paying $24.75 in payroll taxes over three years. Until her death at age 100, Fuller collected over $20,000 in benefits. That over-$19,000 deficit was funded through taxes on the next-younger generation.

The Content of Tax Policy: Administrative Considerations

Defining the Tax Base and Tax Rate

The ATP principle, benefit principle, and different notions of equity have a direct impact on the most important administrative component of any tax policy: definitions of the tax base and the tax rate(s). The tax base is the scope of income, assets, goods, services, or other activities to which the tax is applied. The tax rate is the quantity applied, usually a percentage, to different amounts or quantities of those activities. Policy should offer clear, comprehensible definitions of each element; quite simply, it makes compliance easier.[2]

Defining policy terms is easier said than done. Even a simple tax policy requires hundreds of words to specify. Consider the ordinance passed in 2014 by Berkeley, California, voters that instituted a tax on sugar-sweetened beverages. The ordinance, just over eight pages of single-spaced text, explains the rationale for the tax and contains important information on how the city plans to implement and collect it. As for the tax itself, the ordinance begins innocently enough:

> In addition to any other taxes imposed by the City, the City hereby levies a tax of one cent ($0.01) per fluid ounce on the privilege of Distributing Sugar-sweetened beverage products in the City.

For this particular tax, the definition of "sugar-sweetened beverage" is vital; more than any other term in the ordinance, it must be described clearly so that city officials can determine the tax base and business owners can determine what elements of their inventory may be subject to taxation. Luckily, the ordinance includes a 130-word description:

> "Sugar-sweetened beverage" means any beverage intended for human consumption to which one or more Added caloric sweeteners has been added and that contains at least 2 calories per fluid ounce. "Sugar-sweetened beverage" includes, but is not limited to all drinks and beverages commonly referred to as "soda," "pop," "cola," "soft drinks," "sports drinks," "energy drinks," "sweetened ice teas," or any other common names that are derivations thereof. "Sugar-sweetened beverage" shall not include any of the following: any beverage in which milk is the primary ingredient, i.e., the ingredient constituting a greater volume of the product than any other; any beverage for medical use; any liquid sold for use for weight reduction as a meal replacement; any product commonly referred to as "infant formula" or "baby formula"; or any alcoholic beverage.

"Beverage products" includes liquid sweeteners, which the ordinance refers to as "added caloric sweeteners." But that term also needed defining. According to the ordinance, an added caloric sweetener is:

> any substance or combination of substances that meets all of the following four criteria: is suitable for human consumption; adds calories to the diet if consumed; is perceived as sweet when consumed; and is used for making, mixing, or compounding sugar-sweetened beverages by combining the substance or substances with one or more other ingredients including, without limitation, water, ice, powder, coffee, tea, fruit juice, vegetable juice, or carbonation or other gas. An Added caloric sweetener may take any form, including but not limited to a liquid, syrup, and powder, whether or not frozen. "Added caloric sweetener" includes, without limitation, sucrose, fructose, glucose, other sugars, and high fructose corn syrup, but does not include a substance that exclusively contains natural, concentrated, or reconstituted fruit or vegetable juice or any combination thereof.

These definitions appear very precise, and in most respects they are. However, what the ordinance does not explain is how the city plans to objectively determine whether a beverage "is perceived as sweet when consumed." Without satisfying that perception, the tax cannot be applied.

Compliance and Accountability

Tax policy must also establish how the tax will be collected. Two general approaches may be adopted. Under a taxpayer-passive approach, a government agency determines tax liability. This approach is most common across local governments that levy property taxes; a local assessor determines property value, and an agency sends a tax bill to the owner. Higher compliance costs are at least partially offset by more accurate tax payments and lower evasion.

The alternative is a taxpayer-active approach that delegates responsibility for calculating tax liability to the taxpayer, such as through filing an income tax return. This approach lowers the state's compliance costs but increases the likelihood of errors and tax evasion, thereby lowering revenues. For instance, the IRS audits relatively few tax returns for accuracy, and each year there is a "gross tax gap" and a "net tax gap." The gross tax gap is the IRS's best estimate of the total amount of delinquent taxes; the net tax gap is the amount of delinquent or unpaid taxes that remains after the IRS attempts collections. The tax gap results from three behaviors: taxpayers failing to file a return when they are legally required, taxpayers underreporting income, and taxpayers underpaying taxes due. Estimation of these figures is a significant undertaking, so much so that the IRS usually estimates the tax gap once every five years. In 2006, the most recent year for which data are available, the IRS estimated gross and net tax gaps of $450 billion and $385 billion, respectively.[3]

Efforts to minimize unpaid taxes under either a passive or active approach must focus on accountability. Tax policy should outline and publicize incentives for full compliance (e.g., discounts for early payment) as well as punishments for non-compliance (e.g., late penalties). Policy should also specify who or what institution has interpretive authority for resolving vague legislative language. Feedback mechanisms are also important, such as the procedures through which a taxpayer may appeal their tax liability. Accountability may also mean allowing voters to change or repeal a tax via direct democracy tools, such as the property tax limitations that gained popularity during the 1970s and 1980s.

Sunset Provisions

Some tax policies may include a sunset provision if policymakers intend the tax to be temporary rather than permanent. Sunset provisions should be identified at the outset. Depending on the nature of the tax, policymakers may also wish to include provisions that, if met, automatically delay sunset—a sort of "circuit breaker" provision. In that case, the length of the delay should also be stated along with how determinations will be made as to whether those provisions have been triggered.

Implementing Tax Preferences

Policy choices regarding tax preferences, e.g., reductions or other incentives, are different than those regarding the imposition of new taxes or tax increases. Reduction policies must stipulate how the cut will be applied to existing tax rates, the tax base, or both, and clearly outline who or what qualifies. Incentive policies must specify if the incentive will assume the form of a tax deduction or a tax credit. The difference between deductions and credits is subtle but important. A deduction lowers a taxpayer's taxable income, whereas a tax credit lowers a taxpayer's actual tax liability. Deductions are incorporated before a taxpayer determines their tax liability; credits are subtracted afterward. Both incentives represent a loss of revenue to governments known as a tax expenditure, which itself has budgetary consequences.

The Impact of Tax Policy: Economic and Budgetary Consequences

Behavioral Responses

Tax analyses seek to quantify the impact of tax policies on certain groups in society or on society as a whole. That often entails estimating a tax's deadweight loss, efficiency gains or losses, and other macroeconomic effects. Estimates of tax elasticity are paramount to those analyses. Elasticity estimates are often inconsistent and vary over time and by tax type.

Tax elasticities are fundamentally difficult to pin down because it is impossible to predict with precision how individuals and corporate entities will respond to policy changes. Consider the challenge of predicting how smokers will respond to a tax increase on tobacco products, a matter explored in Chapter 6. Some smokers will reduce their consumption, perhaps even quit. Others will reduce their consumption of legally purchased cigarettes and switch to products obtained through illegal channels (e.g., black market cigarettes). Others will purchase cigarettes from jurisdictions where the tobacco tax is lower, likely by traveling across state lines. Estimating how many smokers fall into each category, not only in the short term but over the long term, is a substantial empirical challenge. A similar challenge awaits any analyst evaluating other targeted taxes, such as those on alcohol, marijuana, or sugar.

Tax elasticity estimates therefore require addressing tax salience, the degree to which individuals incorporate the burden of taxes into decision-making. This, too, is tricky. For instance, consumer reaction to taxes embedded in the cost of certain goods differs from reactions applied separately at the retail level. Research shows that excise taxes included in the price of alcoholic beverages reduce consumption relative to taxes charged at the point of sale (Chetty et al. 2009). The difference results, in part, from imperfect information about which activities are taxed and what the relevant tax rate would be (Zheng et al. 2013).

Or consider behavioral responses to an income tax increase. Income earners may react by earning less, perhaps allocating more time to leisure activities. But responses between tax brackets may differ from behavior when approaching the next highest tax bracket. Some would also respond by underreporting income to evade the tax increase altogether. A more recent and pressing problem for policymakers is the movement of income and assets from high-tax jurisdictions to low-tax jurisdictions. Here the analytical challenge is determining the proportion of income earners (and income) that fall into each category in both the short and long term—no easy task, but one central to quantifying a tax's real-world impact.

Corporate tax responses are similarly difficult. When faced with a tax liability, any corporate entity has a limited set of reactions (Mikesell 2014). One option is to forward-shift the burden to customers through higher prices. The corporation could also backward-shift the burden by lowering the costs of production, e.g., using lower-cost materials, reducing employee wages and/or benefits, and reducing overhead. Still another option is absorption, whereby the corporation assumes the tax liability by reducing profits. A final option is to avoid the tax by restructuring operations to shield business activities from taxation, perhaps through use of tax shelters or by relocating to a lower-tax jurisdiction. Yet each option has a ripple effect to the tax situations of suppliers, employees, and shareholders, respectively, that must also be considered.

Tax Incidence

These examples suggest that beyond elasticity, the incidence of a tax—i.e., where the burden ultimately falls—is also of concern to tax analysis. All taxes have some "trickle down" effects. Corporate taxes eventually fall to individuals (e.g., customers, employees, or shareholders) or to other corporate entities (e.g., suppliers) who, in turn, transfer the burden to their own customers, employees, and shareholders. Taxes to support Social Security and Medicare are levied equally on employees and employers. But most economists believe that employers backward-shift their portion onto employees, who thus pay not the 7.65% that appears on their paychecks, but the full 15.3%. Yet estimating tax incidence is not merely an exercise in economics; incidence relates directly to normative concerns for equity. A tax policy may be developed with one view of equity (and incidence) in mind, but how that tax operates in the real world is always different from policymakers' intention. What seems fair on paper may be unfair in practice.

Budget Impact

Last but certainly not least, evaluating a tax policy requires estimating the policy's budget impact. This monumental task often involves economists and policy analysts working for multiple agencies. For example, tax policy at the federal level is informed by analysis from the Joint Committee on Taxation, the House Ways and Means Committee, the Senate Budget Committee, the Congressional Budget Office, the Office of Tax Analysis, and the Office of Management and Budget, among others.

Despite a bureaucratized structure and access to hundreds of experts, the process of estimating a policy's impact can be alarmingly informal. Bruce Bartlett

(2012), a former congressional staffer, tells this amusing story about tracking down the source of budget estimates used by Congress when debating a proposal for a windfall profits tax on oil companies:

> Curious about the revenue estimate, I called the JCT and was told that on this occasion it had simply used the estimate given to it by Treasury. So I called Treasury and was told that it had simply taken the Department of Energy's forecast for oil production and multiplied it by the tax. In other words, Treasury assumed that a heavy new tax on oil production would have no effect on either supply or demand. I then called DOE to see where its oil production forecast came from and whether this forecast would be affected by the new tax. The person I spoke with said that the forecast came from a private consultant. I called him next. It turned out that the consultant's estimate was a back-of-the-envelope calculation that he gave to DOE over the phone. He was horrified to learn that Congress was about to enact a major tax bill based on his computation.

In fairness, forecasting revenue effects is not an exact science, and estimates can vary wildly based on the nature and content of econometric models and underlying assumptions about individual and corporate responses to policy change. The easiest approach is to assume a static impact—i.e., if a tax rate is cut 5%, then tax revenues will decline 5%; and if the rate is increased 5%, then revenues will increase 5%. But the only thing analysts know for certain when estimating revenue impact is that a static effect will not materialize. The impact will instead be dynamic, a product of policy changes and the sum total of all micro- and macroeconomic changes that occur as a result.

Dynamic Scoring

As econometric methods have advanced over the past century, so has the level of sophistication of estimates regarding tax policies' budget impact, known as "scoring." Analyses of federal tax proposals have, for some time, reflected the fact that taxpayers change their behavior in reaction to tax increases or decreases. But most of those analyses incorporated only microeconomic effects, such as a decline in gasoline consumption after a gasoline tax increase. What analyses often ignored were the much larger—and fiscally consequential—macroeconomic effects.

Beginning in the mid-1990s, Congress began to explore dynamic scoring methods that would incorporate both micro- and macro-economic effects. One might think that changing analytical approaches is a nonpartisan affair, but that has not been the case. Republicans have criticized the widely used nondynamic scoring for failing to integrate the macroeconomic effects of tax cuts, arguing that the method was biased against one of the party's signature policy positions.

Although some Democrats have embraced dynamic scoring, others have been outright hostile. In a 2015 Politico editorial, Representatives Chris Van Hollen and Louise Slaughter, both Democrats, called dynamic scoring "speculative" and said of Republican efforts to change methods,

> they are rigging the rules in favor of windfall tax breaks to the very wealthy and big corporations who can hire high-priced, well-funded lobbyists— once again choosing to leave behind working families.[4]

The progressive Center on Budget and Policy Priorities also argued against dynamic scoring, citing the uncertainty of macroeconomic estimates and the potential for politically motivated manipulation of underlying assumptions (Van de Water and Huang 2014).

Nevertheless, Congress in 2015 mandated that starting with the 2016 fiscal year, the Congressional Budget Office and Joint Committee on Taxation must use dynamic scoring to estimate the 10-year revenue and spending impact of major pieces of legislation when requested by the House of Representatives. However, all such estimates prepared by the Senate are not required to use dynamic scoring. Congress thus relies on two very different methods to ascertain the budget impact of tax policy changes.

Conclusion

The practice of tax policy involves granting due care to several considerations. Some are normative, including addressing underlying motives, equity, and fairness. Others are more quantitative, such as determining tax incidence and budget impact. In many respects, all of these considerations are shaped by politics, and all should be held in mind when evaluating the policy and political aspects of contemporary taxation.

Notes

1 For a more complete discussion of intergenerational equity as it applies to politics writ large, not just taxation, see Gosseries (2008), Tepe and Vanhuysse (2009), and Van Parijs (1998).

2 Some surprising factors outside of policymakers' control affect tax compliance. Based on data gathered from over 30 nations, religiosity was found to increase tax morale— i.e., the intrinsic willingness to comply with tax law (Torgler 2006). Believe it or not, tax morale is higher in the United States than in 15 European nations (Alm and Torgler 2006).

3 See Internal Revenue Service, "Tax Gap for Tax Year 2006: Overview."

4 See "'Dynamic Scoring' Cooks the Books," available at http://www.politico.com/mag azine/story/2015/01/dynamic-scoring-cooks-the-books-113977#ixzz4CfDmkyI6

References

Alm, James, and Benno Torgler. 2006. "Culture Differences and Tax Morale in the United States and in Europe." *Journal of Economic Psychology* 27(2): 224–246.

Auerbach, Alan J., Laurence J. Kotlikoff, and Darryl R. Koehler. 2016. "U.S. Inequality, Fiscal Progressivity, and Work Disincentives: An Intragenerational Accounting." National Bureau of Economic Research Working Paper #22032.

Bartlett, Bruce. 2012. *The Benefit and the Burden: Tax Reform: Why We Need It and What It Will Take*. New York: Simon & Schuster.

Chetty, Raj, Adam Looney, and Kory Kroft. 2009. "Salience and Taxation: Theory and Evidence." *American Economic Review* 99(4): 1145–1177.

Costa-Font, Joan, Filipe De-Albuquerque, and Hristos Doucouliagos. 2015. "Does Inter-Jurisdictional Competition Engender a 'Race to the Bottom'? A Meta-Regression Analysis." *Economics & Politics* 27(3): 488–508.

de Jasay, Anthony. 1998. *The State*. Indianapolis: Liberty Fund.

Gosseries, Axel. 2008. "On Future Generations' Future Rights." *Journal of Political Philosophy* 16(4): 446–474.

Leiser, Stephanie. 2015. "The Diffusion of State Tax Incentives for Business." *Public Finance Review*. doi: 10.1177/1091142115611741.

Mikesell, John L. 2014. *Fiscal Administration*, 9th Edition. Boston: Wadsworth.

Sjoquist, David L., William J. Smith, Mary Beth Walker, and Sally Wallace. 2007. "An Analysis of the Time to Adoption of Local Sales Taxes: A Duration Model Approach." *Public Budgeting & Finance* 27(1): 20–40.

Tepe, Markus, and Pieter Vanhuysse. 2009. "Are Aging OECD Welfare States on the Path to Gerontocracy?" *Journal of Public Policy* 29(1): 1–28.

Torgler, Benno. 2006. "The Importance of Faith: Tax Morale and Religiosity." *Journal of Economic Behavior & Organization* 61(1): 81–109.

Van de Water, Paul N., and Chye-Ching Huang. 2014. "Budget and Tax Plans Should Not Rely on 'Dynamic Scoring'." *Center on Budget and Policy Priorities*. PDF available at http://www.cbpp.org/sites/default/files/atoms/files/10-18-11bud.pdf

Van Parijs, Philippe. 1998. "The Disfranchisement of the Elderly and Other Attempts to Secure Intergenerational Justice." *Philosophy & Public Affairs* 27(4): 292–333.

Zheng, Yuqing, Edward W. McLaughlin, and Harry M. Kaiser. 2013. "Salience and Taxation: Salience Effect versus Information Effect." *Applied Economic Letters* 20(5): 508–510.

PART II
Taxes on Income

3

TAXING INDIVIDUAL INCOME

Misunderstood, but Seldom Forgotten[1]

Before the Sixteenth Amendment was ratified in 1913, federal taxes on individual income were little more than a short-term funding measure for the Civil War. Following ratification, Congress transformed the tax from a levy that applied to very few Americans into one that applies to a majority of the population. In 1913, about 358,000 individuals filed a federal income tax return; by 1945, that number had exploded to nearly 50 million, an almost 14,000% increase.

Tax increases linked to World War I and World War II drove some of that expansion, but tax revenue in the postwar era did not and has not receded to pre-war levels (see Figure 3.1). For over seven decades, income tax collections have contributed between 40% and 50% of all federal revenue, and today, the tax is the single largest contributor to the federal treasury (see Figure 3.2). In 2016 alone, income tax revenue exceeded $1.6 trillion, virtually as much as all other sources of revenue combined.

The two world wars were costly affairs and, unfortunately, were not the only conflicts that entangled the United States. But federal income tax growth is the result of several other factors. Over time, the income tax system has become a complex set of policies that raise revenue but that also bend individual behavior toward ends that policymakers deem appropriate for civil society, regardless of the economic and political consequences. This trend is evident at the federal, state, and municipal levels of government.[2]

More than with any other form of taxation, political clashes over the income tax echo the underlying conflict between classical liberalism's emphasis on private property rights and progressives' emphasis on collectivism. The income tax has been the subject of over a century of ideological tit-for-tat policy decisions about tax rates, incentives, and the appropriateness of using the tax to achieve larger social objectives.

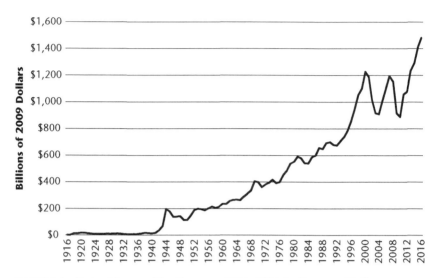

FIGURE 3.1   Federal Income Tax Revenue, 1916–2016, in Constant Dollars

Sources: Author's analysis of data reported by the Department of the Treasury, the Office of Management and Budget, and in the *Historical Statistics of the United States, Colonial Times to 1970, Part 2.*

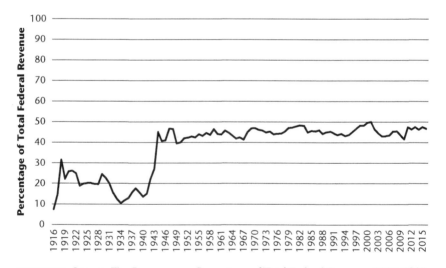

FIGURE 3.2   Income Tax Revenue as a Percentage of Total Federal Revenue, 1916–2015

Sources: Author's analysis of data reported by the Department of the Treasury, the Office of Management and Budget, and in the *Historical Statistics of the United States, Colonial Times to 1970, Part 2.*

This chapter surveys individual income taxes in the United States, including federal and state taxes and payroll taxes.[3] The survey includes an explanation of how income taxes function, from defining income to subtracting exemptions, deductions, and credits. It also includes a discussion of how the income tax interacts with other political conflicts, especially income redistribution and the evolving role of the federal government in society, and what data indicate about tax burdens and inequality. But before tackling those issues, it is important to understand the income tax's historical trajectory, beginning with the immediate aftermath of the Sixteenth Amendment's ratification.

The First Century of the Federal Individual Income Tax: Older but Not Wiser

Since the federal income tax became a permanent fixture of American life in 1913, its most debated aspect has been the number and size of marginal tax rates (MTRs): the rates applied to different income levels that are also referred to as "tax brackets." Pre-1913 iterations of the income tax were not structured consistently; both flat and graduated rates were tried during the Civil War, and the 1894 rate was flat. The income tax enacted in 1913 instituted a graduated MTR structure wherein higher rates were applied to higher income levels, a system that endures today. Graduated rates reflect the ability-to-pay principle as well as progressives' desire to use tax policy to reduce inequality.

Over the past 100+ years, the number of MTRs in the federal income tax code has expanded and contracted, and so have the rates themselves. The 1913 income tax consisted of seven MTRs: 1%, 2%, 3%, 4%, 5%, 6%, and 7%. And while the 2016 income tax also consisted of seven MTRs, the rates were significantly higher: 10%, 15%, 25%, 28%, 33%, and 39.6%. For most of the intervening period, the income tax code contained more rates—as many as 56 during the 1920s.

Contemporary income tax history can be divided into two periods. The first period, lasting from 1913 through the mid-1960s, was characterized by increases to both MTRs and the number of people paying income taxes. The second period, lasting from the mid-1960s to today, has been marked by reduced rates and an evolution in the ranks of who does, and does not, pay the income tax.

The Early Decades: Tax Rates, the Tax Base, and Revenues Increase

The first major post-1913 income tax change was enacted through the Revenue Act of 1918, which raised the top MTR to 77%. Practical reasons for the increase were twofold. First, the American entry into World War I created substantial national defense costs to the federal government. Second, the war reduced tariff revenues which, at that time, were a major source of federal revenue. But political concerns for equality and fairness also shaped congressional decision-making. Whereas the earlier justifications for graduated income tax rates were tinged with reducing economic inequality, the tax system was now positioned as a way to balance the sacrifices made disproportionately by lower- and middle-class men volunteering for, or conscripted into, military service (Scheve and Stasavage 2016).

The 1918 tax increase and the revenues it yielded the treasury changed the federal government from one dependent almost entirely on consumption taxes (e.g., tariffs and excises) to one directly reliant on individuals' income. That change had a ripple effect that reached other areas of American politics. Once the federal government was less dependent on alcohol excise taxes, for example, the political feasibility of national alcohol prohibition increased (see Chapter 6).

After the end of World War I, debate centered on whether high MTRs were sustainable. Many economists advanced a supply-side argument that higher rates discouraged labor, wealth accumulation, and other tax-generating activities, thus hampering economic growth and yielding lower revenues. In other words, high income tax rates were inefficient. Treasury Secretary Andrew Mellon (1924) wrote:

> It seems difficult for some to understand that high rates of taxation do not necessarily mean large revenue to the government and that more revenue may often be obtained by lower rates.

But deliberations over tax cuts were complicated by the fact that, to members of Congress, income tax policy could not be separated from corporate income taxes, estate taxes, tariffs, and excises. Because most World War I-era taxes were paid by high-income earners, reducing their burdens was a nonstarter for progressives. Nevertheless, Congress enacted limited tax cuts in 1921, 1924, 1926, and 1928.

Those reductions did not last. Ballooning budget deficits and growth in the national debt during the Great Depression raised calls for tax increases, and Congress responded in kind. The Revenue Act of 1932 raised the highest MTR from 25% to 63%. Three years later, the Federal Insurance Contributions Act (FICA) introduced another income-based tax to working Americans: a payroll tax to support the newly minted Social Security program.

Income taxes were a campaign issue even during the period in which few people had to pay them. *The Truth About Taxes*, a 1940 film made for Republican presidential candidate Wendell Willkie, warned viewers about the encroachment of taxes on their everyday lives and noted how poorly revenues were spent. The film cautioned viewers about the harm caused by a lack of military spending, juxtaposing the need to prepare for World War II—which the United States had yet to join—against wasteful New Deal infrastructure projects.

The American entry into World War II in 1941 brought sizable defense outlays financed in part through tax increases on nearly every income-earning individual, not just those with high incomes—a first in American history.[4] The Revenue Act of 1942 raised the top MTR to 88% and introduced a "victory tax" of 5% on all incomes over $624, the equivalent of about $9,200 in 2016 dollars.[5] To educate citizens on paying taxes, the federal government turned to popular culture. At the government's request, Walt Disney produced and released *The New Spirit* in January 1942, less than two months after the attack on Pearl Harbor. The seven-minute cartoon depicted a conversation between Donald Duck and an authoritative radio voice that guided Mr. Duck through the process of completing his federal income tax return. Care was taken to ensure exemptions were claimed for his beloved nephews Huey, Dewey, and Louie. Throughout the cartoon, emphasis was placed on the simplicity of filing a return. Most of the content, however, highlighted the importance of taxes to "beat," "bury," and "sink" the Axis powers by funding all manner of weaponry. "Guns" were mentioned eight times in seven minutes.

Widespread income tax withholding began in 1943, although the Victory Tax and Social Security Tax were already collected through withholding at that point. Treasury officials believed that withholding would simplify the process of paying taxes which, for millions of Americans, was still a new experience. It also provided a more rapid stream of revenue to the federal treasury; taxes would otherwise be remitted annually. Withholding had many advocates, including economist Milton Friedman, who would later regret his support.[6]

As World War II continued, Congress raised tax rates further, but rates did not fall significantly after the war ended. The top MTR was increased to 94% in 1944 and was only reduced to 86.45% in 1945. The cost of fighting World War II was far greater than the revenues raised by the income tax, and the national debt had exploded, thereby serving as a barrier to immediate tax reductions. In the immediate aftermath of the war, congressional Republicans favored spending reductions and tax cuts, but President Harry Truman, a progressive Democrat, disagreed. He stated:

> In my judgment, high taxes contribute to the welfare and security of the country. Under the wartime tax system, millions of taxpayers with small incomes are called upon to pay high taxes. When the time comes for taxes to be reduced, these taxpayers will have a high priority among the claimants for tax relief.[7]

To some extent, the postwar partisan conflict was moot. Taxes were raised again during the Korean War, and rates remained high through the 1960s. But for all of the emphasis on high rates, growth in the number of tax deductions and credits meant that few people actually paid those rates. Still, effective tax rates—i.e., the rate paid after deductions and credits—remained around 40% for the highest income earners for most of the immediate postwar period (Scheve and Stasavage 2016).

The Latter Decades: Tax Rates Fall but Revenues Continue to Increase

In his 1963 State of the Union speech, President John F. Kennedy, a not-so-progressive Democrat, proposed across-the-board tax cuts. The Kennedy Administration was motivated to cut tax rates by the same supply-side principle advocated by former Treasury Secretary Andrew Mellon some 40 years earlier: that reducing taxes would increase economic activity and bolster revenues. Kennedy proposed a top rate of 65%, down from 91%, and a bottom rate of 14%, down from 20%.

But Kennedy did not live to see the cuts become law. Under President Lyndon Johnson, a much more progressive Democrat, Congress reduced the top MTR to 70% and the bottom MTR to 14%. Despite income tax cuts, payroll taxes were increased. The payroll tax rate moved higher still after the creation of Medicare in 1965.

In 1969, Secretary of the Treasury Joseph Barr informed Congress that 155 individuals with income over $200,000, the equivalent of about $1.4 million in 2016 dollars, in 1966 owed no federal income taxes. Those individuals had not done anything illegal; rather, they had taken advantage of deductions and credits added to the tax code by Congress. Still, the fact that dozens of individuals earned so much income yet paid so little in taxes struck many policymakers as unfair. In response, Congress passed, and Republican President Richard Nixon signed, the Tax Reform Act of 1969. The Act instituted a "minimum tax" designed to prevent high-income earners from escaping federal income taxation. Provisions of the minimum tax were adjusted four times until 1978, when Congress enacted additional changes and gave the levy a new name: the alternative minimum tax (AMT). Each tax functioned alongside the traditional federal tax code. High-income earners were required to calculate their standard tax liability, then use a different set of rules to calculate an alternative liability, and then pay the IRS the higher of the two figures.

The 1980s ushered in an era of unprecedented tax reform. Republican President Ronald Reagan pushed the same supply-side philosophy that Kennedy had 20 years earlier.[8] Under the Economic Recovery Tax Act of 1981, the top MTR dropped from 70% to 50%. The Tax Reform Act of 1986, enacted with strong bipartisan support including a 97–3 vote in the Senate, reduced the top rate again to 28% while limiting and reducing several tax deductions. But the Act also expanded the deductibility of home mortgage interest and created new tax deductions, and once again, some of the Reagan-era income tax cuts were offset by four increases to the payroll tax rate.

The trend toward lower MTRs reversed under President Bill Clinton, a Democrat. Entering the 1992 election cycle, voters were angry over a recession, rising budget deficits, and incumbent Republican George H. W. Bush's broken "no new taxes" pledge. As a candidate and later as president, Clinton offered tax increases, particularly on "the rich," as a solution. The Omnibus Budget Reconciliation Act of 1993 raised the top MTR to 39.6%, adjusted the income ranges to which each rate applied, eliminated certain payroll tax limits, and increased taxes on Social Security benefits. The Act passed Congress only after a tie-breaking vote from Vice President Al Gore, also a Democrat.

Income tax rates during the first two administrations of the new millennium moved away from and then partially returned to Clinton-era policy. As a candidate and as president, conservative Republican George W. Bush advocated for lower taxes. Two major tax cuts passed during his tenure. In 2001, the Economic Growth and Tax Relief Reconciliation Act reduced the top MTR to 35% and created a new 10% rate for low-income taxpayers. In 2003, the Jobs and Growth

Tax Relief Reconciliation Act kept the MTR structure unchanged but altered the income ranges to which the rates applied. Although the 2001 law reduced tax rates across the board and cut the rate on low incomes from 15% to 10%, Democrats for the next decade derided the policy as "tax cuts for the rich."

In contrast to Bush, Democrat Barack Obama, the United States' most progressive president in decades, sought to increase taxes on high-income earners; recall Obama's benefit principle comments discussed in Chapter 2. By law, the 2001 tax cuts were due to sunset at the end of 2010, and Obama openly supported letting some of those cuts expire, especially cuts that benefited "the richest Americans." But the Tax Relief, Unemployment Insurance Reauthorization, and Job Creation Act signed into law by Obama after passing a Democrat-controlled Congress in 2010 kept the MTRs in effect for two years and included a temporary, two-year reduction in payroll taxes. Maintaining the existing rates while cutting the payroll tax was sold as a way to boost economic growth following the Great Recession. Amid the apparent recovery in 2012, Obama signed the American Taxpayer Relief Act, which preserved the Bush-era tax cuts for low-income earners but raised the top MTR back to the Clinton-era high of 39.6%. Other tax provisions expired, including the payroll tax reduction, and the AMT was reformed to avoid entrapping middle-class income earners.

Overall, federal income taxes have a long, illustrious, and politicized history. Figure 3.3 illustrates the highest and lowest MTR since 1862, the first year in which the United States experimented with a federal income tax, and Figure 3.4 illustrates the number of MTRs over the same period.

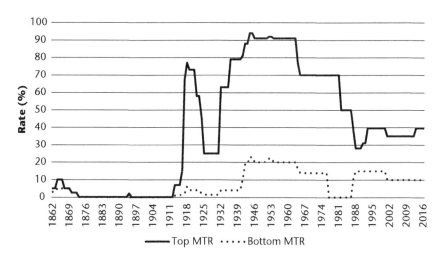

FIGURE 3.3   Highest and Lowest Marginal Income Tax Rates, 1862–2016

Sources: Internal Revenue Service and the Tax Foundation.

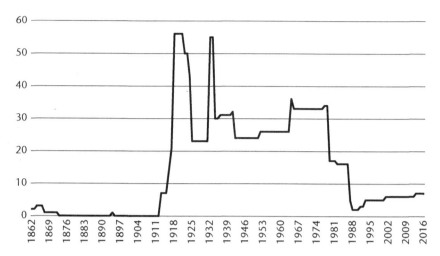

FIGURE 3.4 Number of Marginal Income Tax Rates, 1862–2016

Sources: Internal Revenue Service and the Tax Foundation.

FIGURE 3.5 Percentage of Income Tax Returns with Zero or Negative Tax Liabilities, 1918–2010

Source: Internal Revenue Service Statistics of Income.

Although MTRs in 2016 ranged from 10% to 39.6%, millions of income earners each year have no federal income tax liability. Those individuals file a "zero return" in which they have calculated that they owe no taxes or a "negative return" that indicates the federal government owes them a net refund. The percentage of all income tax returns classified as zero or negative has increased since the mid-1980s, reaching 41% in 2010 (see Figure 3.5).

Two factors affect the number of zero and negative returns. First, the federal income tax code is based on a noncomprehensive definition of income, meaning that billions of dollars per year in economic income are not considered taxable. Second, and more importantly, the tax code includes countless deductions, credits, and other tax preferences. For many individuals, the value of those tax preferences adds up, reducing or completely eliminating their income tax liability—but in the process, raising questions about equity, fairness, and the role of the state in individual affairs.

Demystifying Individual Income Taxes

One of the roadblocks to comprehending the income tax is a poor grasp of how income taxes "work." Tax code intricacy has turned calculating income taxes into the multistep procedure outlined in Figure 3.6.

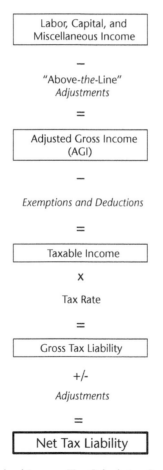

FIGURE 3.6   Outline of Federal Income Tax Calculation Process

Each individual must first identify and sum their taxable sources of income and then reduce that figure by the sum of several "above-the-line" adjustments. The remainder is the taxpayer's adjusted gross income (AGI). The AGI is then further reduced by exemptions and deductions, yielding taxable income. This figure is multiplied by the relevant tax rates to determine gross tax liability, which is then modified higher or lower by one last round of adjustments. The final result is the individual's net tax liability, the amount of money they owe to the federal government or perhaps that the federal government owes them.

For most individual taxpayers, each step of this process requires documentation on IRS Form 1040, 1040A, or 1040EZ and, most likely, completion of several additional forms. As the tax code has grown more complicated, Form 1040 has densified and the number of supporting forms has increased (see Figure 3.7).

Needless to say, income tax preparation is a time-consuming and expensive process, and no two tax situations are alike. In 2015, the IRS estimated that the average individual filing Form 1040, which represented 69% of all returns, spent eight hours on recordkeeping, two hours on tax planning, four hours on completing tax forms, and one hour on all other tax-preparation activities, for a grand total of 15 hours. The average tax-preparation cost for individuals filing Form 1040 was $270. Individuals filing the "simpler" Form 1040EZ faced an average time burden of five hours and $40 in preparation fees. The total compliance burden on individuals has been estimated to exceed 2.5 billion hours of labor and $100 billion in costs (Hodge 2016). Yet 44% of respondents to a 2015 Pew Research Center poll said they either liked or were ambivalent about filing their

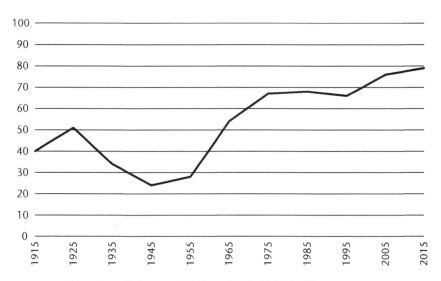

FIGURE 3.7   Number of Lines on IRS Form 1040, 1915–2015

Source: Author's analysis of historic tax forms available from the Internal Revenue Service.

taxes, although the specter of a refund likely alters opinions on the subject, especially if the refund is greater than the cost of filing.

Determining the Taxpaying Unit

The unit to which income tax liabilities accrue is any individual person with some form of income within a calendar year. In practical terms, income taxpayers mostly consist of working or retired adults with wage or retirement plan income, but minors with certain forms of income may also be liable for taxes.

Each individual does not necessarily file their own, separate income tax return. In 1948, Congress passed legislation allowing married couples to file a joint return of their combined income, therefore changing the taxpaying unit from an individual to a pair of individuals that have sought and received legal permission to function as a single social unit. Beginning in 1952, taxpayers could claim "head of household" status if they met certain qualifications, such as having one or more dependents (e.g., grandchildren or a disabled adult). Married and head of household status proffer certain tax benefits compared to filing as a single, unmarried individual with no dependents.

There are now four tax filing options: single, married filing a joint return, married filing a separate return, or head of household. Filing status alters applicable tax rates, and the types and amounts of credits and deductions a taxpayer may claim. Consequently, filing status—and especially marital status—affects tax liabilities and ultimately tax revenues.[9] For instance, legalization of same-sex marriage will likely reduce federal income tax collections and reduce some state income tax collections but raise state tax collections elsewhere (Alm et al. 2014).

Estimating Gross Income

The individual income tax base is not grounded in a comprehensive, or Haig-Simons, definition of income. Comprehensive income is the sum of how much an individual spent in a particular year plus any changes to their net worth. The definition is comprehensive in the sense that it captures the entirety of an individual's income from any potential source by measuring how much that person spent and how much their net worth changed, and then adding the two amounts together. No income is left unaccounted for.

But comprehensive income is immensely difficult to measure. As a result, most governments worldwide, including the United States, establish their income tax base on a modified definition of income. The modified definition combines three categories of income.

The first and largest category of income for most taxpayers is labor income. This includes the taxable portion of salaries, wages, tips, and other compensation remunerated in exchange for labor. The taxable portion often differs from gross income because the earner takes pretax deductions. Common pretax deductions include amounts contributed to retirement plans and amounts paid toward health insurance premiums. For example, if an individual earns a salary of $50,000 but contributes $1,000 to a retirement plan, such as a 401(k) account, and pays $1,000 toward their employer's health insurance plan, the taxable portion of that individual's salary—i.e., the amount used for income tax calculations—is actually $48,000.

The second category is capital income. Whereas labor income is compensation paid in exchange for labor, capital income includes earnings generated by assets, investments, or other forms of wealth. Examples include interest, dividends, and capital gains from the sale of stocks, bonds, mutual funds, land, and other assets. Capital income also includes royalties and earnings produced by certain small businesses, farms, and real estate holdings. Because capital assets fluctuate in value, many taxpayers can, to a point, deduct capital losses from their taxable income. For example, if an individual earns $75,000 but sells an investment for a loss of $1,000, that individual's taxable income is reduced to $74,000.

The third category comprises miscellaneous income sources that affect a relatively small proportion of taxpayers. There are countless examples and exceptions. Individuals withdrawing money from a tax-deferred retirement plan, such as a 401(k) account, must report the withdrawals as income. Depending on marital status and household income, some individuals must pay taxes on Social Security benefits received from the federal government. Alimony is considered income. Most unemployment benefits are taxable. Worker's compensation benefits are not. With rare exceptions, punitive damages received as the result of litigation are taxable. Jury duty compensation is also taxable.

Although these categories appear fairly comprehensive, several sources of income are excluded. Amounts paid by employers on behalf of employees for fringe benefits, such as health insurance, are not currently subject to federal income taxation, a point discussed later in this chapter. Housing allowances for clergy are not taxable. Amounts paid by government transfer programs, including Temporary Assistance for Needy Families benefits, and other welfare programs, including Supplemental Security Income, are not currently taxable. Some forms of income are simply not reported to the IRS, such as trivial amounts of bank account interest (usually less than $10 annually). Other types of income are excluded because they are difficult to track or measure, such as the value of unrealized capital gains and losses and the value of income-in-kind.

Above-the-Line Adjustments

Taxpayers do not pay the income tax on their total income. Before calculating their bottom line, or the income on which they will be taxed, they may claim multiple "above-the-line" adjustments. This yields their AGI. For instance, just as alimony is a source of taxable income for the recipient, alimony paid is an income reduction for the payer. Contributions to tax-deferred retirement plans also reduce taxable income. Some business expenses and moving expenses can also be deducted. Several other adjustments are education-related. Teachers can use a portion of classroom expenses to reduce their taxable income. Some taxpayers can also deduct amounts paid for college tuition, fees, and student loan interest.

Deductions and Exemptions

After calculating their AGI, a taxpayer reduces that amount by subtracting one or more exemptions and one or more deductions. For most taxpayers, the exemption is based on the number of individuals filing the tax return and their number of legal dependents. A single individual with no dependents would claim one exemption, whereas a married couple with three children that files a joint tax return would claim five exemptions. The number of exemptions is multiplied by an amount set annually by the IRS, currently $4,000 for 2016. That sum is subtracted from the taxpayer's AGI. A single individual's AGI would be reduced by $4,000, whereas a married couple with three children would reduce their AGI by $20,000. These exemptions are phased out at higher income levels.

Exemptions may be straightforward in computation, but tax deductions are anything but. The "easy" route is to claim a standard deduction based on the taxpayer's marital status. Standard deductions range from $6,300 to $12,600 for the 2015 tax year. Claiming a standard deduction requires no additional documentation.

But Congress has added a number of tax preferences to the federal tax code that are intended to incentivize certain activities and reduce the burden of others. If a taxpayer believes they have incurred enough expenses from those activities, then they usually elect to itemize their deductions on a separate form, because doing so will reduce their taxable income more than simply claiming a standard deduction.

There are over a dozen itemized deductions. Taxpayers can deduct a percentage of their own medical and dental expenses as well as those paid on behalf of their dependents. Taxpayers can also deduct amounts paid in state and local income taxes, property taxes, real estate taxes, and some other taxes; annual interest paid on home mortgage loans; certain charitable contributions; losses incurred due to casualty or theft; unreimbursed job expenses; and other miscellaneous expenses, including the cost of renting a safe deposit box at a local bank. Gambling losses are, within certain restrictions, deductible. And conveniently, tax preparation fees are also deductible. Who said Congress is immune to the plight of taxpayers?

Applying Tax Rates

Subtracting exemptions and deductions from the AGI returns the taxpayer's taxable income. Taxable income is the basis for calculating gross tax liability, which may be further adjusted higher or lower before determining final, or net, tax liability. Gross tax liability is based not only on an individual's taxable income, but also their filing status. Table 3.1 and Table 3.2 illustrate MTRs for two of the four filing statuses: single individuals, and married couples filing a joint return, respectively.

Income derived from some capital gains is not taxed according to the rates outlined in Tables 3.1 and 3.2. Taxes on short-term capital gains, i.e., gains realized on the sale of an asset held for one year or less, are taxed at the same rate as the taxpayer's ordinary income. If a taxpayer with an MTR of 39.6% incurs a short-term capital gain, then the gain is also taxed at 39.6%. Tax rates on long-term capital gains, i.e., gains realized on the sale of an asset held for longer than one year, range from 0% to 20%. Taxpayers in the bottom MTRs have a long-term capital gain tax rate of 0%; those in the highest MTR have a tax rate of 20%. All others have a long-term capital gain tax rate of 15%.

Of course, there are exceptions. Capital gains from the sale of collectible items are taxed at higher rates, ranging from 10% to 28%. Any taxpayer with an income of $200,000 or more if single or $250,000 or more if married and filing a joint return must pay a 3.8% Net Investment Income Tax (NIIT) on investment

TABLE 3.1 Federal Individual Income Marginal Tax Rates and Tax Liability Formulas for Single Income Tax Filers, 2016

Taxable Income	Tax Liability
< $9,275	10% of taxable income
$9,276—$37,650	$927.50 + 15% of taxable income over $9,275
$37,651—$91,150	$5,183.75 + 25% of taxable income over $37,650
$91,151—$190,150	$18,558.75 + 28% of taxable income over $190,151
$190,151—$413,350	$46,278.75 + 33% of taxable income over $190,150
$413,351—$415,050	$119,934.75 + 35% of taxable income over $413,050
> $415,050	$120,529.75 + 39.6% of taxable income over $415,050

Source: Internal Revenue Service.

TABLE 3.2 Federal Individual Income Marginal Tax Rates and Tax Liability Formulas for Married Individuals Filing a Joint Return, 2016

Taxable Income	Tax Liability
< $18,550	10% of taxable income
$18,551—$75,300	$1,855 + 15% of taxable income over $18,550
$75,301—$151,900	$10,367.50 + 25% of taxable income over $75,300
$151,901—$231,450	$29,517.50 + 28% of taxable income over $151,900
$231,451—$413,350	$51,791.50 + 33% of taxable income over $231,450
$413,351—$466,950	$111,818.50 + 35% of taxable income over $413,350
> $466,951	$130,578.50 + 39.6% of taxable income over $466,950

Source: Internal Revenue Service.

earnings. The NIIT is a relatively new levy, taking effect in 2013, and was one of the tax increases included in the Affordable Care Act. Proceeds are used to fund Medicare. Overall, high-income earners have a long-term capital gains tax rate of 23.8%, the sum of the standard 20% rate and the 3.8% NIIT.

Final Adjustments

Gross tax liability may be altered by several other adjustments before a taxpayer can calculate their net tax liability. If a taxpayer owes self-employment taxes or owes taxes under the Affordable Care Act, those amounts are added to their gross tax liability. If the taxpayer paid foreign taxes or incurred child or dependent care expenses, they may be able to deduct those amounts. Many taxpayers also qualify for additional incentives for retirement savings, education costs, and certain energy expenses. The taxpayer may also qualify for a Child Tax Credit and/ or an Earned Income Tax Credit. Once those final adjustments have been made, a taxpayer calculates their net income tax liability.

Many taxpayers have a portion of their estimated income tax liability withheld from their labor earnings, and some make quarterly payments to the IRS. If the sum of those payments is greater than the taxpayer's net tax liability, they may elect to receive a cash refund from the IRS or have the overpayment applied to future tax liability. If the sum of periodic payments is less than the net tax liability, or no periodic payments have been made at all, then the taxpayer must remit the difference to the IRS. Failure to pay may result in late penalties and incarceration.

Tax Preferences, Part I: Exemptions from Income

How did the income tax reach the point of such offending complexity? The answer ultimately lies within the political system, especially with Congress and the president. For all of the ire directed at the IRS, the agency's primary mission is to implement tax policies that pass Congress and receive the president's signature.

Policy changes over time have accumulated to make the income tax what it is today. Exemptions, deductions, credits, and so on—collectively referred to as "tax preferences"—have existed nearly as long as the federal income tax itself. In the Revenue Act of 1913, for instance, Congress exempted certain organizations, including nonprofit and charitable organizations, from the federal income tax.

The creation of a tax preference is typically motivated by three policy considerations (Hyman 2011). First, it is difficult, if not impossible, to measure the value of certain types of income and activities, and even if the value could be determined, the cost of doing so may be cost prohibitive. Thus, the tax code does not mandate reporting. Second, tax preferences are used to incentivize activities that policymakers believe generate positive externalities. Third, some tax preferences are used to achieve a progressive policy goal: reducing inequality. Of course, there is a fourth motivation for creating and then sustaining any tax preference:

beneficiaries have lobbying influence, of which elected officials and bureaucrats are well aware.

Tax preferences have an important impact on the federal budget. All preferences lower revenue below the level that would otherwise be achieved without the preferences in effect. The loss in revenue is called a tax expenditure. The Congressional Budget Office estimates that federal tax expenditures in 2016 would total $1.5 trillion, nearly as much as the federal government would collect through the income tax.[10] Tax preferences for both individuals and corporate entities incentivize behaviors that earn tax benefits, which are often not the most efficient, nondistortionary behaviors (Horpedahl and Pizzola 2012). The largest overall tax expenditures are those that grant preferential tax treatment for certain health care costs and retirement contributions, as well as specific other deductions.

Health Care Expenses

Like most tax preferences, the excludability of health insurance premiums from income taxation began innocently enough. Enacted amid World War II, the Stabilization Act of 1942 sought to control inflation by instituting price and wage controls.[11] An executive order from President Franklin Roosevelt, a progressive Democrat, excluded insurance and pension benefits from wage controls providing that the cost was limited to a "reasonable amount." The National War Labor Board—an unelected body—later defined "reasonable amount" as 5% of an employee's salary. But in practice, employers circumvented wage controls by offering employees more generous, and expensive, fringe benefits.

In 1943, the IRS ruled that the value of employer-sponsored health insurance was not taxable as income, meaning that premiums paid by employers on behalf of employees were not subject to the federal income tax or payroll taxes. Wartime labor shortages, the low cost of health insurance, and tax-favorable treatment led to an explosion in employer-sponsored group health insurance.[12] That trend continued after the Supreme Court ruled in 1948 that labor unions could bargain not only for wages but also for fringe benefits. A Republican-controlled Congress made the tax exclusion permanent in 1954.

Assuming that employer-paid health insurance premiums are a part of an employee's compensation, their exclusion from income taxation has important budgetary consequences. If a company pays an individual a salary of $75,000 but offers no health benefits, that individual more or less pays income taxes on the full $75,000. But if the same company compensates with $10,000 in health insurance premiums and $65,000 in salary, the individual is taxed only on $65,000. Combined with the cost of health care subsidies issued under the Affordable Care Act, tax preferences for health insurance totaled approximately $300 billion in 2016—the federal government's single largest tax expenditure, much larger than any tax expenditure that benefits corporate entities.[13]

The health insurance tax preference is a good example of inequities across income levels. Given the graduated structure of federal income tax rates, excluding health insurance premiums from taxation yields greater dollar-value benefits for higher-income earners. Excluding $10,000 in health insurance premiums from taxation for an individual in the 15% bracket "saves" them $150; excluding the same premiums for an individual earning $500,000 "saves" that person $396. Note that a flat income tax rate eliminates this inequality.

The health tax preference is also inconsistent with other tax preferences and induces market distortions. If the same $10,000 from the preceding example were instead placed into a tax-deferred retirement plan, the compensation would be taxed at redemption, something that does not happen when health benefits are redeemed. Premium payments thus escape all income taxation.

Why have policymakers been reluctant to reform this tax preference? There are several explanations. It is undeniably true that most public policies, once enacted, stay that way. The inertia is hard to overcome. Bureaucrats are often averse to change, and elected officials are reluctant to vote against policies that they may have supported in the past. Both groups worry about how to transition away from the status quo—in this case, exempting premium payments from income—to an alternative that neither they, nor tens of millions of voters, are familiar with.

Moreover, any official that does advocate change opens themselves up to criticism that may reduce the likelihood of their reelection. As a Republican presidential candidate in 2008, Senator John McCain offered a proposal to subject the value of health insurance to income but not payroll taxation, with the tax increase partially offset by a federal tax credit of no more than $5,000 for couples or $2,500 for individuals. An advertisement for his opponent, Democrat Barack Obama, described the proposal as the "largest middle-class tax increase in history."

Retirement Contribution Incentives

Another significant federal tax expenditure results from how the tax code treats contributions to tax-deferred retirement plans. Participants in employer-sponsored retirement plans, including 401(k) and 403(b) plans, may elect to have contributions automatically deducted from their salaries, in which case their taxable income is reduced by the same amount. For example, an individual who earns a salary of $1,000 per week but contributes $100 toward a 401(k) plan has only $900 in taxable income. Individuals may also contribute to plans that are not linked to their employer, such as an Individual Retirement Account (IRA), and deduct the contribution from their taxable income as an above-the-line adjustment. Individuals can take advantage of both employer-sponsored retirement plans as well as IRAs, but the deductibility of contributions is limited. The maximum contribution to employer-sponsored plans and IRAs in 2016 was $18,000 and $5,500, respectively.[14]

Contributions to tax-deferred retirement plans do not escape taxation; income taxes are, as the name implies, deferred until the contributions and investment earnings are withdrawn from the plan. But in the eyes of the federal government, deferred taxes are a tax expenditure. Their rationale? The total amount of taxes deferred on retirement contributions each year for the entire population is greater than the taxes paid each year on retirement withdrawals. Because the revenue lost is greater than the revenue collected, the difference is a sizable tax expenditure.

A contrasting approach to the retirement tax preference is a lifecycle perspective. Rather than looking at taxes lost and gained population-wide in a given year, this perspective focuses on each individual taxpayer. The tax expenditure is simply the difference between the taxes an individual avoided paying because of retirement plan contributions, and the taxes they paid later when withdrawing funds from tax-deferred plans and the inheritance taxes paid when investment balances are bequeathed to the individual's heirs. Utilizing this definition yields a smaller tax expenditure, and would better approximate the individual's ability to pay, but it is exceedingly difficult to implement.

Some taxpayers also qualify for the Retirement Savings Contribution Credit, or "Saver's Credit." Enacted in 2001 and made permanent in 2006, this credit is aimed at encouraging low-income earners to save for their retirement. The credit is based on income, filing status, and the amount contributed to an employer-sponsored retirement plan or an IRA. The credit is limited to $2,000, or $4,000 for a married couple filing a joint return, with incomes at or below $30,750 or $61,500, respectively. The credit only applies to individuals that have a gross tax liability. If the credit is larger than that liability, the difference is nonrefundable.

All retirement tax preferences seek to encourage savings. Tens of millions of individuals take advantage. But this tax preference is far from immune to criticism and special interest group involvement. Some critics argue that the preference is biased in favor of employer-based plans; recall that the maximum IRA contribution is less than one-third of the maximum contribution allowed for employer-based plans. Because the preference is based on an individual's contribution and their MTR, the preference is also biased in favor of those with higher incomes, who can more easily afford to make retirement contributions anyway.

Like the health care tax preferences, the bias is also partially the result of graduated MTRs. One reason why high-income earners receive a larger incentive to contribute to retirement plans is because their MTRs are higher than they are for low-income earners. Consider two individuals who each contribute $1,000 toward an IRA. The first person earns $9,000 per year and the second person earns $500,000 the same year. Because the first person's MTR is 10%, that person avoids $100 in income taxes. But because the second person's MTR is 39.6%, that person avoids $396 in income taxes. The difference is stark—but only because their MTRs are different. Once again, a flat tax rate eliminates the inequity.

Tax Preferences, Part II: Deductions

Two of the most widespread tax deductions are those for charitable contributions and home mortgage interest paid. Each year, taxpayers that itemize deductions claim hundreds of billions of dollars in both charitable contributions and mortgage interest deductions (see Figure 3.8). The average per tax return reaches the thousands of dollars (see Figure 3.9). In 2013, the average charitable and mortgage interest deductions were $8,854 and $5,343 per itemized return, respectively.

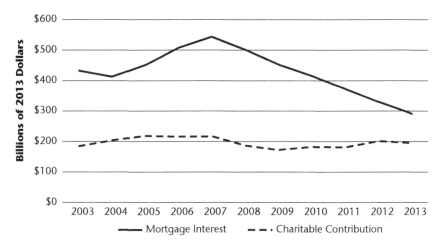

FIGURE 3.8   Total Mortgage Interest Paid and Charitable Contributions Claimed on Federal Income Tax Returns, 2003–2013, in Constant Dollars

Source: Internal Revenue Service Statistics of Income.

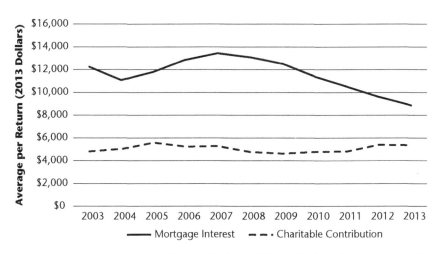

FIGURE 3.9   Average Mortgage Interest Paid and Charitable Contributions per Federal Income Tax Return, 2003–2013, in Constant Dollars

Source: Internal Revenue Service Statistics of Income.

Deduction for Charitable Contributions

With an origin in the 1917 income tax increases, the deduction for charitable contributions is one of the United States' oldest tax preferences. The deduction was made available after lobbying from nonprofit organizations concerned that World War I-era tax increases on high-income earners would reduce charitable contributions. Some of the most prominent advocates for the deduction were presidents of colleges and universities. Others favored the deduction out of fear that, should nonprofit organizations begin to fail due to a lack of contributions, whatever social service functions they provided would fall to government agencies, and thus compel higher taxes. Many studies find that the deduction incentivizes charitable contributions, although the effect varies by type of nonprofit organization (Duquette 2016), and the responsiveness of religiously motivated giving to the deduction is ambiguous (Bradley et al. 2005; Brooks 2007; McClelland and Kokoski 1994).

Despite its popularity, the deduction has not been without criticism. The question of what does, and what does not, constitute a charitable "contribution" has reached the Supreme Court.[15] Because it is only available to taxpayers that itemize deductions, anyone instead claiming a standard deduction cannot take advantage. The deduction has also been criticized for its nondiscrimination with respect to the recipient organization. A $100 contribution to a nonprofit soup kitchen is granted the same tax preference as a $100 contribution to an art gallery with a million-dollar endowment and support from admissions fees, an incentive design that is clearly at odds with the principle of vertical equity. Furthermore, donations to partisan think tanks are deductible, but donations to political parties are not. And because high-income earners are more likely to donate to charity, to itemize deductions, and to pay higher tax rates, the charitable donation incentive provides them with a disproportionately large benefit.

Criticism has led to calls for reform. In 2010, the National Commission on Fiscal Responsibility and Reform proposed limiting charitable deductions. Two years later, presidential candidates Democrat Barack Obama and Republican Mitt Romney both suggested limiting the deduction. As president, Obama repeatedly sought to limit the deduction, arguing that it disproportionately benefited high-income earners. But so far, little has changed. Countless philanthropic organizations lobby against most reforms, including the United Way, American Red Cross, American Jewish Committee, the Independent Sector, and the Alliance for Charitable Reform. Perhaps more importantly, the charitable deduction remains a favorite among the public. A 2012 Marist Poll found 69% of registered voters oppose eliminating the deduction. Opposition was generally bipartisan but was highest among those who described themselves as "liberal" or "very liberal."

Deduction for Mortgage Interest Paid

Starting in 1894, loan interest could be used to reduce federal income tax liability. The rationale was that, since most people ensnared by the income tax were business owners, the interest they paid on loans was a cost of business that reduced profits and should therefore be excluded from determining taxable income. Credit cards did not exist at that time, and personal loans were few and far between. But gradually, more and more individual taxpayers without businesses used credit cards and personal loans. The interest they paid was, by law, deductible. It was not until the Tax Reform Act of 1986, over one century later, that this "loophole" was eliminated.

More significantly, the deductibility of interest paid also applied to mortgages. Once again, few taxpayers carried mortgages in the late nineteenth century, and few therefore had any interest to deduct. But that, too, would not last for long. Several New Deal-era agencies, including the Federal Housing Authority, Federal National Mortgage Association, and Home Owners' Loan Corporation, were created for the express purpose of incentivizing homeownership during and after the Great Depression. They were aided by the GI Bill of Rights, which incentivized postwar homeownership by guaranteeing certain mortgages. That drove the rate of homeownership higher, and after Congress raised taxes on most Americans, more individuals had a tax liability from which to deduct the interest paid on their mortgage.

Conversations about the growth in mortgage interest deduction, and its distortive effect on housing, began in the 1950s and have never abated (Ventry 2010). Debates from the 1970s forward have especially focused on the inequity of the preference, which benefits individuals with higher incomes who can afford more expensive homes with larger mortgages and consequently deduct larger interest expenses. Although the Tax Reform Act of 1986 eliminated the deductibility of some interest expenses and added new rules, it did not eliminate the deduction for mortgage interest. Making matters worse, beginning in 1987, Congress allowed taxpayers to deduct interest paid on home equity loans. Because the proceeds from home equity loans could be used to purchase the same goods typically purchased with credit cards or personal loans, many analysts viewed this policy as a restoration of the personal interest deduction that had been eliminated just one year prior.

Regardless of party control, Congress has been reluctant to curb the mortgage interest deduction.[16] The public is generally supportive but divided over the question of imposing limits.[17] Several interest groups have lobbied in favor of the deduction, arguing that homeownership and the overall economy would suffer if the deduction were reduced or eliminated altogether. These groups include the National Association of Home Builders, the Mortgage Bankers Association, and the National Association of Realtors. According to the Center for Responsive Politics, the National Association of Realtors alone spent over $55 million on lobbying in 2014. The group's top issue area? Taxes.

In contrast, interest groups against the mortgage deduction span the political spectrum but have spent relatively little on lobbying. The liberal National Low Income Housing Coalition spent less than $100,000 on lobbying in 2014. The conservative FreedomWorks spent nothing.

Tax Preferences, Part III: Tax Credits

Whereas deductions allow taxpayers to reduce the portion of income subject to taxation, tax credits allow taxpayers to reduce their tax liability. Federal and state tax codes contain many different tax credits, but at the federal level two are most common: the Earned Income Tax Credit (EITC) and the Child Tax Credit (CTC). Both attract notice from policymakers and interest groups.

The Tax Reduction Act of 1975 established the EITC as a temporary credit, but Congress made the credit permanent three years later. The credit is available to low- and moderate-income taxpayers that fulfill income and dependent requirements. Individuals with no earned income do not qualify for the EITC. The credit is refundable, meaning that if a taxpayer qualifies for a credit that is greater than their tax liability, the federal government refunds the difference in cash. For instance, a taxpayer may calculate a gross tax liability of $2,000, but if, based on income, filing status, and household size, they qualify for a $3,000 EITC, their net tax liability is a negative $1,000 and they will receive a $1,000 refund. Consequently, the EITC is classified as a form of direct cash assistance intended to incentivize work and offset the burden of payroll taxes which, as discussed below, are regressive.

The CTC was established by the Taxpayer Relief Act of 1997. The credit was intended to reduce the financial burden of having children (e.g., biological children, adopted children, stepchildren, and foster children) and is given in addition to dependent tax exemptions. Assuming the taxpayer and dependent(s) satisfy seven qualification requirements, including income, residency, and age requirements, the taxpayer can claim up to $1,000 per child. In contrast to the EITC, the CTC is nonrefundable unless the taxpayer has responsibility for three or more children, in which case they may receive a refund.[18]

Figure 3.10 illustrates the history of EITC and CTC tax expenditures. Since the EITC's inception, annual EITC expenditures have exploded by 1,158%, even after adjusting for inflation—an increase that can only partially be traced to a 364% increase in eligibility. Child Tax Credit spending is essentially flat, even though the number of tax returns claiming the credit has declined by about 13%.[19] In 2013, taxpayers claimed $68 billion and $23 billion in EITCs and CTCs, respectively.

Both Republicans and Democrats have supported the EITC and CTC, but for different reasons. Republicans favor the ETIC's emphasis on labor; Democrats favor the credit as an element of state-funded welfare programs. Because both credits confer lower taxes or outright refunds to low-income earners, and middle- to high-income earners do not qualify, they satisfy any adherent to the philosophy of using the income tax code for redistribution.

Results on EITC impact offer reasons for everyone to be supportive.[20] The EITC reduces but does not eliminate economic insecurity among recipients (Bird 1996) and also reduces the number of welfare caseloads (Grogger 2004). Some recipients use the credit to build their personal savings (Mendenhall et al. 2012). But some merely use their EITC refund to pay state and local taxes (Shipler 2004).

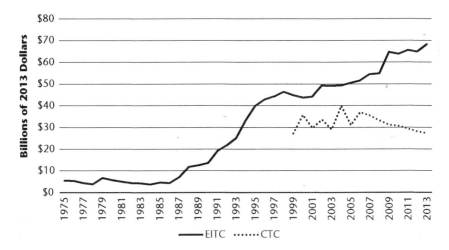

FIGURE 3.10 Federal Tax Expenditures on the Earned Income Tax Credit (1975–2013) and Child Tax Credit (1999–2013), in Constant Dollars

Source: Internal Revenue Service Statistics of Income.

However, the EITC has been designated a "high error program" due to a high number of improper payments, meaning that the federal government either issues the credit to taxpayers who are not qualified or issues a bigger credit than dictated by law. In 2016, improper EITC payments totaled an estimated $15.8 billion, yielding an improper payment rate of 24%. In other words, about one in every four EITC dollars is not paid in accordance with federal law. This circumstance is not a one-time fluke; the improper payment rate has exceeded 23% every year since 2009.[21] Circumstances are not much better for the CTC. The Treasury Department estimates that improper CTC payments totaled between $6 billion and $7 billion in 2013, an improper payment rate of 25% to 30%.[22]

Multiple factors contribute to the high improper payment rates of both credits. Eligibility is anything but transparent. Taxpayers who are uncertain of whether or not they qualify for the EITC must work through IRS Publication 596, a 37-page document. At the same time, the IRS does not verify that the tax credits claimed on every income tax return are accurate. Not surprisingly, a 2014 report from the Treasury Inspector General for Tax Administration found that the IRS' EITC oversight procedures were lacking.[23] Research based on interviews with EITC recipients also reveals that some—illegally and with intent—reallocate their children across multiple tax returns in order to maximize refunds (Edin et al. 2014).

Additional Taxes on Income

Completing IRS Form 1040, 1040A, or 1040EZ is not an individual's only exercise in income taxation. Employed Americans also encounter payroll taxes, and many owe additional income taxes to state and local governments.

Payroll Taxes

Most individuals with wage income must have payroll taxes withheld by their employer. The proceeds are used to fund Social Security and Medicare.[24] Since those programs' creation, payroll taxes have become a significant source of federal revenue (see Figure 3.11). Since 1983, payroll taxes have contributed at least one-third of all revenue to the federal treasury (see Figure 3.12). In 2015 alone, Social Security and Medicare taxes totaled $1.1 trillion. That's a lofty sum, yet insufficient to cover the programs' $1.4 trillion net cost.

There are a number of differences between payroll taxes and income taxes. Payroll tax rates are flatter—there is no complicated set of graduated MTRs—but the rate has increased during the time period in which income tax rates generally declined (see Figure 3.13). There are no exemptions or deductions from the payroll tax. But the greatest difference is that there is a limit on the wages to which Social Security, but not Medicare, taxes are applied. Clearly, there is no such limit to income taxation.

Payroll taxes are divided equally between employees and their employer, although most economists believe the incidence is backward-shifted to employees. Self-employed individuals are responsible for paying the full tax.[25] Rates currently range from 15.3% to 16.2%, but the amount depends on several factors and, for some individuals, tax filing status (see Table 3.3).

Payroll taxes do not apply to all wage and other income earners. For example, many state and local government employees do not pay the Social Security tax. Members belonging to religious sects that meet IRS requirements may apply for a payroll tax exemption. If the IRS grants the exemption, the member loses Social

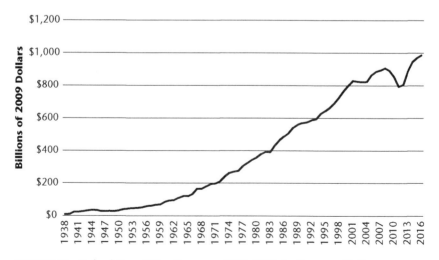

FIGURE 3.11 Federal Payroll Tax Revenue, 1938–2016, in Constant Dollars

Sources: Author's analysis of data reported by the Department of the Treasury, the Office of Management and Budget, the Congressional Budget Office, and in the *Historical Statistics of the United States, Colonial Times to 1970, Part 2.*

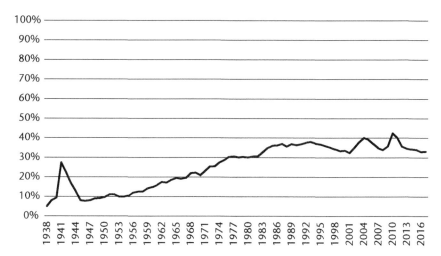

FIGURE 3.12 Federal Payroll Tax Revenue as a Percentage of Total Federal Revenue, 1938–2016

Sources: Author's analysis of data reported by the Department of the Treasury, the Office of Management and Budget, the Congressional Budget Office, and in the *Historical Statistics of the United States, Colonial Times to 1970, Part 2.*

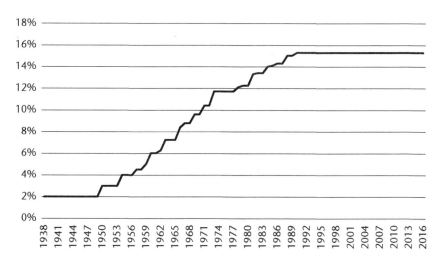

FIGURE 3.13 Combined Payroll Tax Rate, 1938–2016

Source: Social Security Administration.

TABLE 3.3 Payroll Tax Rates, 2016

Payroll Tax	Computation
Social Security	12.4% on earnings up to $118,500 (in 2016) • 6.2% paid by employer • 6.2% paid by employee

(Continued)

TABLE 3.3 (Continued)

Payroll Tax	Computation
Medicare	2.9% on all earnings • 1.45% paid by employer • 1.45% paid by employee Plus an additional 0.9% on earnings above $200,000 (for single and head of household filers) or $250,000 (for married individuals filing a joint return)

Sources: Social Security Administration and the Internal Revenue Service.

Security and Medicare benefits.[26] Certain nonresident employees and student workers may also be exempt.

Furthermore, payroll taxes are not levied on capital income, such as that produced from investments, prompting accusations of unfairness. If Person A earns $50,000 in wages and Person B earns $50,000 in investment income—likely needing millions in assets to do so—only Person A owes payroll taxes. That seems unfair, but only at first glance. Person B accrues no Social Security benefits on their earnings, but Person B does.

Payroll taxes have attracted their share of critics for other reasons. One problem is the intergenerational equity issue discussed in Chapter 2. Since benefits paid depend on the length of time spent between retirement and death, individuals belonging to groups with shorter life expectancies—e.g., blacks, males—receive smaller payouts.[27] Adding insult to injury, the Supreme Court has ruled that individuals paying payroll taxes have no private property right to the funds they remit, a matter discussed in Chapter 10.[28] In other words, the federal government coerces wage earners to pay for a program from which they cannot expect a payout.

Payroll taxes are also regressive. The rate paid by individuals earning less than $118,500 in 2016 is 15.3%, but because wages above the cap are exempt from Social Security taxes, the effective rate declines as income increases (see Figure 3.14). On balance, however, those at higher incomes do not continue to earn unlimited Social Security benefits. Those, too, are limited.

State Income Taxes

The federal government is not alone in levying a tax on income. As of 2016, 45 state governments also levy an income tax. State income taxes can be traced as far back as the colonial era. Whereas many colonies enacted taxes on land and other property, some also charged residents an income tax, then known as a "faculty tax." During the mid- to late-nineteenth century, several states pursued their own income taxes in parallel to the federal government.

State income tax revenues have increased since the end of World War II, even after adjusting for inflation (see Figure 3.15), but revenues have grown more unstable since 2000. No two state governments have identical tax systems. State

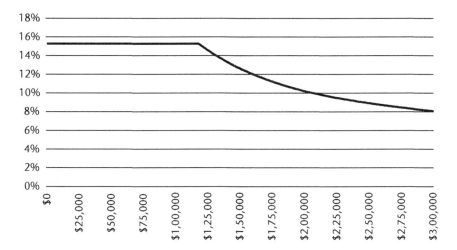

FIGURE 3.14 Effective Payroll Tax Rate Across Income Levels

Source: Author's analysis based on current payroll tax rate.

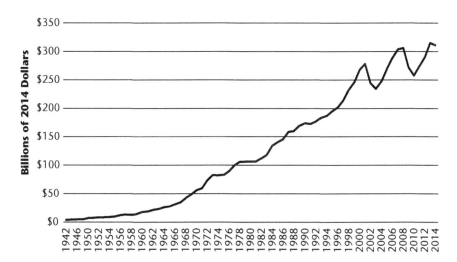

FIGURE 3.15 Aggregate State Income Tax Revenue, 1942–2014, in Constant Dollars

Source: United States Census Bureau Annual Survey of State Government Finances.

income tax codes differ widely in the number of MTRs they contain and the top MTR charged (see Table 3.4). Many have flat, as opposed to graduated, tax rate frameworks. States also differ in their treatment of short- and long-term capital gains. States face many of the same tax policy challenges as the federal government, including an increase in the number and cost of tax preferences.

State and federal tax policy are inextricably linked. Most state and local income tax policies use the federal government's definition of income. In fact, in many

TABLE 3.4 Highest Individual Income Marginal Tax Rate and Number of Rates by State, 2015

State	Highest MTR	# of MTRs
Alabama	5%	3
Alaska	0%	0
Arizona	4.54%	5
Arkansas	7%	6
California	13.3%	10
Colorado	4.63%	1
Connecticut	6.70%	6
Delaware	6.60%	6
Florida	0%	0
Georgia	6%	6
Hawaii	11%	12
Idaho	7.40%	7
Illinois	3.75%	1
Indiana	3.3%	1
Iowa	8.98%	9
Kansas	4.60%	2
Kentucky	6%	6
Louisiana	6%	3
Maine	7.95%	2
Maryland	5.75%	8
Massachusetts	5.15%	1
Michigan	4.25%	1
Minnesota	9.85%	4
Mississippi	5%	3
Missouri	6%	10
Montana	6.90%	7
Nebraska	6.84%	4
Nevada	6.84%	4
New Hampshire	5.00%	1
New Jersey	8.97%	6
New Mexico	4.90%	4
New York	8.82%	8
North Carolina	5.75%	1
North Dakota	3.22%	5
Ohio	5.33%	9
Oklahoma	5.25%	7
Oregon	9.90%	4
Pennsylvania	3.07%	1
Rhode Island	5.99%	3
South Carolina	7.00%	6
South Dakota	0	0
Tennessee	6%	1
Texas	0	0
Utah	5	1

State	Highest MTR	# of MTRs
Vermont	8.95%	5
Virginia	5.75%	4
Washington	0	0
West Virginia	6.50%	5
Wisconsin	7.75%	4
Wyoming	0	0

Sources: The Federation of Tax Administrators and the Tax Foundation.

cases, a taxpayer begins their state or local tax return by entering their federal AGI. Consequently, if Congress enacts changes to how taxpayers determine their AGI, it will have a ripple effect across other governments that levy an income tax unless those governments enact countervailing policies. Federal taxpayers that itemize deductions are allowed to deduct the amount they paid in state and local taxes. Consequently, holding all else equal, an individual living in a state with a state income tax pays less in federal income taxes than an individual living in a state without an income tax, although they likely pay more in taxes overall.

The deductibility of state and local taxes also puts taxpayers that pay for services with direct fees at a disadvantage to those who pay for services through local taxes. If Individual A lives in a city where street lights are paid for with a $100 property tax assessment, then they can claim a federal tax deduction. If Individual B lives in a different city where street lights are paid for with a $100 fee remitted to the local electric company, then they cannot claim the same federal tax deduction.

State governments also have to contend with horizontal tax competition with other states.[29] If citizens find one state's tax burden too onerous and believe they can obtain a similar qualify of life in a different state that offers a lower tax burden, some will elect to move from the former to the latter. Policymakers consequently must respond to market signals when pricing public goods and services through taxes and user fees. This process is known as Tiebout sorting, named after economist Charles Tiebout (1956), whose early work developed the underlying theory.

Outmigration of income is not merely an exercise in theory. According to a Hoover Institution study, between 2004 and 2012, high taxes and housing costs in California drove a sizeable exodus to other states. That exodus was concentrated among employed individuals, those of middle income, and those with children— in other words, the proverbial middle class.[30] From 1993 to 2014, even as California gained taxable income from the migration of individuals from other high-tax states, including New York, Illinois, and New Jersey, the state's outmigration was greater, and income drifted to low-tax states, including nearby Nevada and Arizona as well as Texas.

California is not the only state with this pattern of income migration. From 1993 to 2014, high-tax New Jersey lost some $15 billion in AGI to lower-tax

Florida. Connecticut lost billions of dollars in resident income to Florida and North Carolina. A similar movement out of New York has also been documented.[31]

The flow of income and labor sets off policy debates at the state and local level regarding the nature of tax competition and how best to respond. Those debates are rarely only about taxes. Instead, policymakers must consider a mosaic of distinct metrics that influence both individual and corporate location decisions, including the cost of living and state and local regulatory burdens. Inevitably, some policymakers refuse to accept that income is drifting to low-tax states. They reply to such data by claiming, correctly in some cases, that the state's population is growing. Yet data on income migration often incorporates population changes. If data continue to show that a state is leaking income to another area despite population growth, it suggests that the remaining population is poorer. That shift, in turn, will likely reduce tax collections and increase welfare spending.

Effective Income Tax Rates

One of the most unfortunate elements of income-based taxes is their lack of holistic transparency. An individual pays income taxes to the federal government, payroll taxes to the federal government, and perhaps also an income tax to their state and/or local government. Certain amounts are withdrawn each time that individual receives their wages, and the pay slip most likely reports dollar amounts rather than percentages. The individual then files annual federal and state income tax returns that summarize this information, once again in dollar terms rather than percentages. They may receive additional credits or have additional taxes added. At no point does a taxpayer combine everything into a single effective tax rate, a measure of their total tax burden after all taxes have been paid and all deductions and credits have been taken.

Since state income tax rates vary, an individual with the same income and deductions could very well have a different effective tax rate depending on the state in which they live. Table 3.5 illustrates the effective federal and state income tax burden in the five largest states by population.

TABLE 3.5 Comparison of Effective Individual Income Tax Rate in Five Largest States, 2015

	Federal Income Tax	*Federal Payroll Tax*	*State Income Tax*	*Total Effective Rate*
California	18.3%	15.3%	5.48%	39.1%
Texas	18.3%	15.3%	–	33.6%
Florida	18.3%	15.3%	–	33.6%
New York	18.3%	15.3%	5.49%	39.1%
Illinois	18.3%	15.3%	3.67%	37.3%

Note: Cell entries are based on an assumption of an individual taxpayer with $100,000 in annual wage income, $10,000 in exemptions and deductions, and full payroll tax burden.

Source: Author's calculations based on existing federal and state tax law.

Effective tax rates vary not only by state, but by income level, and are often entangled in any debate about inequality and tax policy. Effective rates also vary by marital status. The effective rate and average MTR across all income quintiles is lower for married taxpayers than unmarried taxpayers, although the tax penalty for being single declines with income (Guner et al. 2014).

Income Taxes, Equity, Fairness, and Redistribution

The crux of most income tax policy discord in the United States is the underlying conflict between classical liberal and progressive theories of the relationship between the individual and the state. The classical liberal belief in natural private property rights that are tied strongly to labor is antithetical to coercive taxation on wages paid in exchange for labor. In contrast, progressive skepticism of private property rights combined with favorability toward a larger state harbors no such philosophical barriers to taxing an individual's income.

The conflict surfaces in partisan policies on income taxation. Republicans are generally opposed to higher taxes on income and to graduated tax rates in particular. Democrats are generally in favor of higher taxes on income. That cleavage is further reinforced by partisan distinctions about the utility of the income tax as a tool of redistribution and its part in broader debates about class warfare. For better or for worse, much of the debate over income taxes adopts an us-versus-them, rich-versus-poor, 1%-versus-99% tone.

Within that partisan context, many individuals believe that income taxes have increased over time. Generally speaking, this belief is accurate. The federal income tax base was indisputably expanded during World War I and World War II. Although both wars ended decades ago and policymakers have lowered wartime tax rates, federal income tax revenues today are over six times what they were during World War II, even after adjusting for inflation. Factoring in both inflation and population growth, revenue has more than tripled to over $4,500 per capita, not including payroll taxes. The trend is compounded by rising state income tax burdens, which grew from an inflation-adjusted $27 per capita in 1942 to $977 per capita in 2014, a growth factor of 36.

But that growing tax burden is paid by a shrinking proportion of the population. In 1984, about 18% of federal tax returns were zero or negative returns; by 2010, that percentage surged to 41% (refer to Figure 3.5). The average taxpayer with an income of $40,000 or less in 2016 had no federal income tax liability at all except for payroll taxes (see Table 3.6). Individuals and couples in that category tended to receive all withheld income taxes back and, because of tax preferences like the EITC and CTC, an additional refund on top.

In other words, effective federal tax rates for many income groups and millions of Americans are negative. For example, the average effective tax rate for someone earning between $30,000 and $40,000 in 2015 was −1.9%. The average rate for earnings between $10,000 and $20,000 the same year was −12.5%. Contrast

TABLE 3.6 Average Federal Individual Income Tax Rate by Income Group, 2015

Annual Income	Average Rate
Less than $10,000	−7.6%
$10,000 to $20,000	−12.5%
$20,000 to $30,000	−5.6%
$30,000 to $40,000	−1.9%
$40,000 to $50,000	0.6%
$50,000 to $75,000	3.8%
$75,000 to $100,000	6.2%
$100,000 to $200,000	9.1%
$200,000 to $500,000	15.5%
$500,000 to $1 million	22.9%
Over $1 million	26.7%

Source: Joint Committee on Taxation, "Overview of the Federal Tax System as in Effect for 2016."

that with someone earning $100,000 to $200,000, who incurred an average rate of 9.1%. Those earning over $1 million had an average effective rate of just over 26.7%, not including payroll or state and local taxes. The effective rate across all tax returns was 10.2%.[32]

It thus comes as no surprise that the public perception of actual tax burdens is profoundly inaccurate. An April 2010 CBS News/*New York Times* poll asked respondents to guess the average federal income tax rate. Just 5% guessed the correct amount, which was less than 10%.[33] About one-third professed not knowing. All other respondents guessed, incorrectly, that the average rate was above 10%. According to a 2011 Rasmussen Reports poll, 64% of American adults believed that the middle class pays a greater share of their income in taxes than the wealthy. Data clearly and consistently show that is not the case.

Within the shrinking ranks of taxpayers, the burden is disproportionately borne by individuals with high incomes. According to the Joint Committee on Taxation, taxpayers with an income of $100,000 or greater represented about one-fifth of all returns filed in 2016. Whereas those taxpayers earned 63% of all reported income, they paid over 95% of all federal income taxes. Taxpayers with earnings over $1 million, which represents the top 0.03%, earned about 12% of reported income, but paid one-third of all federal income taxes. In fact, the Organization for Economic Cooperation and Development (OECD) recently found that the United States' income tax system was the most progressive among its 24 member nations.[34]

That disproportionality is not a recent development. The share of income earned by the top 1% of all earners increased from 11% in 1986 to 19% in 2013, indicative of rising income inequality. Yet over the same period, the share of income taxes paid by the top 1% increased from 26% in 1986 to 38% in 2013 (see Figure 3.16). In fact, some of the largest increases to income earned by the top 1% occurred following the Clinton-era tax increases (Piketty and Saez 2003).

Data notwithstanding, progressives and some conservatives maintain that the federal income tax code remains too favorable toward high-income earners and, consequently, that it remains the optimal tool for reducing inequality. Critics of this theory offer several critiques. First, federal income tax revenues are not linked directly with redistribution. Each dollar of taxes paid by a "have" is not now, nor has it ever been, transferred directly to a "have not." Taxes paid by high-income earners are remitted to the federal treasury and used to fund all programs and the government itself. The system does not directly raise up the "have nots"—it only directly reduces after-tax income among the "haves," thus closing the gap between them. This structure has more or less existed since progressives first won a permanent federal income tax in 1913.

Even if redistribution was direct, it would not occur in a political and economic vacuum. If one class of income earner is made better off as a result of other public policies (e.g., favorable regulations), then the effect of tax policy could be reduced or eliminated. Indeed, Bagchi and Svejnar (2015) found that inequality in general does not harm economic growth, but that inequality facilitated through political connections and favorable regulations does.

Second, a major premise underlying arguments for graduated MTRs—that high-income earners are a fixed class of concentrated economic resources—is demonstrably false. The premise rests on two assumptions: first, that high-income earners continually earn high incomes and thus have a greater ability to pay

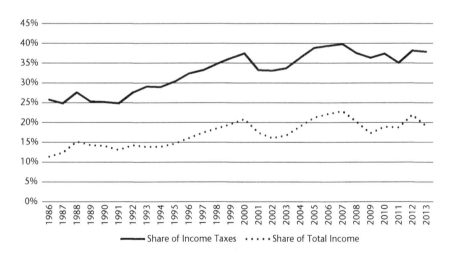

FIGURE 3.16   Share of Total Income and Income Taxes, Top 1% of Earners, 1986–2013

Source: Author's analysis of data reported by the Internal Revenue Service Statistics of Income.

higher income taxes; and second that by instituting higher income taxes on those earners, the state prevents accumulations of income and wealth, serving to limit inequality.

But multiple studies as well as analysis from the Treasury Department find that the American population is characterized by significant income mobility over time, not fixed classes of high and low earners (Auten and Gee 2009; Auten et al. 2013).[35] Lifecycle perspectives that include an examination of income mobility over time are more important to the discussion about inequality than fixed snapshots because, in the words of progressive economist Paul Krugman (1994), "If income mobility were very high, the degree of inequality in any given year would be unimportant, because the distribution of lifetime income would be very even."

For example, research indicates that membership in the oft-derided top 1% is fluid, not fixed. From 1968 through 2011, over one-third of Americans spent at least one year of their working lives in the top 5% of all earners, and over half spent at least one year in the top 10%. Reaching those thresholds is no guarantee of remaining there. Of all the individuals that reach the top 1%, only one in 20 will stay for longer than one year (see Figure 3.17)(Hirschl and Rank 2015).

As for millionaires and billionaires, only about 2% of the top 400 taxpayers between 1992 and 2013 remained for a decade or longer (Rank 2014).[36] Half of the individuals with income above $1 million from 1999 through 2007 were millionaires only once during the same period, and less than 10% were persistent millionaires (Carroll 2010). In the last three decades, the 400 wealthiest Americans have tended to grow up in the middle, not upper, class, and achieved their status by opening their own businesses, a far cry from the Gilded Age (Kaplan and Rauh 2013).

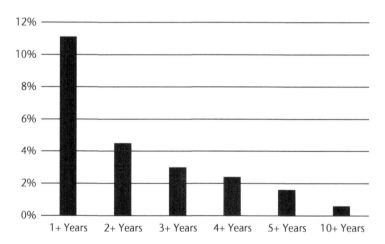

FIGURE 3.17 Percentage of Adults Reaching the Top 1% of Income Distribution for Consecutive Years, 1968–2011

Source: Hirschl and Rank (2015)

At the opposite end of the spectrum, about 62% of Americans will spend at least one year in the bottom fifth of income earners, but for most, their stay is temporary. Less than 6% persist in the bottom fifth for 10 years or longer, and less than 2% are consistently in the bottom tenth of all income earners (Rank and Hirschl 2015).

Third redistribution through the income tax is an overly simplistic solution for the much more complex problems of poverty and inequality of all kinds. Studies of poverty and welfare utilization find the direct cause is not the share of income accrued to a group of individuals in the top 1% in a particular year, but factors within (e.g., marital status, out-of-wedlock births) and not within (e.g., disability, race, parental use of welfare) the control of individuals living below the poverty line (Cellini et al. 2008; Gramlich et al. 1992; Klawitter et al. 2000; Rank and Hirschl 2001, 2015; Thomas and Sawhill 2002). Immigration of low-skill labor has also increased inequality (Xu et al. 2016), an issue well beyond and in some ways more complicated than tax policy, although no less polarizing.

Income redistribution through taxation, however indirect it may be, fails to address those underlying causes. From an economic perspective, graduated MTRs used to fund redistribution programs simultaneously discourage "good" behavior by taxing earnings while encouraging "bad" behavior by transferring the proceeds with few, if any, strings attached. Social welfare programs funded with tax revenues have, at best, a mixed record of success (Bitler and Kalory 2015). The end result is often lower consumption inequality—indeed, the material well-being of the poorest Americans is much better than it was just 30 years ago—but at the expense of disincentivizing economic productivity, which does not discriminate in its depressive impacts (Auerbach et al. 2016).

Conclusion: Income Taxes and the Evolving Role of Government

The imposition of the federal income tax fundamentally altered the relationship between the individual and the state. More than ever before, and ever since, individuals were legally required to report their income and other private activities to the state along with a portion of that income. Tax withholding changed that relationship further still by automating the process and, some research suggests, encouraging higher government spending funded by higher taxes (Dušek 2006). For over 80 years, most working individuals have not been allowed to retain their full earnings and pay taxes later. The government, as Chris Rock said, is paid first.

More broadly, the rise in income tax burdens and its concentration among a smaller, higher-earning segment of the population has correlated with a significant evolution in the role of the federal government in civil society. Beginning in 1954, an increasing share of federal spending has been allocated to nondefense programs, especially Social Security, Medicare, and Medicaid (see Figure 3.18). Those programs have progressive policy roots and, in many ways, conflict with the

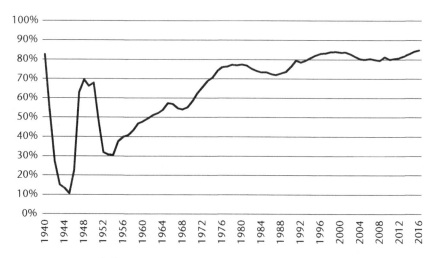

FIGURE 3.18 Nondefense Spending as a Percentage of Total Federal Spending, 1940–2016

Sources: Author's analysis of data reported by the Office of Management and Budget, the Congressional Budget Office, and in the *Historical Statistics of the United States, Colonial Times to 1970, Part 2.*

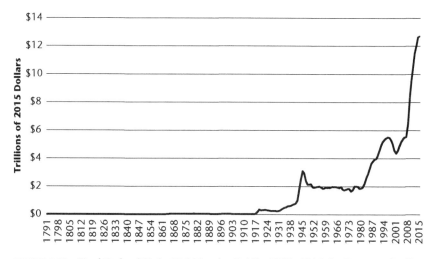

FIGURE 3.19 Total Federal Debt Held by the Public, 1791–2015, in Constant Dollars

Sources: Author's analysis of data reported by the Department of the Treasury, the Office of Management and Budget, the Congressional Budget Office, and in the *Historical Statistics of the United States, Colonial Times to 1970, Part 2.*

classical liberalism that is still very much a part of American political culture. As tax burdens rise but increasingly go to fund programs that taxpayers either don't want, don't agree with, or don't need because private alternatives exist, tax anxiety and political clashes have amplified.

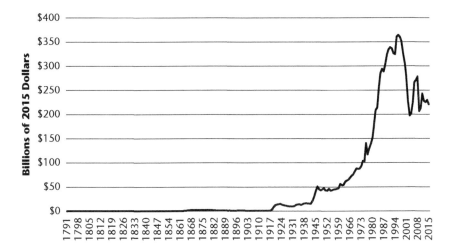

FIGURE 3.20 Federal Interest Payments on the Debt, 1791–2015, in Constant Dollars

Sources: Author's analysis of data reported by the Department of the Treasury, the Office of Management and Budget, the Congressional Budget Office, and in the *Historical Statistics of the United States, Colonial Times to 1970, Part 2.*

By all accounts, the rise in tax burdens has not been matched by fiscal discipline. In the last decade alone, the federal debt held by the public has doubled, with exceptionally sharp gains during the Obama Administration (see Figure 3.19). Concurrently, debt-serving costs have also increased (see Figure 3.20). Long-term liabilities for Social Security, Medicare, and Medicaid have swollen, and with them, a rising likelihood of tax increases. Resistance to tax increases on individuals, coupled with an ever-expanding state, has led policymakers to seek other sources of revenue, including another form of income taxes—those levied on corporations.

Notes

1 The full quote—"Like mothers, taxes are often misunderstood but seldom forgotten"—is credited to George Bramwell, a nineteenth-century English judge.
2 The income tax history included in this chapter is an overview of significant federal developments. Readers interested in a more in-depth study are encouraged to consult Ippolito (2012). The historical evolution of state and local income taxes is, obviously, unique to each jurisdiction.
3 "Individual income tax" and "personal income tax" are interchangeable.
4 Prior to World War II, few individuals paid federal income taxes. Some Americans, in fact, hoped that one day they would have to pay the income tax, because it would mean that their salary put them within the upper tier of income earners.
5 The Victory Tax was temporary and separate from the standard income tax; IRS Form 1040 in 1943 was titled "Individual Income and Victory Tax Return." The taxes were not combined in law or in practice.
6 Friedman later commented, "It never occurred to me at the time that I was helping to develop machinery that would make possible a government that I would come to criticize severely as too large, too intrusive, too destructive of freedom."

7 See "Annual Budget Message to the Congress: Fiscal Year 1948."
8 Although Reagan, a Republican, is often credited as the contemporary father of tax cuts, all policy changes during his tenure as president were passed by a Democratically controlled House of Representatives.
9 For this reason, it can be argued that the taxpaying unit is not the individual, but the household.
10 See Congressional Budget Office, "The Budget and Economic Outlook: 2016–2026."
11 The Revenue Act of 1942 also included, for the first time in American history, a provision for taxpayers to deduct a portion of medical expenses, not just insurance costs.
12 See Hacker (2002) and Starr (1982) for a more comprehensive discussion of the growth of medicine and health insurance, respectively.
13 See Congressional Budget Office, "Private Health Insurance Premiums and Federal Policy" and "The Budget and Economic Outlook: 2016 to 2026."
14 Contribution limits are raised for those closer to retirement (age 55 and older).
15 See *Davis v. United States*, 495 U.S. 472 (1990).
16 In 2005, a panel commissioned by Republican President George W. Bush recommended eliminating the mortgage interest deduction in favor of a credit equal to 15% of mortgage interest paid on homes up to a certain value, based on residence, but no more than $412,000. The proposal was that all taxpayers would qualify, not just those itemizing their deductions.
17 An October 2012 poll from the Pew Research Center found that 47% of the general public favored a cap on the mortgage interest deduction, with 44% opposed.
18 For additional information on the Child Tax Credit, see Congressional Research Service Report R41935, "The Child Tax Credit: Economic Analysis and Policy Options," and R41873, "The Child Tax Credit: Current Law and Legislative History."
19 Comparing similar time periods (1997 forward), EITC spending and eligibility changed 52.4% and 49.6%, respectively.
20 Relative to the EITC, there is little robust peer-reviewed research on the impact of the CTC.
21 See the IRS National Research Program. See also General Accountability Office, "CFO Act Agencies Need to Improve Efforts to Address Compliance Issues," 2016.
22 See Treasury Inspector General for Tax Administration, "Existing Compliance Processes Will Not Reduce the Billions of Dollars in Improper Earned Income Tax Credit and Additional Child Tax Credit Payments," 2014.
23 Ibid.
24 FICA first authorized Social Security tax withholding in 1937; Medicare taxes followed in 1967.
25 Until 1984, self-employed individuals did pay the entire employee and employer portion. It was more than half, but less than the "full" amount.
26 The religious sect must have a "conscientious objection" to any public or private insurance for old age care and health care, must have existed without interruption since December 31, 1950, and must provide a "reasonable level of living" for members. Members must complete IRS Form 4029.
27 Raising the retirement age would exacerbate this inequality. Social Security has a long history of biases, from excluding minority-dominated industries from coverage to excluding males but not females from spousal benefits. See Katznelson (2005), Kessler-Harris (2001), and Mink (1995).
28 *Flemming v. Nestor*, 363 U.S. 603 (1960).
29 Of course, local governments also compete with each other. In many ways, the competition is more intense, as individuals and businesses can relocate to proximate jurisdictions without significant transition costs.
30 See "California's Migration Problem: 'Good Luck Movin' Up Cause I'm Movin' Out'" by Carson Bruno.

31 See, generally, http://www.howmoneywalks.com
32 See "Overview of the Federal Tax System as in Effect for 2016," prepared by the Staff of the Joint Committee on Taxation, Report Number JCX-43–16.
33 About 94% of all income tax returns filed in 2015 had a federal income tax rate of less than 10%.
34 See "Growing Unequal? Income Distribution and Poverty in OECD Countries" (2008).
35 See also Department of the Treasury, "Income Mobility in the U.S. from 1996 to 2005: Report of the Department of the Treasury," 2007.
36 See also IRS, "The 400 Individual Income Tax Returns Reporting the Largest Adjusted Gross Incomes Each Year, 1992–2013," 2016.

References

Alm, James, J. Sebastian Leguizamon, and Susane Leguizamon. 2014. "Revisiting the Income Tax Effects of Legalizing Same-Sex Marriages." *Journal of Policy Analysis and Management* 33(2): 263–289.

Auerbach, Alan J., Laurence J. Kotlikoff, and Darryl R. Koehler. 2016. "U.S. Inequality, Fiscal Progressivity, and Work Disincentives: An Intragenerational Accounting." National Bureau of Economic Research Working Paper #22032.

Auten, Gerald, and Geoffrey Gee. 2009. "Income Mobility in the United States: New Evidence from Income Tax Data." *National Tax Journal* 62(2): 301–328.

Auten, Gerald, Geoffrey Gee, and Nicholas Turner. 2013. "Income Inequality, Mobility, and Turnover at the Top in the US, 1987–2010." *The American Economic Review* 103(3): 168–172.

Bagchi, Sutirtha, and Jan Svejnar. 2015. "Does Wealth Inequality Matter for Growth? The Effect of Billionaire Wealth, Income Distribution, and Poverty." *Journal of Comparative Economics* 43(3): 274–289.

Bird, Edward J. 1996. "Repairing the Safety Net: Is the EITC the Right Patch?" *Journal of Policy Analysis and Management* 15(1): 1–31.

Bitler, Marianne P., and Lynn A. Karoly. 2015. "Intended and Unintended Effects of the War on Poverty: What Research Tells Us and Implications for Policy." *Journal of Policy Analysis and Management* 34(3): 639–696.

Bradley, Ralph, Steven Holden, and Robert McClelland. 2005. "A Robust Estimation of the Effects of Taxation on Charitable Contributions." *Contemporary Economic Policy* 23(4): 545–554.

Brooks, Arthur C. 2007. "Income Tax Policy and Charitable Giving." *Journal of Policy Analysis and Management* 26(3): 599–612.

Carroll, Robert. 2010. "Income Mobility and the Persistence of Millionaires, 1999 to 2007." The Tax Foundation Special Report No. 180.

Cellini, Stephanie Riegg, Signe-Mary McKernan, and Caroline Ratcliffe. 2008. "The Dynamics of Poverty in the United States: A Review of Data, Methods, and Findings." *Journal of Policy Analysis and Management* 27(3): 577–605.

Duquette, Nicholas J. 2016. "Do Tax Incentives Affect Charitable Contributions? Evidence from Public Charities' Reported Revenues." *Journal of Public Economics* 137: 51–69.

Dušek, Libor. 2006. "Are Efficient Taxes Responsible for Big Government? Evidence from Tax Withholding." Unpublished manuscript.

Edin, Katharine, Laura Tach, and Sarah Halpern-Meekin. 2014. "Tax Code Knowledge and Behavioral Responses among EITC Recipients: Policy Insights from Qualitative Data." *Journal of Policy Analysis and Management* 33(2): 413–439.

Gramlich, Edward, Deborah Laren, and Naomi Sealand. 1992. "Moving Into and Out of Poor Urban Areas." *Journal of Policy Analysis and Management* 11(2): 273–287.

Grogger, Jeffrey. 2004. "Welfare Transitions in the 1990s: The Economy, Welfare Policy, and the EITC." *Journal of Policy Analysis and Management* 23(4): 671–695.

Guner, Nezih, Remzi Kaygusuz, and Gustavo Ventura. 2014. "Income Taxation of U.S. Households: Facts and Parametric Estimates." *Review of Economic Dynamics* 17(4): 559–581.

Hacker, Jacob. 2002. *The Divided Welfare State*. New York: Cambridge University Press.

Hirschl, Thomas A., and Mark R. Rank. 2015. "The Life Course Dynamics of Affluence." *PLoS ONE* 10(1): e0116370.

Hodge, Scott A. 2016. "The Compliance Costs of IRS Regulation." The Tax Foundation Fiscal Fact No. 512.

Horpedahl, Jeremy, and Brandon Pizzola. 2012. "A Trillion Little Subsidies: The Economic Impact of Tax Expenditures in the Federal Income Tax Code." Mercatus Center, George Mason University, Report.

Hyman, David N. 2011. *Public Finance: A Contemporary Application of Theory to Policy*, 10th Edition. Mason, OH: South-Western Cengage Learning.

Ippolito, Dennis S. 2012. *Deficits, Debt, and the New Politics of Tax Policy*. New York: Cambridge University Press.

Kaplan, Steven N., and Joshua D. Rauh. 2013. "Family, Education, and Sources of Wealth among the Richest Americans, 1982–2012." *American Economic Review* 103(3): 158–162.

Katznelson, Ira. 2005. *When Affirmative Action Was White: An Untold History of Racial Inequality in Twentieth-Century America*. New York: W.W. Norton.

Kessler-Harris, Alice. 2001. *In Pursuit of Equity: Women, Men, and the Quest for Economic Citizenship in 20th-Century America*. New York: Oxford University Press.

Klawitter, Marieka, Robert D. Plotnick, and Mark Evan Edwards. 2000. "Determinants of Initial Entry onto Welfare by Young Women." *Journal of Policy Analysis and Management* 19(4): 527–546.

Krugman, Paul. 1994. *Peddling Prosperity: Economic Sense and Nonsense in an Age of Diminished Expectations*. New York: Norton.

McClelland, Robert F., and Mary, F. Kokoski. 1994. "Econometric Issues in the Analysis of Charitable Giving." *Public Finance Review* 22(4): 498–517.

Mellon, Andrew W. 1924. *Taxation: The People's Business*. New York: Macmillan.

Mendenhall, Ruby, Kathryn Edin, Susan Crowley, Jennifer Sykes, Laura Tach, Katrin Kriz, and Jeffrey R. Kling. 2012. "The Role of Earned Income Tax Credit in the Budgets of Low-Income Households." *Social Service Review* 86(3): 367–400.

Mink, Gwendolyn. 1995. *The Wages of Motherhood: Inequality in the Welfare State, 1917–1942*. Ithaca, NY: Cornell University Press.

Piketty, Thomas, and Emmanuel Saez. 2003. "Income Inequality in the United States, 1913–1998." *Quarterly Journal of Economics* 118(1): 1–39.

Rank, Mark R. 2014. "From Rags to Riches to Rags." *The New York Times*, April 18, 2014.

Rank, Mark R., and Thomas A. Hirschl. 2001. "The Occurrence of Poverty across the Life Cycle: Evidence from the PSID." *Journal of Policy Analysis and Management* 20(4): 737–755.

Rank, Mark R., and Thomas A. Hirschl. 2015. "The Likelihood of Experiencing Relative Poverty over the Life Cycle." *PLoS ONE* 10(7): e0133513.

Scheve, Kenneth, and David Stasavage. 2016. *Taxing the Rich: A History of Fiscal Fairness in the United States and Europe*. Princeton, NJ: Princeton University Press.

Shipler, David K. 2004. *The Working Poor: Invisible in America*. New York: Vintage.

Starr, Paul. 1982. *The Social Transformation of American Medicine*. New York: Basic Books.

Thomas, Adam, and Isabel Sawhill. 2002. "For Richer or for Poorer: Marriage as an Anti-Poverty Strategy." *Journal of Policy Analysis and Management* 21(4): 587–599.

Tiebout, Charles. 1956. "A Pure Theory of Local Expenditures." *Journal of Political Economy* 64(5): 416–424.

Ventry, Dennis J., Jr. 2010. "The Accidental Deduction: A History and Critique of the Tax Subsidy for Mortgage Interest." *Law and Contemporary Problems* 73(1): 233–284.

Xu, Ping, James C. Garand, and Ling Zhu. 2016. "Imported Inequality? Immigration and Income Inequality in the American States." *State Politics & Policy Quarterly* 16(2): 147–171.

4

TAXING CORPORATE INCOME
Are They People, Too?

The income taxes levied on corporations are not altogether different from the income taxes levied on individuals. Both function in the same manner; the state applies a specified tax rate or rates to a specified definition of income, subject to tax preferences. At one time, each tax was offered as a solution to problems in the once-dominant tariff system. Both taxes are also an enduring constituent of progressive policy agendas. Indeed, among the many charges directed at late-nineteenth-century monopolies was that those corporations controlled too many resources but paid too little in taxes, the same indictment that was—and still is—applied to wealthy individuals. Income taxation on individuals and corporate entities alike was supported as a worthy tonic for the discontent wrought by inequality.

The central difference between individual and corporate income taxes, one that cannot be overstated, is the taxpaying unit. Rather than an individual or a married couple, corporate income taxes apply to certain corporate entities. From this point of distinction spring all manner of policy questions. From small "mom and pop" businesses to much larger multinational corporations, corporate entities are rather heterogeneous, but should those entities be taxed the same? Given the diversity of corporate organizational forms, policymakers also disagree on if and how to integrate vertical and horizontal equity as well as the ability-to-pay and benefit principles into corporate income taxation. Further disagreements are sourced in the definition of "corporation" and its association to the individual as well as the degree to which private property and other rights binding on the latter apply to the former. That some corporate entities operate in multiple states and nations adds a degree of complexity to corporate taxes that far exceeds anything found in the individual income tax code.

Corporate income tax politics have not prevented the levy from becoming a generally reliable source of revenue. Since being made permanent in 1909—yes, the federal corporate income tax predates the individual income tax—revenues have increased, but annual collections are both lower and more cyclical compared to the individual income tax (see Figure 4.1 and also refer to Figure 3.1). Annual revenues have displayed greater volatility since 2000, indicative of the dot-com bubble burst and tepid economic growth following the Great Recession.

Corporate income taxation is alive and well below the federal level of government; over 40 state governments and many municipalities levy their own taxes on corporate entities. Much like the federal situation, state corporate income tax revenue has not traced the same pattern as states' individual income tax revenue (see Figure 4.2 and also refer to Figure 3.15). Aggregate state revenues nearly tripled between 1955 and 1973. But in contrast to the federal trend, state revenues declined sharply during the late 1970s and early 1980s. On an inflation-adjusted basis, annual collections today are lower than they were in 1942.

For all of the attention paid to corporate taxes, the levy is not a major supplier to either the federal treasury or to state treasuries. In 2016, corporate taxes represented about 11% of all federal revenue and about 5% of states' own-source revenue. Recall that the federal government collects the bulk of its revenue from

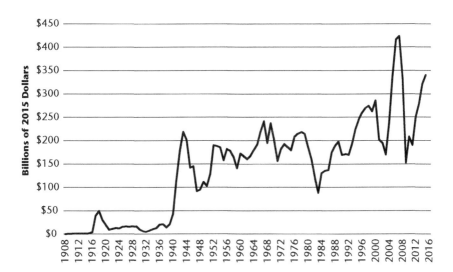

FIGURE 4.1   Federal Corporate Income Tax Revenue, 1908–2016, in Constant Dollars

Note: Early years of corporate income tax revenues are not included because data from the Department of the Treasury do not differentiate between corporate and personal income until 1909.

Sources: Author's analysis of data reported in the *Historical Statistics of the United States, 1789–1945*, the *Historical Statistics of the United States, Colonial Times to 1970, Part 2*, and by the Office of Management and Budget.

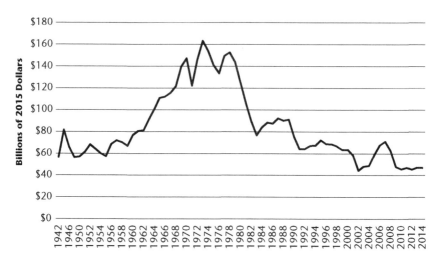

FIGURE 4.2 Aggregate State Corporate Income Tax Revenue, 1942–2014, in Constant Dollars

Source: United States Census Bureau Annual Survey of State Government Finances.

individual income and payroll taxes (refer to Figure 3.2 and Figure 3.12), and whereas state and municipal governments also depend on individual income taxes, they collect proportionally greater revenues from consumption and property taxes as well as user charges.

This chapter examines the function of corporate income taxes in the United States, including a discussion of how corporate entities and their income is defined, how that income is taxed at the federal and state levels, and what that means for American tax competitiveness. Like any income tax, corporate taxes provoke debates about equity and fairness, tax preferences, and tax avoidance, issues that are discussed in turn. Before turning to those matters, the following section outlines the tax's historical development.

Historical and Legal Development of the Federal Corporate Income Tax

The first federal corporate income tax was enacted during the Civil War. The Revenue Act of 1862 encompassed several different taxes, including levies on railroads, banks, and other financial institutions. After the Civil War ended, most of those taxes were repealed or expired (Ippolito 2012). But the corporate income tax was not long in its policy grave before a late-nineteenth-century resurrection facilitated by the rise of progressivism, populist contempt for trusts and other large corporations, and calls for tariff reform. The Wilson–Gorman Tariff Act of 1894, which brought back the individual income tax, applied the same 2% flat tax to corporations. The Supreme Court overturned the entire Act in 1895, effectively ending all income taxes despite the fact that the majority opinion, which focused on the individual income tax, did not resolve the constitutionality of a corporate levy.[1]

Consequently, the policy window remained open to a corporate income tax even as policymakers were uncertain about the constitutionality of an individual income tax. The Payne–Aldrich Tariff Act, also referred to as the Corporate Tax Act, resurrected the tax again in 1909. As before, congressional interest in a corporate levy was a product of progressive and populist demands and dissatisfaction with the tariff system. The Act specified that for-profit corporations operating within the United States "shall be subject to pay annually a special excise tax with respect to carrying on or doing business." The rate was a flat 1% on net corporate income over $5,000, the equivalent of about $123,000 in 2016 dollars. All corporate income derived within the United States was subject to the tax, regardless of where the corporation was chartered. Congress explicitly characterized the measure as an "excise tax" to avoid entanglement with then-unresolved ambiguity over direct and indirect taxes and their respective apportionment requirements. Because a corporate income tax was positioned as a solution to federal tariffs, Congress also had little interest in redistributing any such revenues to the states.

The federal corporate income tax was subject to legal challenges but was eventually upheld by the Supreme Court.[2] The landmark case involved two substantive arguments against congressional authority to enact a tax on corporate entities.[3] The first challenge was that the levy was a direct tax and therefore no different than the individual income tax the Court declared unconstitutional in 1895. The Court disagreed and classified the corporate income tax as an indirect excise tax, both of which were well within congressional authority to enact. In this particular case, the Court ruled that the tax was an excise on the "privilege of doing business in a corporate capacity," aping the law's actual phrasing.

As for the character of the privileges that justify taxation, the Court held:

> These advantages are obvious, and have led to the formation of such companies in nearly all branches of trade. The continuity of the business, without interruption by death or dissolution, the transfer of property interests by the disposition of shares of stock, the advantages of business controlled and managed by corporate directors, the general absence of individual liability, these and other things inhere in the advantages of business thus conducted, which do not exist when the same business is conducted by private individuals or partnerships. It is this distinctive privilege which is the subject of taxation, not the mere buying or selling or handling of goods, which may be the same, whether done by corporations or individuals.

The second challenge was that the tax interfered with state governments' authority to charter corporations. This allegation raised an intriguing constitutional question: if the federal government levies a tax on an entity organized under the auspices of state law, does that tax violate state sovereignty? The Court ruled in the negative, citing the interstate component of many business activities that thereby place those activities within congressional jurisdiction. The majority decision cited prior cases in which congressional authority to tax state-sanctioned entities was upheld, and further noted congressional authority to levy indirect taxes, such as the excise taxes on alcohol and tobacco that had been, at that point, collected for some time.

Despite gaining Supreme Court approval in 1911 and later ratification of the Sixteenth Amendment in 1913, Congress did not immediately increase the corporate income tax. The rate remained a flat 1% until 1916, but amid World War I, Congress implemented a series of increases. The rate was raised to 2% in 1916, 6% in 1917, and 12% in 1918. Some of those increases were defined as an "excess profits" tax on weapons manufacturers. As was the case with individual income taxes on high-income earners during that period, corporate taxes were supported as a fair policy to both raise revenue for World War I and discourage profiteering off the war effort.

And just as with the individual income tax, the termination of World War I did not bring about an elimination or even a significant decrease in corporate taxes. The tax rate remained above 10% until the Great Depression, when Congress and the Roosevelt Administration increased the rate and subsequently introduced a graduated rate structure on higher corporate income levels. An "unjust enrichment tax" went into effect in 1936. Those increases were benign compared to the increases enacted during World War II. Between 1939 and 1942, the highest marginal tax rate (MTR) on corporate income rose from 19% to 53%. Congress also reintroduced an excess profits tax that, from 1942 through 1945, generated more revenue for the federal treasury than the standard corporate income tax. Although some cuts were enacted after the end of World War II, the top MTR remained around 50% until 1979.

Corporate income tax policy evolved markedly during the Reagan Administration. The Economic Recovery Act, enacted in 1981, and the Tax Equity and Fiscal Responsibility Act, enacted in 1982, changed MTRs and modified the rules for calculating corporate income. The most recent significant change to corporate income tax policy occurred during the Clinton Administration. The Omnibus Budget Reconciliation Act of 1993 changed the number of MTRs and added new MTRs of 35% and 38%. Subsequent policy changes have been incremental, such as altering tax preferences, while leaving the 1993 tax rate structure unchanged.

The highest and lowest corporate income MTR and the number of MTRs over time are illustrated in Figure 4.3 and Figure 4.4, respectively. The highest rate was relatively low throughout the Great Depression but, as noted, rose steeply during World War II and remained elevated through the 1980s. The lowest corporate income rate of 15% has not changed since 1983. Relative to the individual income tax, the corporate income tax has never included a significant number of MTRs; by comparison, from 1918 through 1923, there were over 50 different

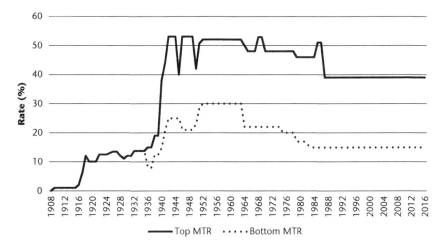

FIGURE 4.3 Highest and Lowest Federal Corporate Income Marginal Tax Rates, 1908–2016

Source: Internal Revenue Service.

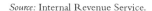

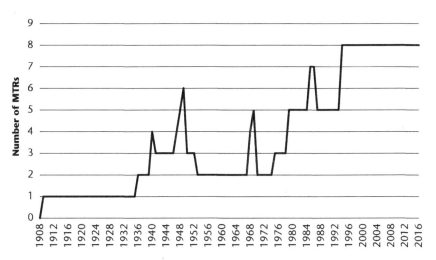

FIGURE 4.4 Number of Federal Corporate Income Marginal Tax Rates, 1908–2016

Source: Internal Revenue Service.

tax rates for individuals (also refer to Figure 3.4). Regardless, with eight different MTRs, the current rate structure is the most complicated in American history.

Defining "Corporation"

Establishing the unit of taxation for the individual income tax is relatively straightforward; each person with income may incur a tax liability determined by their filing status, level of income, and tax preferences. It may likewise appear equally forthright to define the unit of taxation for the corporate income tax. Intuitively, the unit of taxation is any corporation. But that raises several questions: what is a "corporation?" How is a corporate entity, regardless of how it is defined, contrasted legally from an individual? Are all corporations recognized equally under the law?

Simply stated, a corporation (or "business" or "firm") is nothing more than an organized group of individuals that act as a single legal entity in the performance of some function. A corporate entity may be for-profit or not-for-profit; indeed, that nonprofit organizations do not organize for profit-earning does not render them the legal equivalent of an individual.[4] A corporation may have a small number of owners or perhaps millions of owners. A corporation is not a naturally occurring phenomenon like an individual, meaning that, strictly speaking, it enjoys no natural rights. Whereas a corporation is distinct in form and in legal recognition from an individual person, many nations grant corporate entities the same types of rights and privileges enjoyed by individuals. Recognition of corporate personhood raises delicate legal questions, including the extent to which a corporate entity has a right to free speech or a right against self-incrimination.[5]

How a corporation is defined has critical implications for tax policy, regardless of the theories and motives that shape those policies. For starters, only corporations that operate for profit are singled out for taxation.[6] If the corporate organizational form is distinct from its constituent owners or operators, then a legal and perhaps moral case exists for that organization to be taxed separately from those owners or operators. But if the organization is not distinct, then the case for corporate-level taxation is much weaker; owners and operators should instead be taxed individually, and all separate corporate taxes should be eliminated.

In the United States, corporations are considered distinct legal entities and enjoy varying degrees of corporate personhood. All corporations are chartered under state law. In fact, one of the first steps to establishing a corporate entity is for the owners or other decision-makers to decide the jurisdiction in which the entity will incorporate. State laws of incorporation differ, but for tax purposes, two broad organizational forms are most common: S Corporations and C Corporations. These entities are treated differently under federal tax law and may receive differential treatment under state tax laws as well.

S Corporations

A for-profit corporate entity can elect to be recognized as an S corporation ("S corp") if the entity has fewer than 100 owners (or "shareholders"), and all the shareholders are individual American citizens as opposed to noncitizens and/or other corporate entities. The defining trait of an S corp is that the entity, despite being corporate in organizational and legal form, does not incur a federal corporate income tax liability. Instead, S corp income and losses are divided among shareholders, who are then liable for individual income taxes on their earnings.[7]

S corps are known as "pass-through entities" because, although corporate in form, all their income, losses, and taxes are passed through and levied at the shareholder level. The principal benefit of organizing as an S corp is avoidance of double taxation. In the absence of pass-through, corporate income is taxed first at the corporate level and then again at the shareholder level.

Other corporate structures are considered pass-through entities for tax purposes but, because of legal peculiarities, are not classified as an S corp per se. Compared to S corps, limited liability companies (LLCs) have altered governance and management requirements, but income is passed through to shareholders. LLC shareholders owe personal income taxes on their earnings. Limited partnerships and general partnerships also have different governance and management structures, but earnings likewise pass through to shareholders. Because a sole proprietorship by definition has only one shareholder, it is not incorporated as a legal entity distinct from that shareholder. All sole proprietorship income is reported on the shareholder's individual income tax return. Corporate income does not pass through to the shareholder because the corporation and the shareholder are, legally, one and the same.

C Corporations

For-profit entities that do not seek recognition as an S corp are normally classified as a C corporation ("C corp"). C corps do not have the same ownership restrictions as S corps. Unlike S corps, C corps are required to pay federal corporate income taxes. Under a C corp, the entity's income is taxed at both the corporate level and at the shareholder level. For example, individuals that own dividend-paying shares of stock in a C corp must pay taxes on the dividends they receive. But those dividends are paid out of the net income that remains after the C corp has already paid its own federal taxes. Because shareholders pay income taxes on post-tax corporate earnings, the C corp structure facilitates the double taxation that is avoided by organizing as an S corp or another pass-through entity.

Evolution of Corporate Structure in the United States

Although the number of corporate entities in the United States has increased overall, the gains are entirely among S corps and partnerships (see Figure 4.5).[8] Between 1995 and 2013, the number of S corps and partnerships grew by millions but the number of C corps contracted by almost a half million. Correspondingly, the proportion of all corporate entities classified as S corps, C corps, and partnerships has changed. In 1995, 37% of corporate entities filed taxes as an S corp, 35% filed as a C corp, and 27% filed as a partnership. By 2013, the proportions shifted to 46%, 17%, and 37%, respectively.

Aggregate net income reported under each designation has not changed as abruptly (see Figure 4.6). Whereas most corporate income from 1995 to 2013

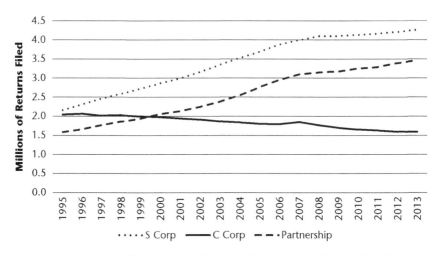

FIGURE 4.5 Number of S Corp, C Corp, and Partnership Federal Tax Returns, 1995–2013

Source: Internal Revenue Service Statistics of Income.

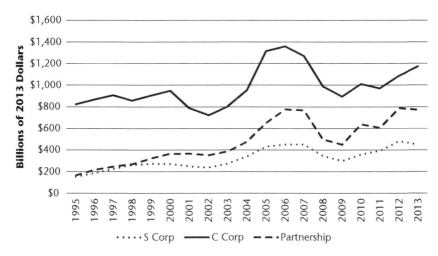

FIGURE 4.6 Aggregate Net Income Reported on S Corp, C Corp, and Partnership Federal Corporate Income Tax Returns, 1995–2013

Source: Internal Revenue Service Statistics of Income.

was earned by C corps, S corp income nearly tripled and partnership income nearly quadrupled. In 1995, 72% of all corporate net income was reported by C corps, 13% by S corps, and 14% by partnerships. By 2013, it was 49%, 19%, and 32%, respectively.

At first glance, the implication for tax policy is clear: if corporate income is increasingly passed through to individuals with lower tax rates than the rate applicable to the relevant corporate entity, then federal and perhaps state governments are not collecting as much corporate income tax revenue as they would otherwise. Upon deeper reflection, however, more questions surface. Is the evolution of corporate structure reflective of a broad tax-avoidance strategy, one resulting from an uncompetitive or overly burdensome tax structure? And is double taxation of C corp income fair?

Demystifying Corporate Income Taxes: Not As Bad As You Think

Calculating Taxable Income

In some respects, the method followed by a C corp to determine its tax liability is similar to the method used by individuals: income is added, certain deductions are subtracted, and the difference is then subject to taxation.[9] Of course, the types of income earned and the tax preferences available to corporations is different. A C corp does not file IRS Form 1040; instead, it files Form 1120. Remarkably, Form 1120 is only half as long as Form 1040. Despite a simpler return, the overall corporate tax compliance burden is massive, estimated in excess of 3 billion hours of labor and $200 billion in costs (Hodge 2016).

A C corp's taxable income is the simple difference between total income and total deductions. A corporation must report to the IRS the total value of the goods and services it sold to customers, investment income received (e.g., interest, dividends, and capital gains), and miscellaneous income collected (e.g., rent and royalties received). Various deductions reduce total corporate income to net, or taxable income—similar to a profit. These deductions include the cost of goods and services sold, employee salaries and benefits, overhead, marketing and advertising costs, charitable contributions, taxes paid to other governments, and capital depreciation expenses.

Federal and State Tax Rates

Table 4.1 outlines the current federal corporate income tax structure. Similar to individuals, C corps are taxed according to a system of graduated MTRs. Unlike the individual income tax, corporate income tax rates do not increase in a linear fashion (refer to Table 3.1 and Table 3.2). The rate increases on net income up to $335,000, is lower on income between $335,000 and $10 million, increases on income up to $18.3 million, and then decreases and remains flat on income over $18.3 million. This configuration is the product of reforms passed in 1984 and 1993.[10]

The rationale for graduated MTRs on corporate income is no different than the rationale for graduated MTRs on individual income: higher corporate income is conceptualized as implying a greater ability to pay taxes. Moreover, as

TABLE 4.1 Federal Corporate Income Marginal Tax Rates, 2016

Taxable Income	MTR
< $50,000	15%
$50,000 to $75,000	25%
$75,000 to $100,000	34%
$100,000 to $335,000	39%
$335,000 to $10 million	34%
$10 million to $15 million	35%
$15 million to $18.3 million	38%
> $18.3 million	35%

Source: Internal Revenue Service.

discussed in Chapter 2, some progressive arguments in favor of corporate taxation are predicated on a variant of the benefit principle.

In addition to federal taxes, corporations may owe state and even local taxes on income generated within those jurisdictions. No two state corporate income tax systems are identical (see Table 4.2). Over half of all state governments have instituted a flat corporate tax rate; the rest have graduated MTRs with higher rates applied to higher income levels. Just two states (South Dakota and Wyoming) have no corporate income tax at all. In all 50 states, corporate entities are liable for state and local property taxes as well as state and local business, user, and other fees.

Even within each state, rate structures may vary. For example, in California a flat rate of 8.84% applies to most C corps and a flat rate of 1.5% applies to most S corps. If the corporation is a bank or financial firm, the income tax rates are 10.84% and 3.5% for C and S corps, respectively.

An Alternative to Corporate Income Taxation: The Gross Receipts Tax

Four state governments (Nevada, Ohio, Texas, and Washington) and some local governments tax corporations with a gross receipts tax (GRT), also known as a gross excise tax or a turnover tax. As the name implies, a GRT is levied on business receipts—i.e., revenues from the sale of goods and services—rather than net income. GRT frameworks usually include a percentage-based tax on receipts with few, if any, tax preferences. Salient features of current state-level GRTs are summarized in Table 4.3.

Although many states experimented with GRTs throughout the twentieth century, especially during the Great Depression as property and individual income tax revenue plunged, most abandoned them by 2000. But by 2015, the tax had undergone a minor resurgence. Nevada is the most recent state to pursue a GRT—legislators there enacted the tax after voters rejected a similar levy in

TABLE 4.2 Highest Corporate Income Marginal Tax Rate and Number of Rates by State, 2016

State	Highest MTR	# of MTRs
Alabama	6.5%	1
Alaska	9.4%	9
Arizona	5.5%	1
Arkansas	6.5%	6
California	8.84%	1
Colorado	4.63%	1
Connecticut	9%	1
Delaware	8.7%	1
Florida	5.5%	1
Georgia	6%	1
Hawaii	6.4%	3
Idaho	7.4%	1
Illinois	7.75%	1
Indiana	6.25%	1
Iowa	12%	4
Kansas	7%	2
Kentucky	6%	3
Louisiana	8%	5
Maine	8.93%	4
Maryland	8.25%	1
Massachusetts	8%	1
Michigan	6%	1
Minnesota	9.8%	1
Mississippi	5%	3
Missouri	6.25%	1
Montana	6.75%	1
Nebraska	7.81%	2
Nevada	★	★
New Hampshire	8.5%	1
New Jersey	9%	3
New Mexico	6.6%	3
New York	6.5%	1
North Carolina	4%	1
North Dakota	4.31%	3
Ohio	★	★
Oklahoma	6%	1
Oregon	7.6%	2
Pennsylvania	9.99%	1
Rhode Island	7%	1
South Carolina	5%	1
South Dakota	None	0
Tennessee	6.5%	1
Texas	★	★

(Continued)

TABLE 4.2 (Continued)

State	Highest MTR	# of MTRs
Utah	5%	1
Vermont	8.5%	3
Virginia	6%	1
Washington	★	★
West Virginia	6.5%	1
Wisconsin	7.9%	1
Wyoming	None	0

Note: States marked with (★) levy a gross receipts tax.

Sources: The Tax Foundation and the Federation of Tax Administrators.

TABLE 4.3 Summary of State Gross Receipts Tax Systems

State	Tax Name	Tax Structure
Nevada	Commerce Tax	Applies to revenues in excess of $4 million Tax rate depends on nature of industry; 26 different rates ranging from 0.051% to 0.331%
Ohio	Commercial Activity Tax	$150 plus 0.26% of receipts above $1 million
Texas	Texas Franchise Tax	0.375% to 0.75% depending on type of business
Washington	Business and Occupation Tax	Tax rate depends on nature of industry; 35 different rates ranging from 0.13% to 1.5%

Sources: Individual states' websites.

2014—and as recently as 2016, a legislator in Oregon proposed eliminating that state's business tax and replacing it with a GRT.

Advocates argue that the GRT has much to recommend it. Compared to traditional corporate income taxes, a GRT is straightforward. A business has to do little more than calculate their receipts and remit a percentage to the state government. States usually apply the GRT to a broad tax base, thereby avoiding the politically difficult question of determining what goods and/or services should be singled out for taxation and what tax preferences should be made available. The hidden nature of the GRT—by nature, it is embedded in the cost of goods, lowered profits, or lower employee pay—makes it more politically feasible than more visible forms of taxation, like an income or retail sales tax (Due 1957).

There are strong arguments against GRTs. Their hidden nature means, obviously, that the tax burden is anything but transparent to the public. Because a GRT applies to receipts, not net income, it does not treat businesses consistently (Mikesell 2007). The most distortionary effect of a GRT is a phenomenon known as tax pyramiding—paying a tax on a tax—because the taxes are often charged to unfinished goods passing between production intermediates. Not surprisingly, the GRT incentivizes tax-avoidance behaviors, such as establishing out-of-state subsidiaries or pursuing vertical integration, whereby corporations eliminate the number of "steps" in production to limit GRT liabilities.

Many policymakers are aware of GRT-induced tax pyramiding and pursue incremental policy changes to lessen the effect. The solutions typically include exemptions and deductions or applying different tax rates to different industries. For example, the Texas Margin Tax requires corporate taxpayers to first determine which of four different tax bases are applicable to their receipts, then determine what proportion of those receipts originated in Texas, then determine which of two tax rates apply, and then determine which, if any, tax credits apply. The Nevada Commerce Tax classifies each of the state's businesses into one of over two dozen different categories, each of which carries a specific tax rate. These adjustments only serve to make the GRT more complicated, neutralizing any theoretical argument in their favor based on simplicity (Chamberlain and Fleenor 2006).

Other Taxes Paid by Corporations

Two other taxes on corporations are worth noting. First, businesses selling certain goods are required to collect tariffs and excise taxes and remit the proceeds to federal, state, and local governments, e.g., a tax added to tobacco products or alcoholic beverages. Those taxes are often passed through to consumers in the form of higher prices, but the responsibility for collecting the tax falls on corporate entities. Second, corporations engaged in international commerce face income and other taxes in the nations in which they transact business. What remains unique about the existing domestic federal corporate tax system is that the United States is the only developed nation that attempts to tax both domestic and foreign income. Most other nations only apply corporate taxes to income earned within their jurisdiction. The same is true for state-level corporate income tax systems within the United States.

Effective Corporate Income Tax Rates

Few corporate tax liabilities are determined solely by the system summarized in Table 4.1. Tax preferences adjust income and tax liabilities and lead to lower effective tax rates, just as they do for individual taxpayers. In 2013, C corps reported $20.2 trillion in income to the IRS. Just over 90% of that income came from the sale of goods and services. All other sources of income (e.g., investment income and capital gains) contributed less than 10%. About $19 trillion was deducted for business costs, leaving taxable corporate income of about $1.2 trillion. Of that amount, C corps paid $266.2 billion in taxes, which yields an effective overall corporate income tax rate of 22.7%, not including state and local income taxes, GRTs, property taxes, or other fees. For comparison, the Joint Committee on Taxation estimates the effective individual income tax rate is less than half the corporate rate, about 10.2%.[11]

Interestingly, effective corporate tax rates vary by industry (see Table 4.4). Corporations in the health care, education, and transportation sectors have the highest effective rates, all in excess of 30%, whereas mining, manufacturing, and food service firms have the lowest, all under 20%. Effective rates vary because each industry has unique revenue sources and cost structures and, as a result, do not qualify for the same tax preferences. Note that the effective tax rate paid by corporations in the information, mining, manufacturing, and food services industries is lower than the effective rate paid by individuals earning over $500,000 per year (refer to Table 3.7).

Taxes also vary across individual corporations. An investigation by finance website 24/7 Wall Street found that the 10 largest corporate taxpayers in the United States in 2013 were recognizable brand names (Hess and Sauter 2014). The 10 largest taxpayers were, in order: ExxonMobil, Chevron, Apple, Wells Fargo, Walmart, ConocoPhillips, J.P. Morgan, Berkshire Hathaway, IBM, and Microsoft. Each is a multinational, highly profitable conglomerate; that they incurred substantial tax burdens is not surprising. Yet the 10 smallest corporate taxpayers that year were also recognizable brand names. They were, in order: General Motors, Bank of America, Verizon, AMR

TABLE 4.4 Effective Federal Corporate Tax Rate by Industry, 2013

Industry	Rate (%)
Health Care	33.4
Education Services	32.3
Transportation	31.9
Wholesale and Retail Trades	29.9
Construction	29.8
Utilities	29.8
Real Estate	29.2
Arts and Entertainment	29.0
Agriculture	28.9
Waste Management	28.3
Professional Services	27.9
Finance and Insurance	27.6
Information	24.9
Mining	18.8
Manufacturing	18.6
Accommodation and Food Services	17.0

Source: Author's analysis of data reported in the Internal Revenue Service Statistics of Income.

Corporation, Hartford Financial, Morgan Stanley, Bristol-Myers Squibb, Rite Aid, Bunge Limited, and United Continental Holdings. Each of these corporations is also multinational, although they are less consistently profitable compared to the 10 largest corporate taxpayers. All 10 reported negative income tax expenses in 2013, meaning that the corporate entity paid no income taxes and, in fact, received a net refund from federal, state, and/or local governments. Thus, overall, some large, recognizable, multinational corporations pay tens of billions of dollars in income taxes, but other large, recognizable, multinational corporations pay nothing.

The Question of Fairness

The most reliably combative aspect of corporate income tax policy is the widespread belief that corporations do not "pay their fair share." Some 64% of respondents to a 2015 Pew Research Center poll agreed that they were bothered "a lot" by the sense that "some corporations don't pay their fair share." Individuals are understandably frustrated by stories about a particular corporation avoiding taxation by taking advantage of tax preferences or by shifting income outside of the United States. Few of those tax-avoidance strategies are available to the average individual.

Yet it is also too easy to paint all corporations with the broad stroke of unfairness. Most corporations do, in fact, pay federal income taxes as well as a host of other state and local taxes. Indeed, as discussed in the previous section, the average effective corporate income tax rate is double the average effective individual income tax rate.

Regardless of what data show, the belief in tax unfairness is facilitated by media attention to corporate scofflaws and longstanding progressive disdain for corporate tax burdens that are perceived as too low. A 2016 release from Citizens for Tax Justice, a progressive think tank and lobbying group, noted that federal corporate tax burdens in the United States, when measured as a percentage of gross domestic product (GDP), were below the average burden in other developed nations—2.3% versus 2.7%.[12] Americans for Tax Fairness, another progressive group, often points out that a significant portion of Fortune 500 companies pay no federal income taxes at all. The progressive Economic Policy Institute has argued that "It's time to raise, not lower, corporate income taxes." Over the course of his campaign, one-time 2016 presidential candidate Bernie Sanders, a socialist, repeatedly called for higher taxes on "Wall Street" and "large corporations." His opponent in the primaries, Hillary Clinton, echoed that refrain.

Of course, corporate leaders disagree with the sentiment that their employers are not paying sufficient income taxes. Defending his company's use of offshore tax structures, Apple CEO Tim Cook told a Senate committee in 2013 that his company was "the largest corporate taxpayer in America." Cook remarked that Apple paid $6 billion in federal income taxes, an effective tax rate of 30.5%.[13] That payment alone is nearly enough to fund the entire National Science Foundation.

The inherent challenge to resolving any claim about corporations or individuals not "paying their fair share" is that the phrase has no objective meaning. Federal corporate income tax collections reached $344 billion in 2015, not including income taxes paid on earnings from S corps and other pass-through entities. It is therefore undeniable that at least some corporate entities are paying federal income taxes, not to mention tens of billions of additional dollars in state and local taxes and fees. When the average federal and state corporate income tax rates are combined, corporations doing business in the United States face the highest tax burden among OECD nations (see Table 4.5). The OECD data do not include

TABLE 4.5 Top Corporate Income Marginal Tax Rate by Nation, 2016

Country	Rate (%)
United States	38.9
France	34.4
Belgium	34.0
Germany	30.2
Australia	30.0
Mexico	30.0
Japan	30.0
Portugal	29.5
Luxembourg	29.2
Greece	29.0
New Zealand	28.0
Italy	27.5
Canada	26.7
Austria	25.0
Israel	25.0
Netherlands	25.0
Norway	25.0
Spain	25.0
Korea	24.2
Chile	24.0
Denmark	22.0
Slovak Republic	22.0
Sweden	22.0
Switzerland	21.1
Estonia	20.0
Finland	20.0
Iceland	20.0
Turkey	20.0
United Kingdom	20.0
Czech Republic	19.0
Hungary	19.0
Poland	19.0
Slovenia	17.0
Ireland	12.5

Note: Includes average subnational tax burden where present.

Source: OECD Tax Database.

property taxes, local corporate income taxes, or other taxes and fees. Whether that is "fair" or not is in the eye of the beholder.

Major Federal Corporate Income Tax Preferences

Whereas many corporations pay income taxes, it is also irrefutably the case that certain corporations, in any given year, pay little or no taxes at all. This is not the result of wanton, illegal tax deceit, but a consequence of qualifying for and taking advantage of tax preferences embedded in the federal tax code by Congress. Corporate tax preferences are often christened "loopholes"—another nebulous term—but were created by the very same legislative and executive branches which, ironically, many people expect to reform corporate taxes toward a fairer orientation. "Loopholes" are little more than an unintended consequence of having a tax code in the first place. The only way to avoid them entirely is to eliminate taxes altogether.

Because tax preferences depress tax revenue below the level it would be otherwise, the value of lost revenue is considered a tax expenditure. According to the Office of Management and Budget, the cost of all federal tax expenditures for both individuals and corporations exceeded $1.3 trillion in 2015. Whereas there are over 150 separate corporate tax preferences, those preferences amounted to only about 10% of all tax expenditures. Fully 90% of all federal tax expenditures are allocated to individuals.[14]

Analysis from the Tax Foundation notes that four corporate tax preferences are most common.[15] First, the largest tax expenditure, amounting to an estimated $68 billion in 2016, results from the deferral of domestic corporate taxes on foreign earnings. American corporations that earn net income abroad do not have to pay domestic taxes on that income until the funds are repatriated to the United States. But for accounting purposes, the federal government considers taxes on foreign earnings due as soon as the income is earned. Allowing domestic corporations to hold earnings overseas and defer payment of federal taxes on those earnings until repatriation is classified as a tax expenditure.

Many other developed nations as well as American state governments do not approach corporate taxation with the global definition of income currently used by the federal government. Instead, they use territorial systems of taxation, meaning that taxes are due to the jurisdiction where income was earned. Because corporate MTRs in the United States are high—again, according to the OECD, currently the highest in the developed world—domestic corporations with foreign earnings have little incentive to repatriate those funds to the United States. High tax rates thus create a corporate income "lockout effect."

Second, some corporations deduct expenses associated with domestic production activities. This tax preference, which amounted to a tax expenditure of about $16 billion in 2016, is assumed to incent corporations to produce and manufacture goods within the United States. It allows certain corporate taxpayers to deduct 9% of either the income they earned from qualified activities or their overall taxable income, whichever is smaller. Many industries take advantage of this preference, including energy production, manufacturing, and film production. Due to the nature of their business, other industries often do not qualify, such as food and beverage sellers and real-estate firms.

Third, corporations can exclude from taxation interest earned on state and municipal bonds. Corporations have invested hundreds of billions of dollars in those bonds, and the interest they are paid in return is substantial. In 2016, this tax expenditure amounted to an estimated $11 billion for interest earned on public purpose bonds and another $3 billion for interest earned on targeted municipal bonds (e.g., those bought by corporations to construct airports, hospitals, schools, and so on). The federal government classifies this tax preference as "general purpose fiscal assistance" for state and local governments because it incentivizes corporate bond buying, thereby making it easier for state and local governments to obtain credit. At the same time, the tax incentive is also criticized for encouraging those governments to finance infrastructure projects with debt.

Fourth, some corporations take advantage of a deduction for accelerated depreciation. This deduction, which amounted to a tax expenditure of about $12 billion in 2016, allows the corporation to write off the value of certain capital assets at a faster rate than the assets actually lose value. Instead of writing off the value of a machine that lasts 10 years over a period of 10 years, for instance, accelerated depreciation might allow the corporation to write off the value over five years instead. The result is lower taxable income in the first five years and higher taxable income in the following five years, unless the corporation buys another machine at the end of the initial five-year period. That's one motivation for allowing accelerated depreciation: it incentivizes higher capital goods turnover, theoretically providing economic stimulus in the process. Far from criticizing this tax expenditure, the Congressional Budget Office suggests expanding the accelerated depreciation deduction as a way to support domestic manufacturing.[16]

Other Corporate Tax Preferences

Congress has enacted several other corporate tax preferences. Among the more popular tax deductions are those allowed for corporate investments in low-income housing (a $7.5 billion tax expenditure in 2016), charitable contributions (a $3 billion tax expenditure in 2016), and research on treatments for rare diseases, known as "orphan drugs" (a $1.8 billion tax expenditure in 2016). There are dozens of other incentives that only benefit one particular industry, inspiring accusations of unfairness. For example, net income earned by credit unions is exempt from federal corporate taxation. That tax expenditure alone amounted to $2.3 billion in 2016. The exemption's largest supporter is, as expected, the National Credit Union Association.

Corporations may also deduct the interest costs from taxable income, but this distorts purchasing decisions and results in a lack of horizontal equity. All else equal, a corporation that finances capital investments with debt incurs a lower federal income tax liability than a corporation that finances investments with cash, because they can deduct interest paid on debt from their income. If a company pays cash, they clearly do not pay any interest and hence cannot take an interest deduction. Their effective tax rate is therefore higher, which strikes many observers as unfair.

Much is often made about tax breaks for oil companies, but the tax preferences in question are nearly always open to any industry. Incentives for domestic production or depreciation may be used widely by oil companies, for example, but those deductions are not oil-specific or even energy-specific tax breaks. Any production- and capital-intensive industry will necessarily reap proportionally larger benefits from both tax preferences.

Still, the legislative and executive branches have crafted tax incentives for the benefit of specific corporations. Any C corp is allowed to offset its current income tax liability with losses incurred in earlier years. For example, if a corporation earns $1 billion this year but lost $1 billion last year, the loss may be carried forward to reduce or eliminate this year's income tax. That tax preference is usually lost if the corporation files for bankruptcy. But there is a recent, prominent exception to the rule: bankrupt corporations that received funding under the federal Troubled Asset Relief Program (TARP), more commonly known as the recession-era "bailouts." TARP participants were allowed to carry forward previous losses despite having filed for bankruptcy.

General Motors (GM) was a noteworthy beneficiary of this preference. GM's "ordered bankruptcy" process, facilitated by the Obama Administration, allowed the "new" GM to reduce its federal corporate income tax liability by carrying forward losses from the "old" GM, which was liquidated. According to the *Wall Street Journal*, regulatory filings estimated that this tax preference alone benefited the new GM to the tune of $45 billion (Smith and Terlep 2010). Not only did GM benefit from carrying forward old losses, but the Obama Administration conferred special tax treatment on the corporation's pensions, property, and equipment. Beyond all that, the Congressional Budget Office now estimates that the automotive industry bailouts were a $17 billion net loss for the federal government.[17]

Fairness and Tax Preferences in Context

Among the four largest corporate tax expenditures, three resulted from congressional efforts to shape corporate behavior toward domestic production, state and local bond investment, and capital goods purchases. The largest expenditure is driven by the United States' world-high corporate income tax rates. In utilizing these incentives, corporations are not stealing money or engaging in illegal tax maneuvers; they are operating within the tax code developed and authorized by elected officials and bureaucrats.

That has not stopped some policymakers and media outlets from suggesting otherwise. Against the backdrop of the Deepwater Horizon disaster, a front-page

TABLE 4.6 Operating Subsidies for Largest Public Transit Systems, 2015

City and System	Operating Subsidy (billions of dollars)
New York (Metropolitan Transportation Authority)	$7.6
Los Angeles (Metropolitan Transit Authority)	$3.8
Chicago (Transit Authority)	$1.2
Houston (Metropolitan Transit Authority of Harris County)	$0.8
Philadelphia (Southeastern Pennsylvania Transportation Authority)	$1.1

Source: Individual transit systems' Comprehensive Annual Financial Reports for Fiscal Year 2015.

New York Times article noted that oil companies had taken advantage of billions of dollars in subsidies they did not need (Kocieniewski 2010). An informative piece in the progressive *Mother Jones* decried tax "loopholes" that subsidize the oil industry for an estimated $3.8 billion per year (Kroll et al. 2014). President Barack Obama, during a Rose Garden news conference in 2012, called for an end to those tax breaks with the savings redirected toward clean energy development.

What is curious about corporate tax subsidies, not only for oil companies but in general, is that critics avoid criticizing subsidies for other industries. Television and film productions receive tens of millions of dollars in federal tax subsidies, but they attract no attention. Or consider the subsidies pumped into public transit systems—infamous "money pits" that do not come close to covering their operating costs through passenger fares. Their operating deficits are subsidized through ever-increasing taxes, grants, and other funding sources. Those subsidies easily reach the tens of billions of dollars. Table 4.6 lists the operating subsidies for each of the United States' five largest cities' transit systems. The total subsidy for these five systems alone was $14.5 billion in 2015, nearly four times the oil subsidies criticized by *Mother Jones*.

Corporate Tax Policy Issues: Avoidance and Competition

Widespread utilization of corporate tax preferences and the related question of their fairness, or lack of it, has fed into a much larger debate about corporate income tax reform. Federal and state deliberations have centered on two dimensions: regulating corporate tax-avoidance strategies and maintaining competitiveness with other governments.

Targeting Tax Avoidance by Regulating Tax Inversions

A tax inversion, sometimes referred to as a corporate inversion, is a relatively recent approach to reduce corporate income tax liabilities. The strategy involves moving a corporation's headquarters to a nation with lower taxes, thus shifting the corporation's tax residence from the United States to a "tax haven" or other nation with lower tax rates. The move is often technical and legal only; most, if not all, employees and operations remain located in the United States.[18] Following inversion, the "new" corporation is headquartered in another country and can minimize exposure to American corporate income taxes.

Whereas the United States has had a permanent corporate income tax since 1909, the first inversion is widely reported to have taken place in 1982. That year, an American construction company with a subsidiary located in Panama, McDermott Incorporated, "inverted" its corporate structure by turning its subsidiary into McDermott's parent company. The entire transaction was motivated by a desire to avoid domestic taxes.

Corporations can achieve a tax inversion through either a self-inversion or through a merger or acquisition. Self-inversion entails reincorporating the American entity in another nation, similar to the McDermott inversion. Another strategy is for an American corporation to merge with a foreign counterpart and establish the new entity's headquarters in the nation with lower taxes. Under both approaches, foreign earnings are locked out of the United States.

Tax inversions have recently gained notoriety. When United States-based Burger King announced its intention to merge with Canada-based Tim Hortons in 2014, and to headquarter the new entity in lower-tax Canada, it did not take observers long to note that the inversion would reduce Burger King's corporate tax burden. "Tax Dodging Whopper?" wondered news website Democracy Now.

The burger merger was nothing compared to the firestorm that erupted in 2016 when Pfizer, a corporation headquartered in the United States, announced a merger with Allergan, an Irish corporation. Ireland, not coincidentally, has the world's lowest corporate income tax rate. With headquarters in Ireland, the inverted Pfizer–Allergan corporation would incur hundreds of millions of dollars in lower taxes compared to a United States-centered operation.

Progressives were apoplectic. At a news conference, President Barack Obama described corporate tax inversion as an "insidious tax loophole." Democratic presidential candidate Hillary Clinton told the audience at a labor union gathering in Pennsylvania, "They call it an inversion. I call it a perversion." A March 18, 2016, letter from Democratic presidential candidate Bernie Sanders to Treasury Secretary Jack Lew urged the Obama Administration to block the merger. "Large multi-national corporations should not be able to avoid paying U.S. taxes when children in America go hungry" he wrote. "We must demand that these profitable corporations pay their fair share in taxes."

Both before and after the Pfizer brouhaha, the Treasury Department took steps to reduce the benefits of tax inversions and curb corporate tax avoidance. In 2014, Treasury authorized new rules aimed at restricting "hopscotch loans" in which a United States-based corporation could obtain funds from one of its foreign subsidiaries or parent company but avoid taxes, because under then-current law, the loan proceeds were not considered taxable income. A corporation could, shockingly, claim a tax deduction for interest paid on loans to their own subsidiaries.

Treasury issued additional restrictions in 2016 that again targeted hopscotch loans and tax inversions. The most recent set of rules stipulate that if 80% or more of an inverted corporation is owned by American shareholders, then for tax purposes, the inverted entity is considered an American corporation.

Treasury's regulations were not without effect. Pfizer called off the Allergan merger less than two days after the new regulations were issued. In a *Wall Street Journal* editorial, Pfizer CEO Ian Read wrote:

> Surely we benefit from world-class academic institutions, a highly skilled labor force and other attractions of doing business in the U.S. But the key point is so do our foreign competitors. And they pay significantly less for the privilege.

He continued:

> If the rules can be changed arbitrarily and applied retroactively, how can any U.S. company engage in the long-term investment planning necessary to compete? The new "rules" show that there are no set rules. Political dogma is the only rule.

Negative reactions to the Treasury rules were not limited to Pfizer. The Organization for International Investment, a business trade group, said:

> The Administration's sweeping proposal will increase the cost of investing and expanding across the United States for all foreign companies and put at risk more than 12 million American workers that are supported by foreign direct investment in the United States.

Two weeks after the inversion rules were announced, Kevin Brady, Republican chair of the House Ways and Means Committee, suggested in a speech before the United States Chamber of Commerce that the Obama Administration may have exceeded their authority by changing tax policy through regulation, not legislation.

Income-shifting to low-tax jurisdictions is not only an issue with American corporations. Many other nations have found that corporations headquartered within their jurisdiction move some income out of their jurisdiction to avoid taxation. The most popular tax havens are Bermuda, the Cayman Islands, the British Virgin Islands, Liberia, Bahamas, Barbados, and Cyprus. This tax-avoidance practice is more generally known as base erosion and profit shifting (BEPS) because it lowers the tax base in one nation by shifting income to another. The OECD estimates that BEPS strategies lower global corporate income tax revenues between 4% and 10%.[19]

Targeting Tax Avoidance by Regulating the "Double Irish"

Some multinational corporations, particularly those in intellectual property-intensive sectors, avoid income taxes by employing a "double Irish arrangement," a legal restructuring scheme that resembles a tax inversion. Under a double Irish, the corporation remains headquartered in the United States but creates one or more subsidiaries in tax havens. The American corporation licenses its intellectual property (e.g., patents and trademarks) to its subsidiaries for a fee. Those foreign subsidiaries then collect all revenues, pay expenses, and retain net income for goods and services sold internationally. Net income remains locked outside the United States and avoids domestic taxation.

The arrangement is called a "double Irish" because it technically involves two foreign subsidiaries, both of which are established by the American parent corporation. The first subsidiary licenses intellectual property from the American parent. This subsidiary is chartered as an Irish corporation, but it is located and managed in a tax haven like Bermuda or the Cayman Islands. Because the subsidiary is chartered as an Irish corporation but managed elsewhere, the subsidiary incurs no Irish corporate tax, because Irish tax law establishes tax residence based on where a corporate entity is managed. Because the subsidiary is both incorporated and managed outside the United States, it also escapes domestic taxes. At present, the United States does not have a tax treaty or other agreement with Ireland to resolve this inconsistency.

The second subsidiary is an Irish corporation managed in Ireland. It sells products overseas and pays the first subsidiary for the use of intellectual property. But the second subsidiary avoids most, or all, Irish taxes because it is allowed to deduct licensing costs from income. Because the second subsidiary is not chartered as an American corporation and is managed in Ireland, it also avoids domestic corporate taxes.

Both Apple and Google have exploited the double Irish or similar schemes for decades and have been widely criticized for doing so. But as was the case with tax inversions, salience of the tax-avoidance strategy inspired policy change. Ireland announced in 2014 that it would cease to allow new double Irish arrangements, but that corporations using existing schemes could continue until 2020. From that point forward, entities incorporated in Ireland are considered Irish corporations for tax purposes, meaning they can no longer use Irish incorporation but non-Irish management to avoid tax residence.

Irish corporate income tax rates remain well below those in the United States. Irish incorporation under the new rules, which may change again, will grow less beneficial but will remain more advantageous than repatriating earnings under current domestic tax policy.

Tax Competition and Reform

The popularity of corporate tax-avoidance strategies has increased attentiveness to the importance of recognizing global tax competition. Evidence suggests that nations engage in strategic tax policymaking (e.g., Altshuler and Goodspeed 2015; Devereux et al. 2008) and that competition has had a reductive effect on corporate income tax rates globally (Leibrecht and Hochgatterer 2012). It is thus critical to the United States' economic vitality that corporate tax policy remain competitive. Luckily, there is fairly broad, bipartisan consensus that the corporate income tax system needs reform.

While corporations may support tax reform in spirit, in practice most have little incentive to lobby in favor of eliminating parts of existing policy that prove favorable to their bottom line (e.g., beneficial tax preferences). Individual corporations, industry-specific trade groups, and general business groups directly and through political action committees often lobby aggressively to maintain the status quo as it applies to their constituencies. That strategy can prove to be quite lucrative. By one measure, the benefits of corporate lobbying exceed benefits of investing in the stock market.[20]

Interest groups and think tanks offer some counterweight to corporate tax policy influence, and there is, surprisingly enough, agreement across the political spectrum that corporate lobbying is not a net benefit to civil society. Progressive coalitions detest the practice, and so do many libertarian and conservative groups, including the Cato Institute, American Enterprise Institute, Heritage Foundation, and Reason Foundation. "Corporate lobbying is the ultimate tragedy of the commons" wrote the conservative *National Review* in 2015 (Drutman 2015a; see also Drutman 2015b).

Beyond those rare points of agreement, there is insufficient consensus on the best way forward. Within progressive ranks, there is a significant fissure over corporate tax reform. Many progressives favor increasing corporate income taxes. Citizens for Tax Justice, Americans for Tax Fairness, the Economic Policy Institute, and several Democratic candidates for higher office have all called for taxes on corporations that exceed the status quo. But other progressives favor revenue-neutral approaches that eliminate many tax preferences and align MTRs with those in other developed nations.

Conservatives agree with reforming tax preferences and lowering rates, but of course there are disagreements over which incentives to keep, which incentives to eliminate, and how to adjust MTRs. Some conservatives go much further and advocate wholesale elimination of all corporate income taxes, rationalizing that the incidence falls on individuals and that double taxation is unfair, inefficient, and onerous.

Consider the simple illustration in Table 4.7, which shows how the effective tax rate on C corp income can approach 60% as a result of double taxation—or quadruple taxation, depending on one's perspective and whether they live in a state that taxes corporate dividends.[21] Under other scenarios that account for different state-level treatment of corporate income, the effective rate can easily exceed 50%, indicating a significant disincentive for savings and investment and a strategic disadvantage for the United States relative to other OECD nations, where effective rates tend to be lower (Pomerleau 2015).

TABLE 4.7 Simplified Illustration of Double Taxation of Corporate Income

	Tax Rate	Dollar Amount
Corporate Pre-Tax Income		$100.00
Less Federal Corporate Income Tax	35%	$35.00
Less California State Corporate Income Tax	8.84%	$8.84
Equals Distribution to Shareholder		$56.16
Less Shareholder's Federal Dividend Tax	15%	$8.42
Less Shareholder's California State Income Tax	9.3%	$5.22
Equals Net Post-Tax Distribution		$42.52
Addendum: Effective Tax Rates		
Federal	43.42%	
State	14.06%	
Combined	57.48%	

Source: Author's analysis using simplified assumptions regarding an individual California resident with $100,000 in labor income and shareholder participation in a California-headquartered C corp with overall net income in excess of $18.3 million in 2016.

Regardless of partisan differences, federal corporate tax reform remains a herculean task because policymakers must balance domestic policy goals against the reality of a competitive global economic environment. It is exceedingly hard to accomplish domestic reform goals in a global economy populated with nations that want to accomplish their own policy objectives, which necessarily cater to their own domestic preferences. That environment is also constantly affected by geopolitical events, such as the United Kingdom's exit from the European Union. Once the United Kingdom officially severs from European Union tax rules, the tax competition landscape will change in a way that was not anticipated as recently as the day of the "Brexit" vote. Although the OECD and United Nations push members to work together on corporate tax reform, the issue remains an as-yet unresolved collective action problem.

Below federal and international attention, corporate tax competitiveness is a major theme across state governments. State and municipal governments face domestic and international competition over economic development catalysts, including manufacturing facilities and business centers. To "win" such developments, state and municipal officials often promise generous tax incentives and, in many cases, offer direct public investment. Consider the competition in 2014 between Arizona, Texas, California, and Nevada for Tesla Motors' so-called "gigafactory." Nevada ultimately won the bidding competition, but not before offering tax incentives valued at over $1 billion, including millions in tax credits, a 10-year waiver on property taxes, and a 20-year waiver on sales taxes.

Evidence suggests that state corporate tax competition does not pay off. Multiple studies indicate that state tax incentives and income tax rate reductions do not yield sustained, positive economic outcomes. Incentives often have insignificant, null, or negative effects (Peters and Fisher 2004; Thom 2016; Wilder and Rubin 1996). Tax reductions do not increase income, job growth, or gross state product (Prillaman and Meier 2014). Many explanations have been offered to explain these findings, but in general, intergovernmental competition is sometimes a zero-sum game that benefits one jurisdiction at the expense of another (Wilson 2009). It can also provoke a "race to the bottom" (Costa-Font et al. 2015; Zheng and Warner 2010). And as state tax incentives have proliferated, each incentive's marginal benefit has declined (Calcagno and Thompson 2004). Yet state corporate tax incentives remain popular; for many election-minded policymakers, the lure of a ribbon-cutting ceremony is too much to resist.

Conclusion: Who Really Pays Corporate Income Taxes?

Speaking at the Iowa State Fair in 2011, Republican presidential candidate Mitt Romney suggested that one way the federal government could meet Social Security, Medicare, and Medicaid entitlement obligations was to "raise taxes on people." Hecklers interrupted Romney, shouting that taxes should instead be increased on "corporations." His now-infamous retort, "corporations are people my friend," was met with shouts of "no they're not!"

> Everything corporations earn ultimately goes to people. Where do you think it goes? asked Romney.
> Into their pockets!
> Whose pockets? People's pockets. Human beings, my friend.

Although neither the *New York Times* nor the *Washington Post* covered Romney's "human beings" remark, he had a point—perhaps the most important point that any corporate tax policy discussion should address: who actually pays corporate income taxes? If the corporate entity is chartered as an S corp or other pass-through entity, then the point is moot. The corporation doesn't pay taxes; individual shareholders do. Those actual human beings directly and unquestionably pay the "corporate" tax.

A comparable argument can be made about the incidence of taxes on C corps, but the tax-shifting possibilities make tracing the incidence more difficult. Given that C corps are fundamentally organizations of individuals (shareholders and employees) buying materials from another group of individuals (suppliers) in turn serving another group of individuals (customers), their corporate tax burden will be shifted to some combination thereof. If taxes reduce corporate income, then shareholders receive smaller dividends and consequently pay less taxes on those dividends, even as the dividends remain double-taxed.[22] If the corporation raises prices, then the incidence is shifted to customers. If the corporation alters its mix of inputs, then the incidence falls on suppliers. If corporate taxes induce lower wages and benefits, then the incidence falls on employees.[23]

Research generally supports the idea of corporate tax-shifting, although findings are not consistent. Examining data on OECD nations from 1981–2009, Clausing (2013) uncovered little to no evidence that incidence was shifted to employees. Clausing speculated that the null result may be due to enormous challenges in econometric modeling of capital flows and the implications for labor in a global economy, which are further complicated by the reality of tax-avoidance strategies. Time presents an additional challenge to quantifying tax-shifting. If a corporate entity faces tax law changes in a particular month, it likely cannot adjust salaries, benefits, or prices until months, or years, into the future. Looking only at the United States, Liu and Altshuler (2013) found a significant wage effect of corporate taxation. Their analysis suggests that each dollar in corporate taxes reduces wages by 60 cents. Other studies have also found that corporate taxes have a depressive effect on wages (e.g., Hassett and Mathur 2015). However, corporate structure modulates tax incidence. The generally lower tax rates charged to S corps benefit employees and owners, but not customers, compared to C corps (Donohoe et al. 2015).

If corporate income taxes are eventually shifted to individuals, why not abandon the tax completely? One factor working against repeal, not to mention cuts to existing rates, is the perception of unfairness. Recall that a majority of the public believes corporations are not paying their "fair share." Progressives and some conservatives have carried that mantle for over a century. And this, despite the fact that corporations benefit from only 10% of federal tax expenditures and pay, on average, an effective income tax rate that is double the rate paid by individuals.

Another undermining factor is the perception that incidence-shifting does not occur and that corporations are autonomous taxpaying entities. That perception is particularly acute among progressives who, as discussed in Chapter 1, conceptualize the state as a central organism rather than a collection of individuals, and perhaps view corporate entities through a similar lens. Progressives also have a tendency to blame corporate tax problems on corporations rather than on the elected officials and experts who both created the "loopholes" and failed to anticipate them in advance.

Regardless of ideology, many people agree with what the Supreme Court explicitly stated in its 1911 decision upholding the corporate income tax: that corporate entities enjoy unique benefits from being allowed to operate in a corporate capacity. In theory and in accordance with the benefit principle, corporate entities should thus render a portion of their income to the state. In essence, this rationale is a corporate variant of the social contract.[24]

Most importantly, a belief persists that corporate and individual income taxes represent a tradeoff. If corporations pay income taxes, then many individuals assume they personally pay less than they would otherwise. If corporate taxes are reduced or eliminated, then many individuals worry that their taxes will increase. The corporate income tax is likely to continue in some form well into the future, if for no other reason than that people are too afraid of life without it.

Notes

1 *Pollock v. Farmers' Loan & Trust Company*, 157 U.S. 429 (1895).
2 *Flint v. Stone Tracy Co.*, 220 U.S. 107 (1911). Constitutionality of a federal tax on corporate income was bolstered, and all further disputes nullified, by ratification of the Sixteenth Amendment in 1913.
3 The case further alleged that the corporate income tax originated in the Senate rather than the House of Representatives, as required by the Constitution, and was thus unconstitutional. Because the tax resulted from a Senate amendment to a bill that originated in the House, the Court rejected the argument.
4 Under this definition, the state itself and each of its bureaucracies are corporate entities.
5 American courts have generally said that corporate entities do and do not, respectively. Note that some nonprofit corporate entities (e.g., houses of worship) jeopardize their tax-exempt status by commenting on political matters, whereas others (e.g., labor unions) clearly do not. The Supreme Court has further ruled that corporate entities have other rights, such as equal protection. See *Santa Clara County v. Southern Pacific Railroad Company*, 118 US 394 (1886).
6 That does not exempt nonprofit organizations from reporting financial information to the federal government (e.g., IRS Form 990).
7 Capital gains and losses also pass through to shareholders.
8 S corps, C corps, and partnerships file different tax forms with the IRS. Most LLCs file as partnerships, but some file as S or C corps.
9 Most of the remainder of this chapter explores income taxation of C corps. The process for pass-through entities better matches Chapter 3's examination of individual income taxes.
10 Nonlinear corporate income MTRs were first introduced in 1940 and lasted until 1949. The existing rate structure can be traced to the Deficit Reduction Act of 1984, which added a 5% tax to corporate income between $1,000,000 and $1,405,000. The surcharge was intended to compensate for the fact that corporations benefited from the lower MTRs that had been previously implemented to help small businesses, not large corporations. The 5% tax did not apply to income earned above $1.4 million. That MTR system more or less continued through 1993, when the Omnibus Budget Reconciliation Act of 1993 added the 35% and 38% rates in effect today.
11 See Joint Committee on Taxation, "Overview of the Federal Tax System as in Effect for 2016," Report Number JCX-43–16.
12 By this measure, which did not appear to include state and local income tax burdens or other taxes, the domestic corporate tax burden is still higher than the burden in France, Spain, and Germany.
13 At the hearing, Republican Rand Paul defended Apple, remarking "Tell me one of the politicians up here who doesn't minimize their taxes."
14 See Office of Management and Budget, "Analytical Perspectives," 2016.
15 See Alan Cole, "Corporate and Individual Tax Expenditures," The Tax Foundation Fiscal Fact No. 476, 2015.
16 See Congressional Budget Office, "Federal Policies and Innovation," 2014.
17 See Congressional Budget Office, "Report on the Troubled Asset Relief Program," 2015.
18 Wages may also be lowered indirectly. In theory, reallocation of corporate resources from high-tax to low-tax jurisdictions increases labor demand in the low-tax jurisdiction, causing an increase in wages, but decreases labor demand in the high-tax jurisdiction, causing a decrease in wages.
19 See OECD, "OECD/G20 Base Erosion and Profit Shifting Project Explanatory Statement," 2015.
20 See "Money and Politics" in the October 1, 2011, edition of *The Economist*.

21 Under this scenario, the total effective tax rate on corporate income for an individual with an income of $50,000 is 56.7%. For an individual with an income of $500,000, the effective rate is 61.1%.
22 Many of the largest shareholders of publicly traded corporations in the United States are, in fact, pensions and retirement plans; therefore, corporate income taxes harm those plans' financial performance.
23 Obviously, there are additional tax consequences and ripple effects based on the behavioral responses of shareholders, customers, suppliers, and employees to corporate tax-shifting. Those discussed here are only the initial possibilities.
24 One other major institution in civil society that involves two individuals agreeing to work in a collective capacity—marriage—confers lower, not higher, tax liabilities on the participants.

References

Altshuler, Roseanne, and Timothy J. Goodspeed. 2015. "Follow the Leader? Evidence on European and US Tax Competition." *Public Finance Review* 43(4): 485–504.

Calcagno, Peter T., and Henry Thompson. 2004. "State Economic Incentives: Stimulus or Reallocation?" *Public Finance Review* 32(6): 651–665.

Chamberlain, Andrew, and Patrick Fleenor. 2006. "Tax Pyramiding: The Economic Consequences of Gross Receipts Taxes." The Tax Foundation Special Report No. 147.

Clausing, Kimberly A. 2013. "Who Pays the Corporate Tax in a Global Economy?" *National Tax Journal* 66(1): 151–184.

Costa-Font, Joan, Filipe De-Albuquerque, and Hristo Doucouliagos. 2015. "Does Interjurisdictional Competition Engender a 'Race to the Bottom'? A Meta-Regression Analysis." *Economics & Politics* 27(3): 488–508.

Devereux, Michael P., Ben Lockwood, and Michela Redoano. 2008. "Do Countries Compete Over Corporate Tax Rates?" *Journal of Public Economics* 92(5–6): 1210–1235.

Donohoe, Michael P., Petro Lisowsky, and Michael A. Mayberry. 2015. "Who Benefits from the Tax Advantages of Organizational Form Choice?" *National Tax Journal* 68(4): 975–997.

Drutman, Lee. 2015a. "Corporate Lobbying: Bad for Business, Bad for America." *National Review*, July 28, 2015.

Drutman, Lee. 2015b. *The Business of America Is Lobbying: How Corporations Became Politicized and Politics Became More Corporate*. New York: Oxford University Press.

Due, John F. 1957. *Sales Taxation*. Urbana: University of Illinois Press.

Hassett, Kevin A., and Aparna Mathur. 2015. "A Spatial Model of Corporate Tax Incidence." *Applied Economics* 47(13): 1350–1365.

Hess, Alexander E.M., and Michael B. Sauter. 2014. "Companies Paying the Most Taxes." *24/7 Wall Street*. Retrieved from http://finance.yahoo.com/news/companies-paying-most-taxes-174550448.html

Hodge, Scott A. 2016. "The Compliance Costs of IRS Regulation." The Tax Foundation Fiscal Fact No. 512.

Ippolito, Dennis S. 2012. *Deficits, Debt, and the New Politics of Tax Policy*. Cambridge: Cambridge University Press.

Kocieniewski, David. 2010. "As Oil Industry Fights a Tax, It Reaps Subsidies." *The New York Times*, July 4, 2010.

Kroll, Andy, Benjy Hansen-Bundy, and Alex Park. 2014. "Triumph of the Drill." *Mother Jones*, April 14, 2014.

Leibrecht, Markus, and Claudia Hochgatterer. 2012. "Tax Competition as a Cause of Falling Corporate Income Tax Rates: A Survey of Empirical Literature." *Journal of Economic Surveys* 26(4): 616–648.

Liu, Li, and Roseanne Altshuler. 2013. "Measuring the Burden of the Corporate Income Tax under Imperfect Competition." *National Tax Journal* 66(1): 215–238.

Mikesell, John L. 2007. "Gross Receipts Taxes in State Government Finances: A Review of Their History and Performance." Joint Report of the Tax Foundation and the Council on State Taxation.

Peters, Alan, and Peter Fisher. 2004. "The Failures of Economic Development Incentives." *Journal of the American Planning Association* 70(1): 27–37.

Pomerleau, Kyle. 2015. "Eliminating Double Taxation through Corporate Integration." Tax Foundation Fiscal Fact No. 453.

Prillaman, Soledad Artiz, and Kenneth J. Meier. 2014. "Taxes, Incentives, and Economic Growth: Assessing the Impact of Pro-business Taxes on U.S. State Economies." *Journal of Politics* 76(2): 364–379.

Smith, Randall, and Sharon Terlep. 2010. "GM Could Be Free of Taxes for Years." *The Wall Street Journal*, November 3, 2010.

Thom, Michael. 2016. "Lights, Camera, but No Action? Tax and Economic Development Lessons from State Motion Picture Incentive Programs." *American Review of Public Administration*. doi: 10.1177/0275074016651958

Wilder, Margaret G., and Barry M. Rubin. 1996. "Rhetoric versus Reality: A Review of Studies on State Enterprise Zone Programs." *Journal of the American Planning Association* 62(4): 473–491.

Wilson, Daniel J. 2009. "Beggar Thy Neighbor? The In-State, Out-of-State, and Aggregate Effects of R&D Tax Credits." *The Review of Economics and Statistics* 91(2): 431–436.

Zheng, Lingwen, and Mildred Warner. 2010. "Business Incentive Use among U.S. Local Governments: A Story of Accountability and Policy Learning." *Economic Development Quarterly* 24(4): 325–336.

PART III
Taxes on Consumption

5

TAXING EVERYDAY CONSUMPTION

Tariffs, Excises, and Sales Taxes

Individuals are hard-pressed to avoid paying the taxes added to or already factored into the price of certain goods and services, generally referred to as consumption taxes. The chief distinction between income and consumption taxes is the tax base: rather than placing a levy on individual or corporate income, consumption taxes are levied on the good or service price. Funnily enough, consumption taxes are often the first tax an individual ever pays. Long before earning taxable wages, young adults pay sales taxes on the items they purchase.

Many analysts view consumption taxes as the optimal substitute for taxes on income (e.g., Bankman and Weisbach 2005; Goldberg 2013; Seidman 1997).[1] Consumption taxes do not harbor the disincentives for labor or savings that are characteristic of income taxes, particularly graduated tax rates, which have been linked to lower economic growth among OECD nations (e.g., Widmalm 2001). Consumption taxes are also simpler in structure and administration. The levy is often a flat *ad valorem*, or percentage-based, tax multiplied by the price of a good or service. The tax is collected by the seller, who then remits the proceeds to the appropriate governmental institution. There are no confusing tax rate structures, complicated forms, or tax preferences.

Consumption taxes are also less coercive than many other forms of taxation, thus avoiding much of the conflict between private property rights and state authority. Rather than taxing resource acquisition, consumption taxes are levied on voluntary resource exchanges. Small wonder that Hobbes wrote in *Leviathan*: "when impositions are laid on those things which men consume, every man pays equally for what he uses."

Consumption taxes cannot avoid the same normative and economic concerns as income taxation, including fairness, equity, and incidence. A consumption tax on food can yield a stable revenue stream, something policymakers desire, but has a disproportionate impact on individuals of lesser means—the very regressivity that policymakers wish to avoid (Kwak 2013). Consumption taxes also allow policymakers to target certain goods or services with negative externalities—e.g., those that are considered "sins" or "vices"—with a corrective tax, an option that the income tax does not allow. By the same token, vice taxation raises questions about equity and fairness, and a new question about policy efficacy: do taxes on the vices accomplish public health and other hoped-for outcomes?

Consumption taxes span the governmental spectrum. Some are exclusively federal (e.g., tariffs), some are used at both the federal and state levels (e.g., excise taxes), and some are prevalent at the state and local levels (e.g., retail sales taxes). This chapter explores standard, everyday consumption taxes, with an emphasis on the history, impact, and political and policy implications of tariffs, excise taxes, and various forms of retail sales tax. The following chapter emphasizes taxes on particular vices, including tobacco products, alcoholic beverages, marijuana, and sugar.

Tariffs

Background and Structure

A tariff, also referred to as a duty, a customs duty, a customs tax, or an import tax, is a targeted consumption tax or fee added to the price of imported goods by the recipient nation.[2] Tariffs in the United States are administered by Customs and Border Protection (CBP), a federal agency housed within the Department of Homeland Security, as well as the federal Department of Commerce. Tariffs are usually applied to dutiable goods, a classification that includes international purchases brought into the United States as well as the value of alterations or other improvements made abroad to domestic goods. Dutiable goods' value must be declared to CBP by the importer within 15 days of arrival.[3] In general, tariffs are levied on goods ranging from food and beverages to live animals, jewelry, clothing, artwork, ammunition, and natural resources. Tariff rates are published in the Harmonized Tariff Schedule of the United States, a document that exceeds 2,700 pages in length.

Tariffs on a specific good vary by nation of origin, thereby entangling federal tax law and trade policy. For example, the United States does not charge a tariff on orange juice imported from Australia, but orange juice imported from Morocco carries a tariff of 1.2 cents per liter. The tariff on orange juice imported from any other nation is 4.5 cents per liter unless that nation has a trade agreement with the United States that stipulates otherwise. Similarly, there is no tariff on a goat imported into the United States from Bahrain or Chile, but goats imported from several other nations are charged a tariff of either $0.68 or $3.00 each. Depending on the nation of origin, green tea could have no tariff at all or a tariff as high as 20%; conversely, there are no tariffs on imported black tea.

History

Tariffs are one of the world's oldest forms of taxation, but they are more accepted today than in ancient times. As described in the New Testament, the apostle Matthew was a wealthy but unpopular tariff collector in Capernaum. Tax collectors in those days were often the subject of public hatred for collecting more than their legal mandate and pocketing the difference. When challenged for associating with "tax collectors and sinners," Jesus Christ did not exactly leap to Matthew's defense.[4]

Tariffs are also one of the oldest sources of revenue in the United States. Before the nation existed as a sovereign entity, many colonies charged tariffs on European imports. One of the first major pieces of legislation enacted by the United States federal government was, in fact, the Tariff Act of 1789. The Act established tariff rates ranging from 5% to 20% and included rewards for individuals that reported smuggling or inaccurate invoicing to the government (Studenski and Krooss 1952). One early argument in favor of tariffs was the ability to pay principle. Since those of higher economic means were more likely to purchase imported goods, tariff incidence fell on them rather than those of lesser means (Bartlett 2012).

For over 100 years, tariffs supplied nearly all revenue to the federal treasury. Until 1907, tariffs provided at least half of all federal revenue and, as recently as 1936, provided one out of every five federal dollars. But their proportional contribution to the treasury dropped rapidly after the close of World War II. By 2015, around 1% of federal revenue was derived from tariffs (see Figure 5.1).

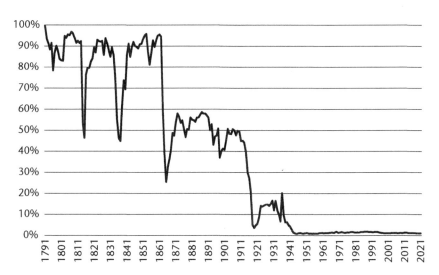

FIGURE 5.1   Tariffs as a Percentage of Total Federal Revenue, 1791–2016 with Projections to 2021

Sources: Author's analysis of data reported in the *Historical Statistics of the United States, 1789–1945*, the *Historical Statistics of the United States, Colonial Times to 1970, Part 2*, and by the Office of Management and Budget.

FIGURE 5.2   Federal Tariff Revenue, 1791–2011, in Constant Dollars

Sources: Author's analysis of data reported in the *Historical Statistics of the United States, 1789–1945*, the *Historical Statistics of the United States, Colonial Times to 1970, Part 2*, and by the Office of Management and Budget.

Tariffs' declining proportional contribution is not the result of declining revenue. On the contrary, tariff revenue has increased, even after adjusting for inflation, reaching just over $35 billion in 2015 (see Figure 5.2). Tariffs' reduced share has more to do with other tax policy changes, especially the large postwar income and payroll tax increases.

Tariff Policy and Politics

Tariffs were politicized from the earliest days of the United States. Initial policy conflicts centered on which goods to tax, by how much, and how to adjust tariffs according to revenue demands and a changing geopolitical landscape. Policymakers from northern, manufacturing-heavy states embraced the protectionism inherent to tariffs; policymakers from the agriculture-dominant south were less favorable. By the late nineteenth century, tariffs were fundamental to political party splits over federal income taxes. Many progressives and Democrats favored tariff cuts funded by new personal and corporate income taxes; many Republicans did not subscribe to that approach. The Wilson–Gorman Tariff Act of 1894 reduced tariffs in exchange for new income taxes, but only temporarily.

In the postwar era, tariffs have continued to remain part of the larger conversation about the merits of free trade. Over 80% of economists agree that tariffs and other protectionistic policies, such as import quotas, reduce social welfare (Mankiw 2015). Tariffs raise the price of imported goods above their market price, incentivizing domestic producers to raise their prices and output, thus making them better off. But faced with higher prices, consumers reduce consumption and are worse off. More generally, tariffs distort the allocation of scarce resources and, like any tax, impose deadweight losses on the economy.

On the other hand, protectionists and some economists believe tariffs level the playing field between the United States and other nations that engage in uncompetitive behaviors, such as currency manipulation or domestic industry subsidies. In this view, tariffs serve to protect American corporations and jobs from unfair trade.[5] For example, several American steelmakers filed a complaint with the Department of Commerce in 2015 alleging that certain foreign competitors were engaged in "dumping," a form of predatory pricing in which a producer sells a good below cost in order to increase sales and gain market share. A producer can afford dumping if, for instance, the producer receives a state subsidy. A federal investigation found merit in the steelmakers' complaint, and the Obama Administration announced increased steel tariffs in early 2016. The new duties ranged from 266% on Chinese steel imports, equivalent to the size of China's subsidy of its own steel industry, to less than 10% on imports from nations including Brazil, India, Russia, and Japan.

As this case illustrates, tariff policy is ripe for regulatory capture in which members of Congress or the bureaucracy act in accordance with an industry's demands instead of the public good.[6] Capture renders tariff policy favorable to those with political connections and may rob consumers of lower-priced goods, an economically inefficient outcome. Manipulating policy in this way can have negative consequences. Tariffs placed on goods from a particular nation may prompt that nation to retaliate with tariffs of their own on American goods. If that occurs, policymakers' efforts to protect one domestic industry end up hurting another.

Steel industry tariffs have not received the same level of political attention as the North American Free Trade Agreement (NAFTA). NAFTA, which took effect in 1994, eliminated a host of tariffs between the United States, Canada, and Mexico. Supportive policymakers, businesses, and economists hailed the agreement as a "win" for all three nations. NAFTANow.org, a website maintained jointly by the Canadian, American, and Mexican governments, touts a tripling of trade among the nations as well as strong job growth, among other economic successes.

But NAFTA has committed detractors, including labor unions, environmental protection groups, and consumer rights groups. American union officials have long believed that NAFTA undermined the domestic manufacturing industry, leading to job losses and lower wages. Public Citizen, a prominent lobbying organization, argues that free-trade agreements like NAFTA are a contributing factor to rising income inequality in the United States. Opposition to NAFTA has attracted strange political bedfellows. Two 2016 presidential candidates—Bernie Sanders, a socialist Democrat, and Donald Trump, a Republican—campaigned in their respective primaries against NAFTA, promising audiences to abandon or renegotiate the agreement if elected.

Many of the same tensions surfaced when the Trans-Pacific Partnership (TPP), a trade agreement between the United States and 11 Pacific Rim nations, was signed in 2016.[7] The pact reduced or eliminated some 18,000 tariffs, including those on most agricultural and manufactured goods originating in the United States, a move expected to benefit small- and medium-sized exporters (Gerwin 2015). But progressive economists, including Joseph Stiglitz and Robert Reich, argued TPP would exacerbate income inequality. That position was echoed by progressive think tanks, including the Economic Policy Institute. A legislative alert from the United Auto Workers described the TPP as "worse than NAFTA." Skepticism again reached across the aisle; the conservative American Enterprise Institute characterized the TPP as having "severe weaknesses" (Scissors 2015).

Excise Taxes

Background and Structure

An excise tax is a tax levied on a particular domestic good, service, or activity. Excise taxes are used by the United States federal government as well as all 50 state governments. In a point of contrast with European-style value-added taxes, domestic excise taxes are usually charged at the end of production or at the point of service delivery. Excises vary based on the nature of the good, service, or activity, the price charged, and the quantity sold or consumed. The federal government currently charges over 50 different excise taxes (see Table 5.1).

Because excises are most often embedded in the price of a good or service, they are less transparent to consumers than a retail sales tax. Indeed, many consumers are surprised to find out that certain goods or services are taxed at all. Most common vaccines, including those for MMR, chicken pox, hepatitis A and B, and seasonal influenza, were taxed at $0.75 per dose in 2015. Since the MMR vaccine contains three separate doses (one each for measles, mumps, and rubella), the excise was actually $2.25. But vaccine excises are not reported separately from the vaccine's price. Likewise, the excise on fishing rods in 2015 was an ad valorem tax of 10% with a $10 limit per rod, whereas the excise on tackle boxes was a relatively small 3%. Again, because these taxes are embedded in the cost of a fishing rod and tackle box, respectively, most consumers have no idea the excise exists. Perhaps more surprisingly, private foundations—often

TABLE 5.1 Examples of Goods and Services Subject to Federal Excise Taxation

Fuel and Transportation Taxes:	Goods and Services:
• Petroleum★	• Tires★
• Diesel Fuel★	• Gas Guzzler Vehicle Tax
• Kerosene★	• Vaccines★
• Gasoline★	• Health Insurance Plans
• Liquefied Petroleum Gas	• Fishing Equipment★
• Liquefied Hydrogen	• Electric Outboard Motors
• Compressed Natural Gas	• Archery Equipment
• Other Liquid Fuels★	• Indoor Tanning Services
• Coal★	• Local Telephone Service
• Inland Waterways Fuel★	• Ozone-Depleting Chemicals
• Passenger Transportation by Water	
• Air Transportation	

Note: Asterisk (★) denotes multiple taxes may apply depending on the use or quantity of the good.

Source: Internal Revenue Service.

described as tax-exempt organizations—pay an excise tax of 1% or 2% on net investment earnings, depending on the level of distribution from the foundation to beneficiaries.

The federal government collects tens of billions of dollars in excise taxes each year (see Table 5.2). Fuel excises comprise the largest single generator of tax revenue, but billions of dollars are also collected on alcohol and tobacco taxes, discussed further in Chapter 6, as well as excises on firearms, sports equipment, and coal. About 70% of excise revenues are collected by the IRS; the remainder are collected by other federal agencies, including the Bureau of Alcohol, Tobacco, and Firearms and the Transportation Security Administration.

Some excise revenue, like tariff revenue, is used to support general government operations, but certain revenue streams are directed toward specific programs. Revenue from the tax on fishing equipment, first authorized in 1950 by the Sport Fishing Restoration Act, is pooled with other excise taxes (e.g., levies on small motors and certain types of fuel) in the Sport Fish Restoration & Boating Trust Fund. This federal program allocates funding to coastal state fisheries, conservation programs, and environmental initiatives. Revenue from the vaccine excise tax is allocated to the Vaccine Injury Compensation Trust Fund, a federal program that since 1988 has provided funding for individuals harmed by Centers for Disease Control and Prevention-approved vaccines. Revenue from the excise tax on indoor tanning services is not specifically earmarked to fund Affordable Care Act subsidies, but was nevertheless used in cost estimates to illustrate that the Act would be deficit-neutral.

TABLE 5.2 Largest Federal Excise Taxes by Revenue, 2013

Category	Revenue (in millions)
Gasoline and Diesel Fuel	$ 33,607.92
Tobacco Products	15,146.18
Air Transportation	14,418.94
Alcoholic Beverages	10,028.32
Trucks, Trailers, and Tractors	3,321.70
Other Fuel Taxes	1,745.73
Medical Devices	1,404.28
Telephone	773.70
Firearms and Ammunition	762.84
Coal	570.66
Private Foundations	505.69
Vaccines	313.26
Sports Equipment	163.69
Tanning Services	91.66

Notes: Total for "Alcoholic Beverages" includes taxes on domestic and foreign products; "Other Fuels Taxes" includes excises on kerosene, aviation fuels, and liquid fuels (e.g., hydrogen, natural gas, petroleum gas) in addition to environmental fees; "Air Transportation" revenues do not include Passenger Facility Charges.

Sources: Internal Revenue Service Statistics of Income and the Transportation Security Administration.

History

Much like tariffs, excise taxes were among the federal government's first revenue sources, but their contribution to the federal treasury has traced a different path. The Tariff Act of 1789 included a number of taxes on popular vices, including alcohol, tobacco, and sugar. Because the Act placed greater emphasis on tariffs, excise taxes did not supply large revenues until many were increased during the Civil War. Postwar cuts returned excise contributions to their lower pre-war levels. Subsequent ratification of the Eighteenth Amendment made it impossible to place an excise tax on alcohol, at least until the end of Prohibition. Excise taxes were increased during the Great Depression and, once again, grew to provide a greater share of federal revenue, but only temporarily. Since the end of the Great Depression, excise revenue as a proportion of overall federal revenue has dwindled (see Figure 5.3). Although excise taxes today represent less than 5% of federal revenue, collections in 2015 amounted to nearly $100 billion (see Figure 5.4).

State governments charge excise taxes on everything from alcohol, tobacco, and fuel to insurance plans and real estate. As with the federal government, states previously relied on excise taxes for a greater proportion of revenue, but that reliance has declined (see Figure 5.5). Nevertheless, states collect relatively more revenue from excises taxes than the federal government, both as a percentage of own-source revenue and in dollar terms (see Figure 5.6).

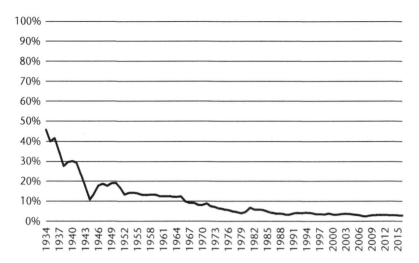

FIGURE 5.3 Excise Taxes as a Percentage of Total Federal Revenue, 1934–2015

Note: Data are either unavailable or unreliable for years prior to 1934.

Sources: Author's analysis of data reported in the *Historical Statistics of the United States, 1789–1945*, the *Historical Statistics of the United States, Colonial Times to 1970, Part 2*, and by the Office of Management and Budget.

FIGURE 5.4 Federal Excise Tax Revenue, 1934–2015, in Constant Dollars

Note: Data are either unavailable or unreliable for years prior to 1934.

Sources: Author's analysis of data reported in the *Historical Statistics of the United States, 1789–1945*, the *Historical Statistics of the United States, Colonial Times to 1970, Part 2*, and by the Office of Management and Budget.

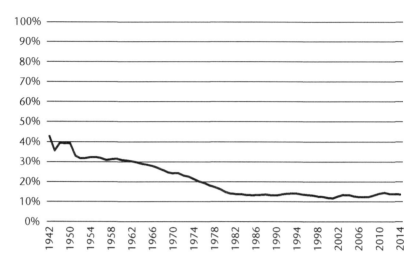

FIGURE 5.5 Excise Taxes as a Percentage of Total State Own-Source Revenue, 1942–2014

Source: United States Census Bureau Annual Survey of State Government Finances.

FIGURE 5.6 State Excise Tax Revenue, 1942–2014, in Constant Dollars

Source: United States Census Bureau Annual Survey of State Government Finances.

A Closer Look at Common Excise Taxes

Motor Fuels

The largest federal excise is the tax included in the price of gasoline and diesel fuel (refer to Table 5.2). The first federal gasoline tax—just one cent per gallon—was enacted in 1932. But it was not until Congress established the Highway Trust Fund in 1956 that revenues were dedicated solely to transportation funding. In the following decades, Congress increased fuel excise taxes several times. By 2016, the tax stood at 18.4 cents per gallon of gasoline and 24.4 cents per gallon of diesel. After adjusting for inflation, excise rates per gallon are at neither their highest nor their lowest historical levels (see Figure 5.7). Note that the diesel tax was first implemented in 1951 and was equal to the gasoline tax through 1983. Beginning in 1984, the diesel tax was raised above the gasoline tax.

Fuel prices paid by consumers also include state and sometimes local excise taxes. State-level fuel taxes predate the federal tax; in 1919, Oregon, North Dakota, Colorado, and New Mexico became the first state governments to tax gasoline. Within a decade, and ever since, all 50 states have charged a fuel tax. State fuel excises assume multiple structures, including a flat rate per gallon, regardless of price; an ad valorem tax based on price, regardless of quantity; a tax on fuel wholesalers; and additional environmental fees. Like the federal government, many states apply different rates to gasoline and diesel fuel (see Table 5.3).

Combined federal and state gasoline tax revenues exceeded $67 billion in 2012, not inclusive of excise taxes on diesel and other motor fuels. States collect more revenue in the aggregate from gasoline taxes than the federal government (see Figure 5.8), which should be expected given that most of their excise rates are higher than the current federal rate (refer to Table 5.3).

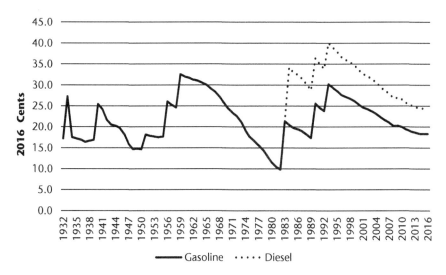

FIGURE 5.7   Federal Gasoline and Diesel Fuel Excise Tax per Gallon, 1932–2016, in Constant Dollars

Source: Federal Highway Administration.

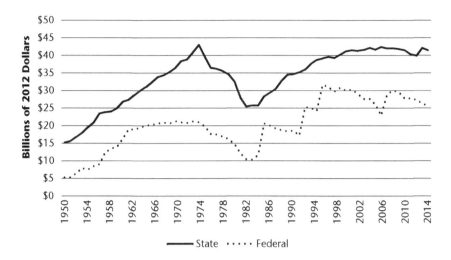

FIGURE 5.8 Federal and State Gasoline Excise Tax Revenue, 1950–2014, in Constant Dollars

Sources: Author's analysis of data reported in the *Historical Statistics of the United States, Colonial Times to 1970, Part 2,* by the Office of Management and Budget, the Federal Highway Administration, and the United States Census Bureau Annual Survey of State Government Finances.

TABLE 5.3 Gasoline and Diesel Excise Taxes by State, 2016

State	Gasoline	Diesel Tax	Gas Rank	Diesel Rank
Alabama	20.87	21.85	40	40
Alaska	12.25	12.75	50	50
Arizona	19.00	27.00	43	29
Arkansas	21.80	22.80	38	38
California	40.62	34.30	5	10
Colorado	22.00	20.50	37	41
Connecticut	37.51	50.30	6	2
Delaware	23.00	22.00	34	39
Florida	36.58	33.77	7	12
Georgia	31.02	34.66	17	8
Hawaii	42.35	39.55	4	5
Idaho	32.00	32.00	14	18
Illinois	30.18	33.40	20	14
Indiana	29.89	38.81	23	6
Iowa	32.00	33.50	15	13
Kansas	24.03	26.03	31	32
Kentucky	26.00	23.00	30	36
Louisiana	20.01	20.01	41	42
Maine	30.01	31.21	21	19
Maryland	32.60	33.35	13	15
Massachusetts	26.54	26.54	29	30

State	Gasoline	Diesel Tax	Gas Rank	Diesel Rank
Michigan	30.54	28.49	18	26
Minnesota	28.60	28.60	25	23
Mississippi	18.79	18.40	45	44
Missouri	17.30	17.30	46	47
Montana	27.75	28.50	27	25
Nebraska	27.70	27.10	28	28
Nevada	33.85	28.56	10	24
New Hampshire	23.83	23.83	33	34
New Jersey	14.50	17.50	49	46
New Mexico	18.88	22.88	44	37
New York	42.64	42.10	3	4
North Carolina	35.25	35.25	8	7
North Dakota	23.00	23.00	35	35
Ohio	28.00	28.00	26	27
Oklahoma	17.00	14.00	47	49
Oregon	31.10	30.36	16	20
Pennsylvania	50.40	65.10	1	1
Rhode Island	34.00	34.00	9	11
South Carolina	16.75	16.75	48	48
South Dakota	30.00	30.00	22	21
Tennessee	21.40	18.40	39	45
Texas	20.00	20.00	42	43
Utah	29.41	29.41	24	22
Vermont	30.46	32.00	19	17
Virginia	22.33	26.03	36	31
Washington	44.50	44.50	2	3
West Virginia	33.20	34.60	11	9
Wisconsin	32.90	32.90	12	16
Wyoming	24.00	24.00	32	33

Note: All taxes are listed as cents per gallon.

Source: American Petroleum Institute.

Air Transportation

The federal government charges several excise taxes on air transportation. For domestic travel within the United States, passengers incur the following charges:

- An ad valorem tax based on the amount paid for air transportation (i.e., the airline ticket price). The rate is currently 7.5% and has been unchanged since 1999.
- A segment fee based on the number of flight segments in an itinerary (i.e., the number of landings per trip). The segment fee is currently $4 and is indexed to inflation. In 2015, the ad valorem tax and segment fee together amounted to over $9 billion in revenue.

- A September 11 Security Fee, also referred to as a Passenger Fee. The fee is currently $5.60 per passenger per one-way trip with a maximum of $11.20 for each round trip. Total September 11 Security Fee revenue in 2015 was approximately $3 billion, an all-time high.
- A Passenger Facility Charge (PFC). The charge varies by airport, with a maximum of $4.50 per passenger per flight segment with a maximum of $9 per one-way trip or $18 per round trip.[8] Total PFC revenue in 2015 was approximately $3 billion.

Excise taxes on international travel and cargo shipments differ from those levied on domestic travel, but generated approximately $3.6 billion in revenue in 2015.

No single federal agency administers air transportation excise taxes. The IRS administers the ad valorem and segment taxes, the Transportation Security Administration administers the September 11 Security Fee, and the Federal Aviation Administration administers the PFC program.[9] The federal government retains all revenues except PFC proceeds, which are reallocated to airports to fund capital projects, increase security, or enhance airport performance. Certain other excise revenues are channeled into the Airport and Airway Trust Fund along with fuel excise revenues. The funds are used to support the Federal Aviation Administration and the Department of Transportation's controversial Essential Air Services Program, which subsidizes air carriers that provide service to rural airports.

Communications

Perhaps the most vexing excise taxes are those added to the monthly price of landline and wireless communication services. It is not unusual for a consumer to notice that their monthly statement itemizes a dozen or more taxes and fees, some of which are federal, some of which are state, some of which are local (either a county-based levy, a city-based levy, or both), and some of which are not taxes at all but provider-specific service charges. Adding to the confusion, communication excise taxes are labeled with a dizzying array of abbreviations that are defined in fine print elsewhere on the statement, if at all.

The most widespread of all voice communication taxes are Universal Service Charges (USC), sometimes labeled as Universal Service Fees (USF) or Universal Connectivity Charges (UCC). The Telecommunications Act of 1996 required that providers, including telephone companies, wireless carriers, and cable television providers that offer voice services, all contribute a percentage of revenues to the federal Universal Service Fund. The proceeds are then allocated to four different programs established by the Federal Communications Commission but administered by a separate entity, the Service Administrative Company. Those programs are aimed at increasing voice and high-speed internet access to rural areas, low-income individuals, schools, libraries, and health care providers. Communications providers pass their federally mandated contributions to customers with a percentage-based

USC, USF, or UCC. To finance the cost of complying with communications taxes, the federal government allows providers to charge an extra fee to customers.

Some state governments maintain their own universal service programs over and above the federal program, with contributions drawn from providers that, in turn, forward-shift the burden to customers. For example, the Texas Universal Service Fund results in an excise tax of about 3% on the price of applicable services. In California, six different taxes for universal service programs add up to a total excise tax of about 8.5%.

Consumers face several other taxes for telephone service. Landline customers are charged a 3% federal excise on local but not long-distance telephone service.[10] Many local governments charge taxes to fund 911 and emergency service costs, which may be a flat rate per household or line of service or an ad valorem tax. Many states add their retail sales tax to the price of wireless service, and over a dozen states charge a higher rate on wireless service compared to the sales tax on other goods and services. Some state and local governments add even more miscellaneous taxes and fees for each extra line of service.

Add all the federal, state, and local wireless taxes together, and the effective tax rate can be astonishingly high. In 2014, for instance, the effective excise tax rate ranged from a low of 7.59% in Oregon to a high of 24.42% in Washington. For consumers with multiple lines of service, the burden is higher yet, as much as 32% in Baltimore and 35% in Chicago (Mackey and Henchman 2014). High local taxes on cellular service have one definite impact: reducing the number of individuals with access to a cellular phone (Mitchell and Stratmann 2015).

Excise Policy and Politics

Revenue Stagnation and Alternatives

One of many ongoing issues faced by policymakers is how to respond in the event that a good or service that generates excise tax revenue is displaced by technology or falls victim to changing consumer demands. Consider the recent history of federal telephone excise tax revenue (see Figure 5.9). After adjusting for inflation, revenue plunged 90% between 2000 and 2013 as landline telephone service was displaced by cellular phones and internet-based communications services.[11] Both federal and state policymakers have likewise realized that fuel tax revenues have stagnated, which constrains the amount of funding available to finance transportation projects and maintain existing assets—the costs of which are anything but constrained. Indeed, Figure 5.8 suggests that states' fuel tax revenues have remained mostly unchanged for nearly 20 years, whereas federal revenues are lower now than they were in 1994. That stagnation is the result of market forces. Revenues are dependent not only on the price of oil, which is dynamic, but also on consumer demand for gasoline and diesel fuel. Efficiency gains in internal combustion engines, the rising electrification of motor vehicles, and dispersion of

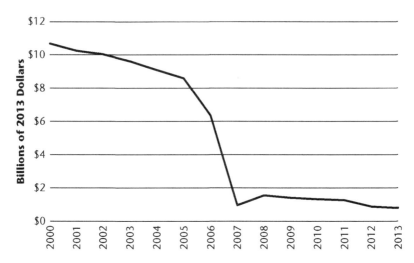

FIGURE 5.9   Federal Landline Telephone Excise Tax Revenue, 2000–2013, in Constant Dollars

Source: Internal Revenue Service Statistics of Income.

mass transit systems have exerted tremendous downward pressure on fuel demand and hence fuel tax revenue.

Consequently, federal and many state policymakers have begun to reconsider the role of fuel taxes as an instrument to fund transportation projects. One obvious solution is a straightforward increase in the existing gasoline tax, but that option is not popular with the public. A 2013 Gallup poll found that 66% of Americans would, given the chance, vote against a 20-cent per gallon tax increase. A 2015 poll conducted by the Mineta Transport Institute found 71% of Americans would favor a smaller 10-cent tax increase, providing that the proceeds were specifically dedicated to road maintenance. If the tax revenue were instead used to fund general transit projects, support for a hypothetical 10-cent increase plunged to 31%.

Another alternative is an excise tax based not on the number of gallons consumed but on the number of miles driven, which reflects a direct application of the benefit principle. Proposals under this approach call for a new tax or charge to replace existing excises, commonly referred to as vehicle-miles traveled (VMT) fees, mileage-based user fees (MBUF), and road usage charges (RUC). A 2016 report from the Congressional Budget Office suggested that federal and/or state governments should recalibrate per-gallon fuel taxes toward a VMT system in which the cost of using roads is more directly charged to the amount a driver uses them.[12] Many state governments are studying this alternative, and two have implemented programs. Oregon initiated a voluntary pilot program in 2015 called "OReGO." Instead of fuel excise taxes, participants pay a fee of 1.5 cents per mile traveled. Illinois has rolled out a similar program, but participation is limited to trucks and certain commercial vehicles.

However, the public is unsupportive of applying the benefit principle to road funding through a usage-based tax (Duncan et al. 2014). A 2016 study from the National Academy of Sciences concluded that the mean level of support across dozens of polls on the subject was just 24%.[13] Given that assessing a tax based on road usage would require a government agency to track a driver's origin, destination, route, distance traveled, and perhaps time traveled, a major source of opposition is worry over a loss of personal privacy. Public opinion polls also reflect concerns about fairness. Some people fear that they would pay more under a usage tax; others complain that they should not be punished for owning and operating a fuel-efficient vehicle.

The cost of administering VMTs, MBUFs, and RUCs is also higher than the existing excise system. A usage tax would require a significantly different administrative infrastructure. Whereas the existing system costs approximately 1% of revenues administer, a usage tax could cost between 5% and 6% (Sorensen et al. 2012). Assuming no change in how revenues are spent and holding all else equal, the tax burden under a VMT-style framework would have to rise to cover the cost of collecting the tax.

Transparency

Excise taxes are often criticized for their lack of transparency, more so than tariffs, which most consumers have less interaction with. Air transportation taxes are a prime example. Federal regulations require that airlines disclose to customers how much of the price of airfare is the actual fare versus how much is government-imposed taxes and fees. But depending on the airline, a consumer may or may not receive a clear, detailed explanation of the taxes included in the price of airfare. Because excise taxes are a mixture of ad valorem and flat taxes, consumers rarely have a sense for the total excise tax burden as a percentage of the ticket price. Just as with individual income taxes, determination of the effective excise tax rate is rare.

Complicating matters further, air transportation excise taxes vary depending on the flight. A passenger paying a base fare of $500 for a non-stop, round-trip ticket from Los Angeles to New York would pay a total of $65.70 in excise taxes, an effective tax rate of 13.1%. If the same passenger pays the same base fare for the same trip that includes a layover in Detroit—or any other city—federal excise taxes increase to $82.70, for an effective rate of 16.5%.[14] In other words, nonstop flights are taxed at a lower rate than flights with layovers.

Confusion over airfare taxes has led to dueling proposals for reform. The Transparent Airfares Act, introduced in 2014, would allow airlines to advertise to customers using base fares (i.e., pretax price) as long as the airline also informs customers of the excise taxes incurred by each trip. The bill was favored by airline industry groups, including Airlines for America, which argue that forcing airlines to advertise the total cost of airfare (i.e., base fares plus all excise taxes) hides the tax burden from consumers, facilitating a lack of transparency. A competing bill, the Real Transparency in Airfares Act of 2016, would leave existing rules in place (i.e., airlines must advertise using the total cost of a ticket) and increase the fine on airlines that fail to advertise using total costs. This particular bill, opposed by Airlines for America, had support from the U.S. Travel Association which, as Elliott (2014) notes, represents hotels that are allowed to advertise pretax rates to customers. Neither bill has made it out of committee.

The Role of Interest Groups

As witnessed in the politics of air transportation excise taxes, no excise would be complete without attracting interest group attention. Some groups lobby in favor of new or reformed excise taxes. For example, road usage fees have their own interest group, the Mileage-Based User Fee Alliance. Other groups lobby against taxes. The Council on Foundations opposes the federal excise on foundations, arguing that the tax and the cost of compliance diminish the resources that foundations can distribute to beneficiaries. The excise tax on tanning services is opposed by Indoor Tanning Association and the American Suntanning Association, which has argued the tax led to a 53% drop in the number of tanning salons and a 51% drop in tanning salon employment, with most of the burden falling on female owners and employees.[15] Americans for Tax Reform also criticized the tanning tax after actual revenues were about two-thirds less than the Obama Administration's original estimates (Anderegg 2015).

Sales Taxes

Most state and local governments in the United States levy sales taxes. But "sales tax" is a broad term. In practice, state and local governments utilize one or more discrete types of sales tax: retail sales taxes, use taxes, and transient occupancy taxes.

Retail Sales Tax

A retail sales tax (RST) is a tax added to the price of goods and services at the point of sale. Since the RST is itemized separately on the transaction receipt or proof of sale, the tax is more transparent to consumers than a tariff or excise. Consumers are also more likely to be directly impacted by a RST. Although most consumers rarely face tariffs and pay excise taxes on only certain items, 45 state governments have enacted a RST. The exceptions are Alaska, Delaware, Montana, New Hampshire, and Oregon.

Whether measured in aggregate or per-capita terms, state RST revenues have grown sharply (see Figure 5.10 and Figure 5.11, respectively). Most states direct RST revenue toward funding general government operations and public education. Many of those states further allow local governments to levy a separate RST on purchases made within their jurisdiction. Such local option sales taxes (LOST) may be charged at the county level, the city level, or both, with revenue often used

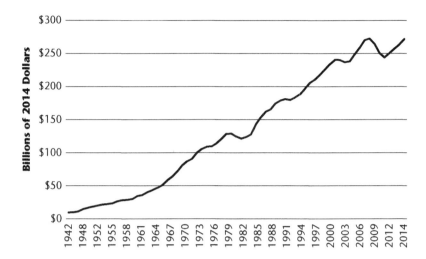

FIGURE 5.10 Aggregate State Retail Sales Tax Revenue, 1942–2014, in Constant Dollars

Source: United States Census Bureau Annual Survey of State Government Finances.

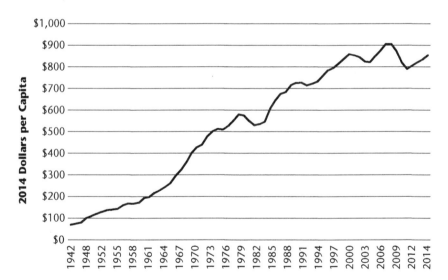

FIGURE 5.11 State Retail Sales Tax Revenue per Capita, 1942–2014, in Constant Dollars

Source: Author's analysis of data reported in the United States Census Bureau Annual Survey of State Government Finances and the Current Population Survey.

to fund local government operations, public education, infrastructure, or mass transit.[16] Local governments may pursue sales taxes in response to limits on their ability to raise other revenue, especially property taxes (Alfonso 2014; Jung 2001). Table 5.4 lists each state's RST rate and, where applicable, LOST rates.

TABLE 5.4 Retail Sales Tax Rates and Local Option Sales Tax Range by State, 2016

State	State Rate	LOST (Low)	LOST (High)
Alabama	4.00%	0.00%	8.50%
Alaska	0.00%	0.00%	7.50%
Arizona	5.60%	0.00%	7.10%
Arkansas	6.50%	0.00%	5.50%
California	6.25%	1.25%	3.75%
Colorado	2.90%	0.00%	8.00%
Connecticut	6.35%	0.00%	1.00%
Delaware	–	–	–
Florida	6.00%	0.00%	1.50%
Georgia	4.00%	1.00%	4.00%
Hawaii	4.00%	0.00%	0.50%
Idaho	6.00%	0.00%	3.00%
Illinois	6.25%	0.00%	4.75%
Indiana	7.00%	–	–
Iowa	6.00%	0.00%	2.00%
Kansas	6.50%	0.00%	5.00%
Kentucky	6.00%	–	–
Louisiana	5.00%	0.00%	7.75%
Maine	5.50%	–	–
Maryland	6.00%	–	–
Massachusetts	6.26%	–	–
Michigan	6.00%	–	–
Minnesota	6.88%	0.00%	1.00%
Mississippi	7.00%	0.00%	1.00%
Missouri	4.23%	0.50%	6.63%
Montana	–	–	–
Nebraska	5.50%	0.00%	2.00%
Nevada	6.85%	0.00%	1.30%
New Hampshire	–	–	–
New Jersey	7.00%	–	–
New Mexico	5.13%	0.13%	6.63%
New York	4.00%	0.00%	5.00%
North Carolina	4.75%	2.00%	3.00%
North Dakota	5.00%	0.00%	3.00%
Ohio	5.75%	0.00%	2.25%
Oklahoma	4.50%	0.00%	6.50%
Oregon	–	–	–
Pennsylvania	6.00%	0.00%	2.00%
Rhode Island	7.00%	–	–
South Carolina	6.00%	0.00%	3.00%
South Dakota	4.00%	0.00%	2.00%
Tennessee	7.00%	1.50%	2.75%
Texas	6.25%	0.00%	2.00%
Utah	4.70%	1.00%	6.25%
Vermont	6.00%	0.00%	1.00%

State	State Rate	LOST (Low)	LOST (High)
Virginia	4.30%	1.00%	2.20%
Washington	6.50%	0.50%	3.40%
West Virginia	6.00%	0.00%	1.00%
Wisconsin	5.00%	0.00%	1.75%
Wyoming	4.00%	0.00%	4.00%

Sources: The Tax Foundation and the Sales Tax Institute.

Use Tax

A use tax is akin to a RST but applies to goods consumed, stored, or otherwise used within a particular jurisdiction that were purchased outside that jurisdiction. The use tax and RST are mutually exclusive, meaning that a good can only incur one of the two. Currently, 45 state governments—all of those that have a RST—have authorized a use tax.

In most cases, a use tax liability is incurred by interstate purchases, such as when a consumer buys goods online from an out-of-state retailer but that retailer does not collect the consumer's applicable RST. This sort of transaction produces a tax disparity versus the alternative, wherein the consumer buys the same good from an in-state vendor and pays the applicable RST. For example, if a consumer purchases a $100 watch in their home state and that state levies a 7% RST, the seller would collect $7 in taxes on the purchase and remit that amount to the state government. But if the consumer purchased the same watch for the same price from an out-of-state retailer, that retailer may or may not collect a sales tax. If the retailer is an online merchant, or "remote retailer," in many cases no RST is collected at all. If the watch were instead purchased from a brick-and-motor retailer while the consumer is traveling, the consumer would more than likely only pay a RST where the purchase was made but not in their home state, where the watch was used or otherwise "consumed."

Use taxes are paid directly by the consumer. The reasons for this structure are both practical and legal. It would be difficult for retailers to keep track of myriad RST and LOST rates, much less collect and remit the proceeds to hundreds of different governments. More importantly, the Supreme Court has ruled that a state government cannot compel an out-of-state vendor, including remote retailers, to collect that state's RST. A state can only require RST and LOST collections of vendors that have a nexus, or physical presence, within their jurisdiction.[17]

Tracking these sorts of purchases, especially for individual consumers, is practically impossible and is not appreciably easier for retailers. State and local governments that levy a use tax consequently rely on voluntary compliance. Technically, consumers are required to keep track of purchases that would normally incur a state RST or LOST but did not, perhaps because of online, catalog, or vacation shopping, and then remit the applicable use tax to their state or local government each year. In 27 states, consumers are supposed to report their use tax liability on their state income tax return.

Compliance with that procedure is very low. According to a report from the Minnesota state legislature, less than 5% of all income tax returns in those states report a use tax liability. The state where participation was highest, Maine, had a compliance rate of just 10.2%.[18] In states without income taxes, such as Texas, consumers are mandated to complete a separate form and remit their use tax to the state government, but few people actually do so.

Transient Occupancy Tax

A transient occupancy tax (TOT), also referred to as a hotel occupancy tax, a lodging tax, or a bed tax, is an ad valorem tax added to the price of temporary accommodations. TOTs may be levied by state and/or local governments. In fact, temporary accommodations in some jurisdictions are subject to state, county, and city TOTs in addition to standard RST and LOST rates (see Table 5.5). Governments typically direct TOT revenues to fund general operations, infrastructure projects, economic development programs, and tourism initiatives.

TOTs may appear straightforward but are often complicated to legislate and implement. Aside from determining a TOT rate, policymakers must pay careful attention to how terms are defined, similar to the sugar-sweetened beverage tax discussed in Chapter 2. In particular, a jurisdiction must define both "temporary"— i.e., what defines whether a person's transiency is, in fact, temporary— and "accommodations"—i.e., the types of lodging or other accommodations that will incur a tax liability. "Temporary" could mean anything from an overnight

TABLE 5.5 Transient Occupancy Taxes in Select Cities, 2016

City	Taxes
New York	8.875% state and county sales tax plus $1.50 flat rate per night of occupancy plus 5.875% city hotel tax and another flat rate of $2.00 per night of occupancy; total is 14.75% plus flat rate
Los Angeles	14.0%, city only
Chicago	6.0% state hotel operators tax + total of 5.9% city tax rates
Houston	6.0% state tax + 4.0% county tax + 7.0% city tax
Philadelphia	8.5% city tax
Phoenix	1.8% county tax + 5.3% city tax
San Antonio	6.0% state tax + 1.8% county tax + 9.0% city tax
San Diego	Between 11.05% and 12.5%, city only
Dallas	6.0% state tax + a city tax of between 7% and 9%
San Jose	10%, city only

Note: In some cities, the retail sales taxes also apply.

Source: Individual city websites.

stopover that is best measured in mere hours, to a relocation, to an extended-stay facility that lasts weeks or months.

The duration element and its relationship to TOT applicability is important. TOTs in some jurisdictions have been the subject of legal challenges on this very question. Critics have argued that some temporary stays are not long enough to establish a taxable nexus and, consequently, TOTs should not be levied on those temporary stays. Others contend that TOTs charged in most jurisdictions are unfair because the tax is disproportionately greater than the public services consumed by the taxpayer (Nemerofsky 2001).

The definition of "accommodations" is even more critical. Historically, TOTs applied to the price of rooms booked at hotels and motels, but more recently policymakers have had to judge whether TOTs should also apply to home rentals, timeshares, and even campsite reservations. Defining the tax treatment of home rentals is imperative, given the popularity of services like Airbnb that allow homeowners to rent their homes, in whole or in part, to travelers, thereby reducing hotel and motel bookings and hence local TOT revenues (Gottlieb 2013). Application of TOTs to nontraditional accommodations raises further issues. For instance, which party is responsible for collecting the tax—the service that facilitates the rental or the property owner? And do nontraditional accommodations qualify for TOTs in the first place if the owner of an Airbnb property is already paying other state and local taxes?

Some state and local governments have also revisited TOT statutes in light of the sustained popularity of online travel reservation services. Some are built on an "agency model" in which the service collects a commission from hotels as compensation for booking rooms on their behalf. But many other online travel services are built on a "merchant model" in which the service purchases a block of rooms from hotels at a discounted rate and resells the rooms to customers at a marked-up price, which includes the room cost and a profit margin. This begs the question of whether TOTs should apply to the discounted rate or the marked-up rate. If the latter, then the TOT functions in part as a corporate income tax. Statutory language on this question is not consistent across governments, and court decisions thus far are ambiguous (Melvin 2012).

One final issue with TOTs, like excise taxes, is a potential lack of transparency. Many travelers have booked accommodations at an advertised price only to find, usually when checking out, that the real price is noticeably higher because TOTs (state, county, and/or local) were not included in the advertised price. The situation is analogous to that involving airfare prices, which federal regulations mandate include base airfare prices as well as all applicable excise taxes.

Additional Retail Sales Tax Policy Issues

Tax Competition and Strategic Behavior

As with corporate income taxation, state and local governments engage in strategic policymaking with respect to RST policy. Local governments may look to consumption taxes as compensation for slack in other revenue streams (Hoene 2004), and decisions regarding state RSTs and LOSTs are affected by policies in effect in other states (Fletcher and Murray 2006; Sjoquist et al. 2007). One of the issues policymakers often confront is that, if the RST (and LOST) burden in their jurisdiction is too high relative to a bordering jurisdiction, then the burden incentivizes cross-border shopping. In other words, if a consumer living in a jurisdiction with a high RST can easily travel to a jurisdiction with a lower tax and obtain the same goods or services, then that consumer can rationally be expected to spend more money in the lower-tax jurisdiction. Research indicates that cross-border shopping to evade taxes is substantial (Fox et al. 2014). But relative to the overall volume of RST-generating transactions, the revenue impact is small, perhaps reducing revenues by less than 1% (Alm and Melnik 2012).

Sales Tax Holidays

For a number of reasons, some state governments regularly institute a sales tax holiday (STH), a limited period of time during which certain purchases do not incur the state's usual RST. Put another way, an STH is a period in which the state suspends its own RST, and perhaps LOSTs as well. The first known tax holiday occurred in 1980, when Michigan and Ohio waived taxes on new vehicle purchases. In 2016, 14 states instituted holidays lasting anywhere from two to seven days. Six of those states instituted multiple holidays.[19]

Some policymakers view a STH as an opportunity to incentivize consumers to buy targeted goods. For example, Texas, Missouri, and Virginia have instituted holidays for the purchase of Energy Star-certified appliances. During the STHs in Louisiana and Alabama, RSTs are waived on the purchase of certain hurricane preparedness supplies. Policymakers also view STHs as a family-friendly tax program, one that benefits those with lower incomes (Ruano 2008). Indeed, many states establish a holiday during the August "back to school" shopping season and exempt clothing, footwear, technology, and other education-related goods from taxation.

Tax competition also plays a role in establishing STHs. When Massachusetts instituted a two-day STH in 2004, in part to keep residents from making purchases in neighboring New Hampshire—which has no sales tax—New Hampshire responded in kind by taking out an advertisement in the *Boston Globe* that read: "365 vs. 002 . . . Tax Free Shopping Days (for those of you keeping score)."

Despite the attractiveness of STHs to policymakers and consumers, observers have questioned the wisdom of STHs. In 2000, two states, Indiana and Illinois, held fuel tax holidays that lasted for four and six months, respectively, and Florida and Georgia held similar holidays in 2004 and 2005, respectively. Whereas these tax holidays reduced consumer gasoline prices, they did so at the expense of reduced transportation funding. The 2015 STHs in Mississippi and Louisiana exempted the purchase of firearms, ammunition, and other hunting supplies, raising the ire of gun control advocates. South Carolina's 2015 holiday exempted school supplies and clothing, but also arguably less essential goods, like shower curtains.

Evidence also indicates that STHs are ineffective at increasing consumer spending and tax revenues (Mikesell 2006), so much so that one analyst described them as "dumber than a bag of hammers" (Brunori 2001). One study found that retailers engage in strategic pricing behavior during STHs, either by raising prices or eliminating or reducing price discounts, thereby capturing about 20% of the benefits that would otherwise flow to consumers (Harper et al. 2003). In retailers' defense, of course, the cost of implementing and complying with an STH falls entirely on them, and disproportionately so on smaller businesses.

Sales tax holidays do not necessarily compel higher consumption, but they are more likely to induce consumers to change the timing of some purchases they already planned on making (Cole 2009). Thus, consumers delay certain purchases or make purchases earlier than they would otherwise, simply to take advantage of the incentive, thereby lowering sales tax revenues. The Massachusetts Department of Revenue estimated that the state's 2013 STH reduced tax revenue by about $25 million, but the added economic activity prompted by the holiday generated less than $3 million (Downing 2014). Thus, the state's STH was a net loss.

Most importantly for tax administrators, implementing STHs requires significant attention to detail. Some policy parameters are fairly basic, such as how many holidays to have, how long they should last, and when they should occur. Policymakers must also determine if the STH is for individual consumers, businesses, or both, and be clear about defining which businesses qualify. Other aspects of establishing an STH are not so simple. For example, is the holiday a one-time affair, one that requires annual reauthorization, or one that is permanent? To what goods or services does the holiday apply? Is there a spending cap and, if so, how much and on what goods? Who is responsible for monitoring compliance and how do they accomplish it? Is the spending cap per-person for all purchases or is the cap a one-time, point of sale cap? How does the STH interact with LOST, where present? Can retailers and/or local governments opt out of participating?[20]

The prospect of an STH attracts attention from think tanks and interest groups. Policy institutes as politically diverse as the Tax Foundation and the Institute on Taxation and Economic Policy have denounced STHs as ineffective. But state and local retailer groups often lobby in favor of tax holidays, believing that their members' sales will increase as a result. In states where a tax holiday is conferred only on certain goods, interest groups associated with industries that do not benefit lobby for their own holiday. The 2010 Massachusetts STH did not apply to purchases at restaurants, leading restaurant advocates to seek legislation exempting restaurant meals from the state's sales tax. "Why would we give Best Buy—a multi-million, multi-national company—a tax break and not a family that runs a diner in Watertown?" asked one business leader (Hatch 2011).

Retail Market Evolution

In addition to contending with tax competition and cross-border purchasing, state and local policymakers have had to confront a significant evolution in how consumers make retail purchases. In the last 20 years, the value of goods and services purchased through remote, online retailers has skyrocketed, often at the expense of brick-and-motor retailers. Holding all else equal, remote retailers have a competitive advantage over brick-and-mortar stores whenever the former does not collect taxes that, by law, the latter are obligated to collect (Hoopes et al. 2015). Not surprisingly, consumers flock to online retailers for both convenience and, of course, tax avoidance (Ballard and Lee 2007).

The inconsistency of collection requirements strikes many as unfair, especially by brick-and-motor store owners, who believe their businesses have suffered as a result. The Supreme Court has ruled on multiple occasions that state governments cannot compel remote retailers without a nexus in their jurisdiction to collect the state's RST (refer to endnote 17). The only constitutional path to compelling RST collection from remote retailers is for Congress to exercise its authority under the Commerce Clause and enact legislation granting states the power to collect RSTs and LOSTs from non-nexus retailers.

A policy to that end, the Marketplace Fairness Act, was first proposed in 2011. The Act would have allowed state governments to require retailers without a nexus in their jurisdiction to collect the state's retail sales and use taxes. The initial proposal as well as subsequent revisions have enjoyed support from both Republicans and Democrats, both in Congress and across state governments. Many interest groups, including the Alliance for Mainstreet Fairness, American Conservative Union, Americans for Limited Government, the National Retail Federation, and the Retail Industry Leaders Association, have also expressed support for the Act. But opponents were also vocal, including the American Catalog Mailers Association, the Direct Marketing Association, eBay, Freedomworks, the Heritage Foundation, and the National Taxpayers Union. Representatives from states without a RST have also expressed opposition. And others have questioned the long-term implications of allowing one state government to alter business practices on entities located outside their jurisdiction.

While the concept of the Marketplace Fairness Act is well-liked—according to a 2015 poll sponsored by the International Council of Shopping Centers, 70% of registered voters think online retailers should collect state sales taxes—the Act has stalled in Congress. A related proposal, the Remote Transactions Parity Act of 2015, has not advanced out of committee. As a result of congressional inaction, various stakeholders formed the Streamlined Sales Tax Governing Board. That organization sought to help states and remote retailers overcome the compliance challenges inherent to collecting sales taxes from customers living in thousands of different tax environments all over the United States. The result of their efforts, the Streamlined Sales and Use Tax Agreement, outlines a series of rules and procedures that simplify sales tax policy and introduces a greater level of uniformity across the states. Participation in the Agreement is voluntary, and to date, 24 state governments have adopted it.

Shifting and Incidence

The burden of consumption taxes, including the excises levied on air transportation and communication services, clearly falls on consumers. Many of the other consumption taxes charged in the production or importation process are forward-shifted into the price of goods, and hence the burden again falls on consumers. Depending on the state and the good or service, most of the burden of RSTs also falls on consumers. Ring (1999) found that nationwide, 59% of the burden falls on consumers, but that state-specific shifting ranged from a low of 28% to a high of 89%.

The most frequent criticism of consumption taxes is their regressivity. Widely paid consumption taxes, particularly federal excise taxes, RSTs, and LOSTs, have a disproportionate impact on individuals of lesser means. The difference across income quintiles is striking (see Table 5.6). In 2013, the average effective federal excise tax rate on taxpayers in the highest income quintile, who had an average pretax income of $265,000, was 0.4%. For those in the lowest income quintile, who had an average pretax income of $25,400, the effective rate was 1.7%, over four times greater.

Relative to federal policymakers, state and local governments have attempted to address the regressive nature of consumption taxes in their jurisdictions by exempting certain vital goods from taxation, including food, water, prescription drugs, and utilities. However, as discussed in the following chapter, the same policymakers often increase taxes on the vices, which are often more regressive than other consumption levies.

TABLE 5.6 Average Federal Excise Tax Rate by Income Quintile, 2013

Quintile	Rate (%)
Lowest	1.7
Second Lowest	1.1
Middle	0.9
Second Highest	0.7
Highest	0.4

Source: Congressional Budget Office, "The Distribution of Household Income and Federal Taxes, 2013," 2016.

Conclusion

Consumption taxes are a ubiquitous part of life as a consumer. Tax analysts tend to favor consumption taxes over those on income, and many individuals don't mind paying excise taxes on fuel or transportation or retail sales taxes because the proceeds are dedicated to funding the public goods they utilize. Consumers that wish to avoid or minimize their RST or LOST liability can seek out substitute goods and services or engage in purchasing from retailers in lower-tax jurisdictions—avoidance strategies that are more difficult to execute with one's income.

But like any tax, consumption taxes are plagued by questions about fairness and equity. Most of the levies have a regressive impact, especially federal excise taxes, and efforts to date to balance that regressivity only go so far. Some consumption taxes are also applied unequally to identical goods; a beverage purchased at a grocery store may not incur a RST or LOST, yet the same beverage purchased in a restaurant does. When consumption taxes are used as a tool of redistribution, such as when certain federal excises are directed to provide communications or air transportation service to select communities, some taxpayers believe they have been treated unfairly. But perhaps the most important question of all is this: why do individuals pay consumption taxes when purchasing goods and services with their take-home pay, which has already cleared one hurdle of taxation?

Notes

1 Perspectives on taxing consumption versus income have survived centuries of evolving economic and political thought. Thomas Hobbes' *Leviathan*, Adam Smith's *Wealth of Nations*, and John Stuart Mill's *Principles of Political Economy* are only three of dozens of philosophical volumes that address the issue.
2 In some instances, a tariff may be placed on exported goods.
3 Not all imported goods are subject to tariffs, but their value must be declared to Customs and Border Protection.
4 See the Book of Matthew, Chapter 9.
5 Tariff policy is arguably a nonviolent strategy to effect regime change. If tariffs on goods imported from a particular nation cause economic harm to that nation, the theory is that citizens will act against the regime in power and demand political reforms.
6 Critics also worry about the loss of sovereignty that results from ceding tax policy authority to agencies like the World Trade Organization.
7 The other TPP signatories were Australia, Brunei, Canada, Chile, Japan, Malaysia, Mexico, New Zealand, Peru, Singapore, and Vietnam.
8 Not all airports levy a Passenger Facility Charge. As of June 2016, five of the 100 largest airports in the United States did not participate in the program.
9 Air carriers are required to self-report excise taxes collected. The Transportation Security Administration does not send them an invoice.
10 Long-distance service was also charged the excise until 2006 when, after losing a series of court cases, the Treasury Department announced it would no longer collect the tax. The IRS was then tasked with administering refunds.
11 Federal telephone excise revenue in 2013 was at its inflation-adjusted lowest point since 1941; the highest point occurred in 1973.

12 See Congressional Budget Office, "Approaches to Making Federal Highway Spending More Productive," 2016.
13 See National Cooperative Highway Research Program, "Public Perception of Mileage-Based User Fees," 2016.
14 In each illustration, the passenger owes the percentage-based tax of $37.50 (7.5% of $500) and a September 11 Security Fee of $11.20. The difference results from the layover. The segment tax on a nonstop, round-trip flight is $8, and the Passenger Facility Charge is $9. But the extra stop increases the segment tax to $16 and the PFC to $18.
15 See American Suntanning Association, "Consequences of the 10% Tan Tax," 2015.
16 One LOST variant, currently used in Iowa, is the School Infrastructure Local Option (SILO) tax. Revenue from this 1% county-level tax is pooled and shared among the state's public school districts to finance capital projects. Research suggests that LOSTs earmarked for transportation projects crowd-in additional spending on those projects at the expense of reductions in other areas (Alfonso 2015).
17 See *National Bellas Hess v. Department of Revenue*, 386 U.S. 753, 87 S.Ct. 1389 (1967) and *Quill Corp. v. North Dakota*, 504 U.S. 298 (1992); see also *Direct Marketing Association v. Brohl* 575 U.S.
18 See Nina Manzi, "Use Tax Collection on Income Tax Returns in Other States," Minnesota House of Representatives Research Department Policy Brief, 2015.
19 The all-time high was 19 states in 2010 (Drenkard and Henchman 2015).
20 Dozens of local jurisdictions in Alabama and Missouri have opted out of those states' tax holidays.

References

Alfonso, Whitney B. 2014. "Local Sales Taxes as a Means of Increasing Revenues and Reducing Property Tax Burdens: An Analysis Using Propensity Score Matching." *Public Budgeting & Finance* 34(2): 24–43.

Alfonso, Whitney B. 2015. "Leviathan or Flypaper: Examining the Fungibility of Earmarked Local Sales Taxes for Transportation." *Public Budgeting & Finance* 35(3): 1–23.

Alm, James, and Mikhail I. Melnik. 2012. "Cross-Border Shopping and State Use Tax Liabilities: Evidence from eBay Transactions." *Public Budgeting & Finance* 32(1): 5–35.

Anderegg, Caroline. 2015. "Obama's Tanning Tax Still Burning Taxpayers." Americans for Tax Reform. Retrieved from https://www.atr.org/obama-s-tanning-tax-still-burning-taxpayers

Ballard, Charles L., and Jaimin Lee. 2007. "Internet Purchases, Cross-Border Shopping, and Sales Taxes." *National Tax Journal* 60(40): 711–725.

Bankman, Joseph, and David A. Weisbach. 2005. "The Superiority of an Ideal Consumption Tax over an Ideal Income Tax." *Stanford Law Review* 58: 1413–1456.

Bartlett, Bruce. 2012. *The Benefit and the Burden: Tax Reform-Why We Need It and What It Will Take*. New York: Simon & Schuster.

Brunori, David. 2001. "The Politics of State Taxation: Dumber Than a Bag of Hammers." *State Tax Notes*, March 12, pp. 48–63.

Cole, Adam J. 2009. "Sales Tax Holidays: Timing Behavior and Tax Incidence." Doctoral Dissertation.

Downing, Neil. 2014. "Last Sales Tax Holiday Cost State $25 Million." *State Tax Notes*, January 6, p. 12.

Drenkard, Scott, and Joseph Henchman. 2015. "Sales Tax Holidays: Politically Expedient but Poor Tax Policy." The Tax Foundation Special Report No. 229.

Duncan, Denvil, John Graham, Venkata Nadella, Ashley Bowers, and Stacey Giroux. 2014. "Demand for Benefit Taxation: Evidence from Public Opinion on Road Financing." *Public Budgeting & Finance* 34(4): 120–142.

Elliott, Christopher. 2014. "Airfare 'Transparency' Gets Cloudier." *USA Today*, May 12.

Fletcher, Jason M., and Matthew N. Murray. 2006. "Competition over the Tax Base in the State Sales Tax." *Public Finance Review* 34(3): 258–281.

Fox, William F., LeAnn Luna, and Georg Schaur. 2014. "Destination Taxation and Evasion: Evidence from U.S. Interstate Commodity Flows." *Journal of Accounting and Economics* 57(1): 43–57.

Gerwin, Ed. 2015. "Small Businesses with a Big Stake in the Pacific Trade Deal." *Wall Street Journal*, November 26.

Goldberg, Daniel S. 2013. *The Death of the Income Tax: A Progressive Consumption Tax and the Path to Fiscal Reform.* New York: Oxford University Press.

Gottlieb, Charles. 2013. "Residential Short-Term Rentals: Should Local Governments Regulate the 'Industry'?" *Planning & Environmental Law* 65(2): 4–9.

Harper, Richard K., Richard R. Hawkins, Gregory S. Martin, and Richard Sjolander. 2003. "Price Effects around a Sales Tax Holiday: An Exploratory Study." *Public Budgeting & Finance* 23(4): 108–113.

Hatch, Kendall. 2011. "Restaurants Seek Their Own Holiday." *The MetroWest Daily News*, February 7.

Hoene, Christopher. 2004. "Fiscal Structure and the Post-Proposition 13 Fiscal Regime in California's Cities." *Public Budgeting & Finance* 24(4): 51–72.

Hoopes, Jeffrey L., Jacob R. Thornock, and Braden Williams. 2015. "Does Use Tax Evasion Provide a Competitive Advantage to E-Tailers?" *National Tax Journal* 69(1): 133–168.

Jung, Changhoon. 2001. "Does the Local-Option Sales Tax Provide Property Tax Relief? The Georgia Case." *Public Budgeting & Finance* 21(1): 73–86.

Kwak, Sunjoo. 2013. "Tax Base Composition and Revenue Volatility: Evidence from the U.S. States." *Public Budgeting & Finance* 33(2): 41–74.

Mackey, Scott, and Joseph Henchman. 2014. "Wireless Taxation in the United States 2014." Tax Foundation Fiscal Fact No. 441.

Mankiw, N. Gregory. 2015. *Principles of Economics.* Stamford, CT: Cengage.

Melvin, Kerra J. 2012. "Technology, Travel Companies & Taxation: Should Expedia Be Required to Collect and Remit State Occupancy Taxes on Profits from Facilitating Hotel Room Rentals?" *Washington Journal of Law, Technology & Arts* 8(1): 43–59.

Mikesell, John L. 2006. "State Sales Tax Holidays: The Continuing Triumph of Politics over Policy." *State Tax Notes*, July 10, pp. 107–112.

Mitchell, Matthew, and Thomas Stratmann. 2015. "A Tragedy of the Anticommons: Local Option Taxation and Cell Phone Tax Bills." *Public Choice* 165(3): 171–191.

Nemerofsky, Jeff. 2001. "Sleepless Over the Hotel Tax." *Southern Illinois University Law Journal* 25(3): 527–562.

Ring, Raymon J., Jr. 1999. "Consumers' Share and Producers' Share of the General Sales Tax." *National Tax Journal* 52(1): 79–90.

Ruano, Martin. 2008. "Stop Whining and Go Shopping Already: Why the Sales Tax Holiday Critics Are Wrong." *State Tax Notes*, September 29, p. 875.

Scissors, Derek. 2015. "Grading the Trans-Pacific Partnership on Trade." American Enterprise Institute. Retrieved from https://www.aei.org/wp-content/uploads/2015/12/Grading-the-Trans-Pacific-Partnership-on-trade.pdf

Seidman, Laurence A. 1997. *The USA Tax: A Progressive Consumption Tax*. Cambridge, MA: MIT Press.

Sjoquist, David L., William J. Smith, Mary Beth Walker, and Sally Wallace. 2007. "An Analysis of the Time to Adoption of Local Sales Taxes: A Duration Model Approach." *Public Budgeting & Finance* 27(1): 20–40.

Sorensen, Paul, Liisa Ecola, and Martin Wachs. 2012. *Mileage-Based User Fees for Transportation Funding: A Primer for State and Local Decisionmakers*. Santa Monica, CA: RAND Corporation.

Studenski, Paul, and Herman Edward Krooss. 1952. *Financial History of the United States*. New York: McGraw-Hill.

Widmalm, Frida. 2001. "Tax Structures and Growth: Are Some Taxes Better Than Others?" *Public Choice* 107(3): 199–219.

6

TAXING SINFUL CONSUMPTION
Tobacco, Alcohol, Marijuana, and Sugar

The consumption of certain goods creates negative externalities—i.e., physical and/or economic harm to an uninvolved third party. Consider an individual who purchases a pack of cigarettes from a convenience store. That individual benefits from the transaction and subsequent consumption by satisfying their craving and relieving stress, and the store owner benefits by incurring an economic profit. But the consequences extend beyond the consumer and seller. Secondhand smoke may intrude on the otherwise good health of individuals in the smoker's vicinity. The smoker's health care costs may increase and at least some of that cost is transferred to other individuals, including taxpayers and participants in the smoker's health insurance plan.

Not only are negative externalities of this sort inefficient, but they also strike many observers as unfair. In a perfect market, the price of cigarettes or any other vice would reflect not only production, distribution, and retailing costs, but also the social cost of their associated externalities. But because vices are not priced in this fashion, their cost appears artificially low and consumption is therefore artificially high. In theory, a tax would help correct the imbalance.

Throughout history, policymakers have appealed to policies shaped by behavioral economics to raise the costs of negative externality-producing goods to both discourage consumption and compensate for negative externalities. While recent efforts include public health education campaigns and policies that restrict access to those goods, the most robust state efforts across time and space involve instituting special consumption taxes on targeted goods. Such taxes are often referred to as Pigovian taxes, named for economist Arthur C. Pigou and his seminal 1920 book *The Economics of Welfare*.

Pigovian taxes are conceptually similar to sin taxes or sumptuary taxes or fees that have long been added to vices not because officials conducted an analysis of their negative externalities, but because the good in question was viewed as morally inferior, corrupting, addictive, or otherwise unnecessary for life.[1] In his *Wealth of Nations*, Adam Smith noted that "sugar, rum, and tobacco are commodities which are nowhere necessaries of life, which are become objects of almost universal consumption, and which are therefore extremely proper subjects of taxation."

The United States has a fascinating history with vice taxation. The federal government in particular has long placed tariffs and excise taxes on tobacco and alcohol. Faced with a limited set of constitutional revenue-raising tools, early policymakers turned to consumers of those commodities to fund government operations. As the tax system evolved and the federal government derived more revenue from income taxes, vice taxes were no longer justified as budget necessities; instead, policymakers now appeal to the health consequences of tobacco and alcohol, and their cost to government-funded health care plans and to private insurance, as a reason to maintain if not increase existing excise taxes.

Policymakers have more recently expanded the reach of vice taxes to include sugar and marijuana. The taxation of sugar, much like that of tobacco and alcohol, is often but not exclusively justified on public health grounds, an easy "sell" in any nation with marked increases in obesity, diabetes, heart disease, and related conditions. Since the health consequences of marijuana consumption remain unclear, policymakers almost exclusively justify tax efforts on the basis of needing revenue for government programs.

Vice taxation is an interesting but complex field within tax policy and behavioral economics. Advocates praise taxes on alcohol, tobacco, sugar, and marijuana as a way to improve health outcomes and raise revenue, although not always in that order of importance. Critics point out that such taxes are often regressive and often have limited impacts on behavior and health. But as this chapter illustrates, the story of vice taxes and their impact depends on the vice itself.

"Hateful to the Nose": The Taxation of Tobacco

History

Tobacco has an illustrious political history. Well before European arrival in the Americas, some Native American tribes used tobacco during pipe ceremonies and many used it as a form of currency. In fact, Webb (1907) notes that some tribes grew nothing but tobacco. After introduction to Europe in the sixteenth century, tobacco was accepted both for recreational and medicinal purposes; Spanish physician Nicolás Monardes claimed the plant could treat or cure dozens of physical ailments.

But tobacco consumption had opponents. King James I wrote that tobacco was a "foolish vanity," "loathsome to the eye, hateful to the nose, harmful to the brain," and "dangerous to the lungs."[2] In 1604, he directed Lord Treasurer Thomas Sackville to implement one of the world's first tobacco taxes.

European demand nevertheless remained strong and grew in other regions, including the Ottoman Empire, which also made use of tobacco taxes.[3] Demand was met in part by the American colonies, where tobacco cultivation—aided by the use of African slaves—became a lucrative industry. When tobacco prices dropped in the mid-eighteenth century, plantation owners, including George Washington and Thomas Jefferson, found it difficult to repay their indebtedness to English banks. The resultant irritation fueled a growing desire to seek American independence.

Perhaps learning from the English experience, Americans imposed tobacco taxes as one of the first excises in the United States. Alexander Hamilton first suggested the tax in 1790.[4] Congress acted on the proposal in 1794, placing a tax on domestic tobacco and sugar of eight cents and two cents per pound, respectively, with higher tariffs charged on imports. That first federal tobacco tax was not universally supported. During a debate in the House of Representatives in early May 1794, James Madison complained that the burden "fell upon the poor, upon the sailors, day-laborers, and other people of these classes, while the rich will often escape it." Because of collection difficulties and pervasive evasion, Congress made changes to the tobacco tax in 1795. But those changes raised the ire of tobacco growers which, coupled with low revenues, led Congress to suspend the tax from 1796–1799 before making repeal official in 1800 (DePew 1895).[5]

Tobacco taxes were not dead for long. To fund the Civil War, Congress resurrected them in 1862. That year's Revenue Act added federal taxes on smoking tobacco, snuff, and cigars. The Act also added excise taxes to alcohol, playing cards, feathers, carriages, umbrellas, glue, newspaper advertisements, and dozens of other goods. Whereas most of the other taxes were eventually repealed, the tobacco levies proved to be a lucrative revenue source. They have remained part of the federal tax system ever since.

Figure 6.1 illustrates federal tobacco tax revenues from 1863 through 2016. The federal government enjoyed robust growth in revenue from World War I through the mid-1960s, after which annual collections tumbled. Following decades of stagnation, revenue peaked in 2010 following tax increases enacted in early 2009. Despite the recent increases, revenue has dropped as tobacco consumption has declined.

Not wanting to miss potential revenue, state and local governments also levy tobacco excises taxes. Compared to the federal government, states began taxing tobacco relatively late. The first state to tax cigarettes, Iowa, did not do so until 1921. Enactment of cigarette taxes by other states was not complete until North Carolina acted in 1949. Today, all 50 states and the District of Columbia levy tobacco taxes. Alabama, Illinois, Missouri, Tennessee, and Virginia allow local governments to collect additional tobacco taxes, similar to a LOST. For example, cigarettes purchased in Chicago include a Chicago city tax, a Cook County tax, and an Illinois state tax, in addition to a federal excise tax. Cities in other states, including Juneau, Alaska, and New York, New York, also levy a local cigarette tax.

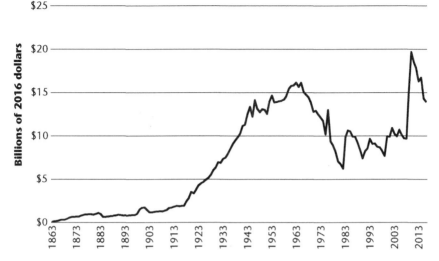

FIGURE 6.1   Federal Tobacco Excise Tax Revenue, 1863–2013, in Constant Dollars

Sources: Author's analysis of data reported by the Office of Management and Budget and in the *Historical Statistics of the United States, Colonial Times to 1970, Part 2.*

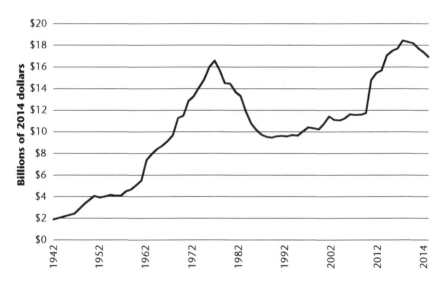

FIGURE 6.2   State Tobacco Excise Tax Revenue, 1942–2014, in Constant Dollars

Source: United States Census Bureau Annual Survey of State Government Finances.

Figure 6.2 illustrates aggregate state tobacco tax revenues from 1942 through 2014. Mirroring the federal trend, state revenues surged through the 1960s and peaked in 1973 before falling throughout the remainder of the 1970s and into the 1980s. After a period of stagnation, collections rose sharply in the early- and mid-2000s. But like federal revenues, state collections have started to decline.

At all levels of government, the enactment of tobacco taxes and subsequent decisions over how high or low those taxes should be have been shaped not only by the desire to raise revenue, particularly for war costs, but also by a desire to improve public health and compensate for the negative externalities of tobacco and nicotine consumption. Cigarette smoking has been linked to higher risks of developing multiple types of cancer, heart disease, and stroke among heavy users, casual users, and even individuals exposed to secondhand smoke. Chewing tobacco has been linked to higher rates of oral cancer. Policymakers view tobacco taxes as a tool to raise tobacco product prices, thus discouraging consumption while making available new revenue to compensate for the health and social costs of tobacco products.

Current Tobacco Tax Landscape

Tobacco excise taxes assume two forms; some are per-unit taxes based on the quantity sold, and others are ad valorem taxes based on price. Tobacco excises also vary by product type. Cigarettes, cigars, "roll your own" tobacco, pipe tobacco, chewing tobacco, snuff, and snus each have specific tax structures applied (see Table 6.1). These taxes were most recently increased in 2009 as part of the Children's Health Insurance Program Reauthorization Act. The Act boosted tobacco taxes moving forward and included a tax on then-current inventory, called a floor stocks tax, equal to the difference between the old and new tax rates. In contrast with most other excises, federal tobacco taxes are remitted to the Alcohol and Tobacco Tax Trade Bureau.

Additional taxes are accrued to anyone importing tobacco products into the United States. As with many other imports, the federal government levies tariffs based on the type of product and its nation of origin. These tariffs vary and are often raised, lowered, or eliminated as part of trade agreements between the United States and the nation of origin. Beyond tariffs, consumers may pay

TABLE 6.1 Federal Excise Taxes on Tobacco Products, 2016

Product	Tax
Class A "Small" Cigarettes	$50.33 per 1,000
Class B "Large" Cigarettes	$105.69 per 1,000
Small Cigars	$50.33 per 1,000
Large Cigars	52.75% of sales price, with a cap of $0.4026 per cigar
Chewing Tobacco	$0.5033 per pound
Snuff	$1.51 per pound
Pipe Tobacco	$2.8311 per pound
"Roll Your Own" Tobacco	$24.78 per pound
Cigarette Paper	$0.0315 per 50
Cigarette Tube	$0.0630 per 50

Source: Alcohol and Tobacco Tax and Trade Bureau.

higher prices for tobacco products originating in certain nations because federal law restricts the total amount of product that may be imported.[6] If demand for tobacco from those areas exceeds the import cap, prices will increase regardless of their tax treatment.

At the state level, most tobacco taxes are an excise on cigarettes (see Table 6.2). Excises range from a low of $0.17 per pack in Missouri to a high of $4.35 per pack in New York. Because some local governments charge their own excise, the total tax burden per pack of cigarettes is higher in certain jurisdictions within each state. For example, a pack of cigarettes purchased in New York City includes the state excise of $4.35 plus an additional city excise of $1.50. Including the federal excise, which works out to about $1.00 per pack, the total tax burden is $6.85 per pack. Likewise, in Chicago, the total tax burden would be $7.16, comprised of the federal excise, Illinois state excise ($1.98), Cook County excise ($3.00), and city excise tax ($1.18).

TABLE 6.2 State Excise Taxes on Cigarettes, per Pack, and Rank among the States, 2016

State	Tax	Rank
Alabama	$0.67	39
Alaska	2.00	12
Arizona	2.00	12
Arkansas	1.15	32
California	0.87	35
Colorado	0.84	37
Connecticut	3.90	3
Delaware	1.60	23
Florida	1.34	29
Georgia	0.37	49
Hawaii	3.20	5
Idaho	0.57	44
Illinois	1.98	17
Indiana	0.99	34
Iowa	1.36	28
Kansas	1.29	31
Kentucky	0.60	42
Louisiana	0.86	36
Maine	2.00	12
Maryland	2.00	12
Massachusetts	3.51	4
Michigan	2.00	12
Minnesota	3.00	8
Mississippi	0.68	38
Missouri	0.17	51
Montana	1.70	20
Nebraska	0.64	40
Nevada	1.80	18
New Hampshire	1.78	19

(Continued)

TABLE 6.2 (Continued)

State	Tax	Rank
New Jersey	2.70	9
New Mexico	1.66	22
New York	4.35	1
North Carolina	0.45	47
North Dakota	0.44	48
Ohio	1.60	23
Oklahoma	1.03	33
Oregon	1.32	30
Pennsylvania	1.60	23
Rhode Island	3.75	2
South Carolina	0.57	44
South Dakota	1.53	26
Tennessee	0.62	41
Texas	1.41	27
Utah	1.70	20
Vermont	3.08	6
Virginia	0.30	50
Washington	3.03	7
West Virginia	0.55	46
Wisconsin	2.52	10
Wyoming	0.60	42

Sources: The Federation of Tax Administrators and the Tax Foundation.

How tobacco tax revenues are spent has varied over time and depends on the level of government. Historically, federal revenues have been used to pay for Civil War costs, to fund general government operations, and to finance the Children's Health Insurance Program (CHIP), which provides funding to state programs that offer health care plans to families with modest incomes that do not qualify for Medicaid. State and local revenues have been allocated to general operations, to close budget deficits, and to fund public education, public health, and smoking cessation programs.

Special Interest Groups and the Taxation of Tobacco

Tobacco taxes are somewhat unique in that policy debates on their merits gain interest not only from the usual suspects—e.g., economists and policymakers— but also from public health groups. These include the World Lung Foundation and the International Union Against Tuberculosis and Lung Disease, both of which have lobbied in favor of tobacco taxes. The World Health Organization's Tobacco Free Initiative, established in 1998, offers resources to assist policymakers reduce tobacco consumption. Among the initiative's policy recommendations is that governments tax tobacco products.[7] To make their case for tobacco taxes more impactful, some interest groups invoke images of children. On its website,

Raise Your Hand for Kids, a Missouri-based group, advocates raising the state's cigarette tax to 60 cents per pack and dedicating the revenue to fund "vital early childhood education programs."

Other interest groups lobby in favor of tobacco taxes not to achieve public health outcomes, but because the group believes that revenues can achieve other policy goals. In 2015 and 2016, Save Lives California, a coalition of health groups, labor unions, and insurance companies, lobbied for a state cigarette tax increase that would fund public health programs, increase the number of practicing physicians, and improve California's dental education system.

The tobacco industry itself has been a powerful lobbying voice on a number of issues, not just taxes, especially within state legislatures (Apollonio and Bero 2007; Givel and Glantz 2001). Tobacco industry campaign contributions, as well as the amount of in-state tobacco production, have a negative influence on state cigarette tax rates (Hoffer 2016) and spending on tobacco cessation programs (Hoffer and Pellillo 2012). But according to the Center for Responsive Politics, tobacco industry spending on lobbying totaled $20.3 million in 2015, the smallest amount since the group began collecting data in 1998. Not only has tobacco lobbying declined, but the industry's major players, including Altria, Philip Morris International, and R.J. Reynolds, do not always speak with a unified voice. Whereas Altria has generally favored Food and Drug Administration regulation of tobacco products, R.J. Reynolds has not. R.J. Reynolds in particular has also lobbied against tobacco tax increases; the company sponsors Transform Tobacco, an initiative that aims to empower consumers to take action against increases.

Public Policy Issues in Tobacco Taxation

The "Quit Smoking, But Keep Smoking" Paradox

Policymakers justify tobacco taxes as a way to reduce tobacco consumption and fund associated public health costs, but they often allocate revenues to programs that have no direct connection to public health. But as fewer people smoke, tax revenue will decline, and programs funded with those revenues will have to implement budget cuts or seek additional taxes on nonsmokers. For example, bootstrapping federal tobacco tax revenues to CHIP funding means that policymakers need a certain percentage of the population to continue consuming tobacco, the very behavior they are ostensibly trying to eradicate. Otherwise, CHIP funding will fall short. Linking state and local tobacco tax revenue to general government operations or public education, as some jurisdictions do, likewise means that policymakers need a persistent number of tobacco users to keep those budgets in balance.

Thus, achieving one policy goal—reduced or total cessation of tobacco consumption—shifts the burden of funding tobacco tax-supported programs onto other taxpayers. Whereas most government agencies stop short of advocating total tobacco cessation, many interest groups, including the Campaign for Tobacco-Free Kids and the Truth Initiative, advocate exactly that, often without offering suggestions on how to compensate for the tax revenue lost if tobacco consumption is eliminated.

Fairness

Whereas health care costs are above average for most tobacco users while they are alive, cost-benefit approaches seldom acknowledge that users' shorter life expectancies represent a substantial cost offset, an arguably positive externality of tobacco consumption. One Dutch study found that lifetime health care costs for smokers were over 20% lower than costs for thin, healthy patients (van Baal et al. 2008). Relatedly, a 2012 report from New Zealand's Treasury Department found that, by dying younger and paying tobacco taxes over the course of their lifetimes, cigarette smokers more than compensate for the social burdens caused by their tobacco use. In the United States, smokers' shorter life expectancies result in lower total lifetime health care costs for both private insurance plans as well as Medicare and Medicaid.

Shorter life expectancies among tobacco users also accumulate savings to Social Security. Using the difference in life expectancies between cigarette smokers and nonsmokers, reported by the Centers for Disease Control and Prevention as 10 years shorter for smokers, and average monthly Social Security benefits, reported by the Social Security Administration as $1,335 per month in 2015, the average smoker saves the federal government just over $160,000 by dying sooner than a nonsmoker.[8] Yet this take on fairness is rarely, if ever, introduced into debates about the merits of tobacco taxation.

Equity

Critics of tobacco taxes often note, and research supports, that the incidence falls disproportionately on lower-income individuals (Farrelly et al. 2012; Remler 2004). Indeed, the regressive nature of tobacco taxes was one of Madison's primary criticisms of them over 200 years ago. Low-income consumers sustain two hits from tobacco and other vices taxes. Centers for Disease Control and Prevention statistics have consistently shown that tobacco consumption is higher among individuals living below the federal poverty line. And holding all else equal, the tobacco tax burden consumes a larger proportion of those individuals' income. Compounding the situation, evidence suggests that tobacco consumption among low-income consumers does not decline when taxes are increased even though consumption among higher-income earners does decline, exacerbating tobacco taxes' regressivity (Franks et al. 2007).

Shifting Marketplace and Substitutes

As the pool of tobacco consumers shrinks and tax revenues dwindle, policymakers in many jurisdictions have considered whether to tax tobacco's logical substitute: vapor products, more commonly known as e-cigarettes. By 2016, four states (Kansas, Louisiana, Minnesota, and North Carolina) and three local governments (Montgomery County, Maryland; Chicago, Illinois; and Cook County, Illinois) had enacted an excise tax on vapor products. Twenty-two additional state legislatures considered e-cigarette taxes during 2015.

Where enacted, vapor product excise taxes are either ad valorem or value-based levies. In Kansas, the tax is $0.20 per milliliter of liquid; in Minnesota, the tax is 95% of the wholesale cost of any tobacco-derived product. Residents that purchase over $50 of taxable products across state lines but consume them within Minnesota are legally obligated to pay a tobacco use tax to the state treasury in the month following purchase.

The Impact of Tobacco Taxation on Consumption and Health

Advocates argue that the tobacco taxes reduce consumption among current users and discourage new users from entering the marketplace. But evidence to that end is mixed. True enough, multiple studies indicate that tobacco products have negative price elasticities, suggesting that higher taxes reduce consumption (Chaloupka et al. 2012; Farrelly et al. 2001), although, as noted, the reductive effect is larger among high-income consumers (Franks et al. 2007).

However, the impact varies not only by income but also across other demographic categories. For instance, younger consumers are more responsive to tobacco price than older consumers (Evans and Farrelly 1998; Zhang et al. 2006). MacLean et al. (2016) found that a tax increase of over 100% reduced consumption among those over age 50 less than 5.2%. Similarly, Callison and Kaestner (2014) found that, at best, doubling cigarette taxes may reduce consumption for some groups by around 5%, but that for most groups the association between taxes and consumption was insignificant or small.

These conclusions should not come as a surprise. Rather than discourage consumption, higher tobacco taxes may instead encourage shifts in consumer behavior. Smokers may respond to tax increases by increasing the intensity of their smoking, such as through extracting more nicotine from each cigarette (Adda and Cornaglia 2006) or by switching to a product with a higher nicotine concentration (Evans and Farrelly 1998). Cigarette users may also practice tax-avoidance strategies, such as buying cigarettes on the black market, cross-border shopping in jurisdictions with lower tax rates, or purchasing cigarettes through online merchants that do not comply with tax law (Merriman 2010; Stehr 2005). Research from the Tax Foundation and the Mackinac Center for Public Policy found a strong relationship between state cigarette tax rates and the proportion of cigarettes smuggled in from other states. States with higher taxes have a much higher share of imported cigarettes.[9] Users may also purchase cigarettes on Native American reservations, where tobacco taxes may not be charged (Carpenter and Mathes 2016). Ultimately, higher tax rates reduce revenue collections, hurt local retailers, and do little to reduce smoking. Worse, high cigarette taxes have also incentivized terror-related criminal activity.[10]

Evidence suggests that if policymakers wish to reduce tobacco consumption, regardless of the revenue implications, other policies would have a greater effect. For example, smoking bans can be more effective than taxes at reducing consumption (Hofmann and Nell 2012; Vuolo et al. 2016), although findings are inconsistent (Adda and Cornaglia 2010). But if policymakers are specifically tied to the notion of taxing tobacco, evidence suggests that optimal tax rates that incorporate the cost of avoidant behaviors are lower than current rates. For many states, tobacco taxes would need to be reduced at least 20% (DeCicca et al. 2013), an option that policymakers and other stakeholders dependent on tobacco tax revenues are not likely to embrace.

Government Hits the Sauce: The Taxation of Alcohol

History

Like tobacco, alcohol and its taxation played a crucial role in early American history. Many colonies experimented with alcohol taxes well before the United States formed. New York first taxed alcohol in 1644, Connecticut followed suit in 1650, and sellers of foreign alcohol in Pennsylvania were taxed starting in 1756 (Cherrington 1920). Alcohol taxation was also among the first issues considered by the United States federal government. After ratification of the Constitution in 1789, Congress had to confront many problems, including the rather important issue of how to resolve the colonies' Revolutionary War debts and the more pragmatic issue of where to locate the national capitol. The Compromise of 1790 solved both issues. Passage of the Residence Act required that the federal capital be located along the Potomac River, and the Funding Act stipulated that the federal government would assume colonial debts. Congress then had to address how to obtain the funds necessary to retire those debts. Alexander Hamilton, then serving as Secretary of the Treasury, proposed a series of excise taxes on alcoholic beverages.

The House of Representatives considered the proposal in January 1791. Supporters argued that the excises functioned as a luxury tax, paid only by those who could afford to purchase alcohol. Dry activists welcomed the taxes for their role in diminishing alcohol consumption.[11] Opponents, including James Jackson of Georgia, complained that the United States was already doing too much to imitate Great Britain and should not follow that nation's lead in taxing alcohol.

Nevertheless, Congress enacted alcohol taxes in 1791, the first federal excise on a domestic product.

Alcohol taxes were unpopular in some areas, particularly those on the western side of the Appalachian Mountains. Citizens in rural spaces rarely, if ever, came in contact with actual paper money or coinage; instead, they used commodities like whiskey as currency, just as many Native American tribes had used tobacco. Alcohol taxes were accordingly viewed as an unfair tax on their currency. Farmers that distilled whiskey from excess grain argued that they, too, were unfairly impacted by the tax. Tensions came to a head in western Pennsylvania one evening in September 1791 when a small gang of men—some in blackface, some wearing dresses—attacked and then tarred and feathered a federal tax collector (Hodgeland 2015). Thus was born the Whiskey Rebellion, which lasted until 1794. Although unpopular and difficult to collect because many opponents refused to pay the levies outright, alcohol taxes survived for several years. As a presidential candidate in 1800, Thomas Jefferson campaigned against the tax and won. It was repealed in 1802.

As with tobacco taxes, the taxes on alcohol would return. Congress brought them back to fund the War of 1812 but repealed them in 1817. In 1862, Congress revived alcohol taxes a third time to fund the Civil War, and they have remained in law ever since. By the late nineteenth century, many state governments began charging excise taxes on alcohol, especially distilled spirits, but their efforts were often hampered by state-level prohibition legislation, which started as early as 1851 in Maine.

By the beginning of the twentieth century, alcohol excise taxes had become entangled with dry activism and the progressive push for taxing individual and corporate income. In the years preceding national prohibition, alcohol taxes contributed a substantial proportion of total federal revenue. From 1910 through 1916, no less than 30% of federal receipts came from taxes on alcohol (see Figure 6.3).

Dry activists knew that their chances of succeeding with a nationwide alcohol ban were limited unless the federal government had another source of revenue that could replace the revenue from alcohol taxes in the event of prohibition. Many lobbied for the Sixteenth Amendment, which would allow Congress to impose a federal income tax (Okrent 2010). For their part, wet activists noted that national prohibition would lower not only federal, but also state and local revenues, raising the likelihood of other tax increases. "Most of our American municipalities are bonded to the limit," said one anti-prohibition text in early 1917, "our cities cannot bear the burden of additional taxes."[12]

As many states expanded alcohol regulations or passed their own dry laws outright, thus depressing legal alcohol consumption, and as Congress passed the Eighteenth Amendment and the ratification process began, alcohol tax revenues dropped markedly beginning in 1917 (see Figure 6.4 and refer also to Figure 6.3). Revenues surged following the end of prohibition, but the advent of income taxes

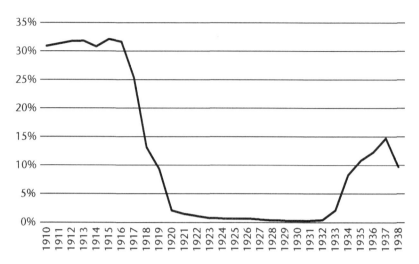

FIGURE 6.3 Federal Alcohol Excise Tax Revenue as a Percentage of Total Revenue, 1910–1938

Source: Author's analysis of data reported in the *Historical Statistics of the United States, Colonial Times to 1970, Part 2.*

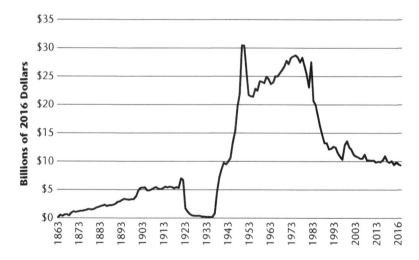

FIGURE 6.4 Federal Alcohol Excise Tax Revenue, 1863–2016, in Constant Dollars

Sources: Author's analysis of data reported by the Office of Management and Budget and in the *Historical Statistics of the United States, Colonial Times to 1970, Part 2.*

and their significant contribution to the federal treasury meant that, proportionally, alcohol taxes carried much less weight. By 2016, the federal government collected just under $10 billion in alcohol taxes, less than one-third of 1% of total revenue.

Alcohol tax revenues are obviously tied directly to consumption. Data suggest that alcohol consumption peaked during the late 1970s and early 1980s, reaching nearly 2.8 gallons per capita.[13] But from 1980 to 2000, consumption per capita dropped 21%, dragging excise tax revenue with it. The decline in consumption was, in part, a product of federal policy: enactment of the National Minimum Drinking Age Act of 1984 pushed states to raise the drinking age to 21 from 18, reducing the pool of legal alcohol consumers.

Evolving consumer tastes are also a factor in changing alcohol tax revenues. The percentage of overall alcohol consumption drawn from beer increased from 50% in 1980 to 56% in 2000, crowding out consumption from wine and distilled spirits, which generally carry higher excise taxes. Growth in home brewing has also had an impact; within some limits, alcoholic beverages produced for personal and family consumption have been exempt from federal taxation since 1979.

The end of national prohibition essentially devolved alcohol regulation to state and local governments, where policymakers assumed varying degrees of control (e.g., blue laws and state monopolies on distribution and retail sales). Over time, many of the control mechanisms implemented in the immediate aftermath of prohibition's end have liberalized. All state and some local governments today collect excise taxes on alcoholic beverages and charge additional license fees on producers, distributors, and retail outlets. Relative to license fees, excise taxes raise more revenue, but collections from both are well below their inflation-adjusted peaks (see Figure 6.5 and Figure 6.6). State alcohol taxes crested at nearly $10 billion in 1973, but by 2014, they totaled just $6.2 billion. License revenues are also relatively lower today, totaling less than $700 million in 2014.

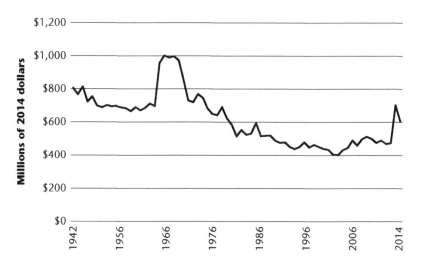

FIGURE 6.5   State Alcohol Licensing Revenue, 1942–2014, in Constant Dollars

Source: United States Census Bureau Annual Survey of State Government Finances.

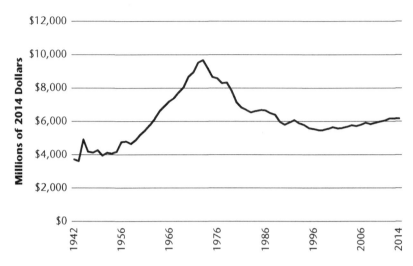

FIGURE 6.6 State Alcohol Excise Tax Revenue, 1942–2014, in Constant Dollars

Source: United States Census Bureau Annual Survey of State Government Finances.

Current Alcohol Tax Landscape

In general, little has changed about alcohol taxation since the end of prohibition; taxation of beverages mostly continues at the federal and state levels of government. Excise tax rates depend on the type of beverage and amount of alcohol (see Table 6.3 and Table 6.4).

Local and other taxes may apply over and above federal and state levies. For example, Cook County, Illinois, levies an excise tax of between six cents and $2.50 per gallon, contingent on beverage type and alcohol content. Chicago, Illinois, levies a liquor tax of 29 cents per gallon of beer and between 36 cents and $2.68 on liquor, also contingent on alcohol content. In Pennsylvania, possibly the state with the most restrictions on alcohol, the retail price of alcoholic beverages includes an 18% "emergency tax." The levy was originally lower (10%) and had a different name, the Johnstown Flood Tax. The eponymous—and, apparently, rather unlucky city—was damaged by floods in 1889, 1894, 1907, 1924, and 1936, and state officials decided in 1936 to fund rebuilding efforts with an excise tax on alcohol. Sufficient funds were raised by 1942, but the tax has remained in effect and, indeed, has nearly doubled from its original level.

Federal, state, and local alcohol taxes are charged at various points in the production stream. Federal excise taxes are typically paid by the producer—i.e., the brewery or the importer of nondomestic products. State and local excise taxes are typically paid by distributors or wholesalers, but they may be charged at the point of sale. In addition to paying excise taxes embedded in the cost of alcoholic beverages, consumers in most states must also pay state and perhaps local retail sales taxes on their purchase. In other words, alcohol consumers are victims of tax pyramiding.

TABLE 6.3 Federal Excise Taxes on Alcoholic Beverages, 2016

Product	Tax
Beer	Either $7 or $18 per 31-gallon barrel, depending on quantity produced by brewer
Wine	$1.07 per gallon (14% alcohol or less) $1.57 per gallon (14–21% alcohol) $3.15 per gallon (21–24% alcohol) $3.30 per gallon (artificially carbonated) $3.40 per gallon (naturally sparkling)
Hard Cider	$0.226 per gallon, subject to credits for some producers
Distilled Spirits	$13.50 per gallon, subject to credits for flavor and alcohol content

Source: Alcohol and Tobacco Tax and Trade Bureau.

TABLE 6.4 State Excise Taxes on Alcoholic Beverages, per Gallon, 2016

	Beer	Wine	Liquor
Alabama	0.53	1.70	18.22
Alaska	1.07	2.50	12.80
Arizona	0.16	0.84	3.00
Arkansas	0.23	0.75	2.50
California	0.20	0.20	3.30
Colorado	0.08	0.28	2.28
Connecticut	0.24	0.72	5.40
Delaware	0.16	0.97	3.75
Florida	0.48	2.25	6.50
Georgia	0.32	1.51	3.79
Hawaii	0.93	1.38	5.98
Idaho	0.15	0.45	10.90
Illinois	0.23	1.39	8.55
Indiana	0.12	0.47	2.68
Iowa	0.19	1.75	12.49
Kansas	0.18	0.30	2.50
Kentucky	0.08	0.50	1.92
Louisiana	0.32	0.11	2.50
Maine	0.35	0.60	5.79
Maryland	0.09	0.40	1.50
Massachusetts	0.11	0.55	4.05
Michigan	0.20	0.51	11.99
Minnesota	0.15	0.30	5.03
Mississippi	0.43	0.35	2.50
Missouri	0.06	0.42	2.00
Montana	0.14	1.06	9.74
Nebraska	0.31	0.95	3.75

(Continued)

TABLE 6.4 (Continued)

	Beer	Wine	Liquor
Nevada	0.16	0.70	3.60
New Hampshire	0.30	–	–
New Jersey	0.12	0.88	5.50
New Mexico	0.41	1.70	6.06
New York	0.14	0.30	6.44
North Carolina	0.62	1.00	12.30
North Dakota	0.16	0.50	2.50
Ohio	0.18	0.32	9.34
Oklahoma	0.40	0.72	5.56
Oregon	0.08	0.67	22.72
Pennsylvania	0.08	–	–
Rhode Island	0.10	1.40	5.40
South Carolina	0.77	0.90	2.72
South Dakota	0.27	0.93	3.93
Tennessee	1.29	1.21	4.40
Texas	0.20	0.20	2.40
Utah	0.41	–	12.18
Vermont	0.27	0.55	7.68
Virginia	0.26	1.51	19.18
Washington	0.26	0.87	35.22
West Virginia	0.18	1.00	1.89
Wisconsin	0.06	0.25	3.25
Wyoming	0.02	0.28	–

Notes: A (-) denotes no excise applies, but other taxes or mandatory price markups may be in effect; local taxes and price markups are above those listed; sparkling wine taxes may differ.

Sources: The Federation of Tax Administrators and the Tax Foundation.

Altogether, the price of an alcoholic beverage is often determined more by taxes and fees than the cost of the beverage itself. North Carolina's Alcohol Beverage Control Commission offers the following illustration.[14] Assume that a distiller prices a 12-bottle case of whiskey at $74.59. To that cost, the state of North Carolina adds the following taxes and fees: a $1.60 "bailment charge" to fund the state's warehouse, an 80-cent "bailment surcharge" to fund the Commission's budget, two different per-bottle fees, a mandatory 39% price markup, a 30% state excise tax, and then, finally, the state's 7% retail sales tax. All told, the cost of that 12-bottle case of whiskey has ballooned to $153.48, assuming the case is bought by an individual. That yields an effective state alcohol excise tax rate of 105.8% on whiskey. If the same case is instead purchased by a retail outlet, the sales tax does not apply but a higher mixed-beverage tax does apply, bumping the price to $188.40 and an effective tax rate of 152.3%.

How alcohol tax revenues are spent depends on the government collecting them. At the federal level, taxes subsidize the cost of the Alcohol and Tobacco Tax and Trade Bureau, which is responsible for collecting the excise taxes and enforcing federal law. But federal alcohol and tobacco tax collections are far greater than the Bureau's budget. In 2014, the Bureau collected over $22 billion in excise taxes, but its budget was only about $100 million, leaving billions of dollars to fund other federal programs that may have absolutely nothing to do with alcohol or tobacco. In many states, revenues are used to fund the very bureaucracy charged with collecting them in the first place (e.g., North Carolina) and to fund general government operations. For instance, California deposits alcohol tax revenues into an Alcohol Beverage Control Fund, from which funds are transferred to the state's general fund.

Interest Groups and the Taxation of Alcohol

The alcohol industry counts among its members some of the most recognizable consumer brands in the world, including Anheuser-Busch InBev, Molson Coors Brewing, and SABMiller. According to the Center for Responsive Politics, industry players and their trade groups, such as the National Beer Wholesalers Association, the Distilled Spirits Council, and the Wine & Spirits Wholesalers of America, made $17.4 million in campaign contributions in 2014 and spent $25.1 million on lobbying in 2015. Roughly 60% of 2014 campaign contributions went to Republicans, although as recently as 2010, a majority was donated to Democrats. The industry's chief concerns are often regulatory but sometimes include changes to alcohol excise taxes.

Industry positions on alcohol taxes vary. Both the National Beer Wholesalers Association and the Wine & Spirits Wholesalers of America have recently focused on federal corporate tax reform more than excise taxes. But most industry groups lobby against alcohol tax increases. The Distilled Spirits Council opposes increases, arguing that alcohol is already among the most taxed consumer goods and that increases will harm the industry through job and wage losses. The Beer Institute and the Brewers Association have lobbied in favor of the Craft Beverage Modernization & Tax Reform Act, which reduces federal beer excise taxes for most brewers. The American Beverage Institute has lobbied against tax increases at the state level. It denounced proposals to increase taxes in Illinois (2011), Maryland (2011), Hawaii (2011), and Minnesota (2013), citing the depressive effect on hospitality industry employment and the likelihood in some states that higher taxes would encourage cross-border shopping.

A number of national groups have fought to increase alcohol taxes. Mothers Against Drunk Driving's official position is that alcohol taxes should be increased and, more specifically, that the rates on beer and wine should be equivalent to the rate on distilled spirits. The progressive Center for Science in the Public Interest advocates for higher alcohol taxes, rationalizing that the burden of alcohol consumption is far greater than excise revenues, and that federal excise rates have not kept pace with inflation.

Some interest groups attempt to sell the public on alcohol tax increases by emphasizing how much revenue the government will collect as a result, as if that itself is a societal gain. The Center on Alcohol Marketing and Youth, housed at the Johns Hopkins Bloomberg School of Public Health and funded by the Pew Charitable Trusts and the Robert Wood Johnson Foundation, argues that higher alcohol prices such as those achieved through excise taxation are good public policy. The Center operates an interactive web tool, funded in part by the Centers for Disease Control and Prevention, wherein the user can select a state, select a tax increase (five cents, 10 cents, or 25 cents per drink, or a 5% retail sales tax), and receive a report on the tax's budget impact. The tool's graphics invariably show that excessive drinkers would bear most of the burden ("non-drinkers pay nothing," the website helpfully informs the user) and that the increase would create jobs, mostly in government. For example, selecting a 5% retail sales tax in California apparently nets 21,912 "general government" jobs and 666 health care jobs.

Alcohol Justice, an anti-industry group, also has an interactive calculator on its website. For each state, the feature tells the user when state excise taxes were last updated and how inflation has eroded the value of the excise over time. The user can input a tax increase for beer, wine, and/or distilled spirits, and the calculator shows the user how much the state will gain in excise and retail sales tax revenue.

Public Policy Issues in Alcohol Taxation

Paradoxes and Inconsistencies

Policymakers and special interest groups often allege that alcohol taxes, like tobacco taxes, are an effective tool to reduce consumption and compensate for alcohol-related negative externalities. But as with tobacco taxes, revenues are infrequently tied to cessation programs. Some may indirectly fund alcohol-related education programs for youth, but most revenues are allocated toward general government operations. At the state and local levels, alcohol taxes are, in practice, not a public health tool but a levy that enables policymakers to balance budgets without spending cuts.

Because policymakers often use alcohol taxes as a budget-balancing measure, it comes as no surprise that the rationale behind the taxes and alcohol policy more generally is not particularly well-conceptualized. Policymakers are often not explicit about their objective: is it to reduce excessive drinking or to reduce all alcohol consumption, even among adults that drink responsibly?[15] Excessive, not casual, drinking presents significant costs, about 40% of which are governmental responsibility (Sacks et al. 2015), but the effective tax rate on one beer is the same as it is on the fifth beer. That begs the question: why do casual drinkers that cause no harm to others have to subsidize treatment and prevention programs or otherwise pay higher taxes over and above standard retail sales taxes?

One of the more glaring inconsistencies is that even as state governments levy excise taxes on alcoholic beverages, many policymakers support granting tax incentives to alcohol producers. New Belgium Brewing Company opened a brewery in Asheville, North Carolina, but only after an estimated $13 million in city, county, and state tax subsidies were approved in 2012. Stone Brewing Company announced in 2014 that it would construct a new facility in Richmond, Virginia, but only after the city agreed to borrow $23 million on the company's behalf, in addition to a city economic development grant of $1.5 million, a sustainable development grant of $500,000, and a Virginia state grant of $5 million. In 2016, Deschutes Brewery announced a new facility for Roanoke, Virginia, made possible by a state grant of $3 million. "Virginia is for beer lovers, folks" remarked Governor Terry McAuliffe, a Democrat.

Fairness and Equity

Because federal, state, and local alcohol excise taxes are embedded in the cost of alcoholic beverages, they are far from transparent; and their incidence falls not on producers and distributors, but on consumers. Shrestha and Markowitz (2016) found that state excise taxes, and more, are shifted directly to consumers: a 10-cent tax increase led to a retail price increase of 17 cents. The incidence is less regressive than tobacco taxes, but still disproportionate across different demographic groups. As with tobacco taxes, alcohol taxes fall disproportionately on heavier users and on those who consume beverages with higher alcohol content, as both federal and state excise taxes tend to increase with content (Daley et al. 2012).

But in contrast to tobacco excises, alcohol tax increases would likely have a disproportionate impact on higher-income households (Naimi et al. 2016), and especially on employed, college-educated white males earning over $50,000 annually (Daley et al. 2012), suggesting that alcohol taxes are perhaps a "luxury tax." Studies that find evidence of a regressive impact of alcohol taxes find the effect is small and concentrated among heavy users (Vandenberg and Sharma 2016).

Shifting Marketplace

Recent changes in the alcoholic beverage marketplace may necessitate attention from policymakers at all levels of government. The growth in popularity of home brewing has clear implications for tax policy. Home production is exempt from excise taxes and, even if governments attempted to levy a tax, it is not feasible to collect. As home brewing spreads, consumers may eschew higher retail prices and taxes in favor of producing their own untaxed substitutes at home.

Even more recently, the Alcohol and Tobacco Tax and Trade Bureau in 2016 approved the sale of powdered alcohol, more commonly known as palcohol. The product works just like powdered energy drinks or lemonade; a consumer simply empties a package of powdered material into a container of water, and the beverage is ready for consumption. Because palcohol is virtually indistinguishable from nonalcoholic powdered beverages, and easier to conceal than bottled alcohol, policymakers are concerned about consumption, especially among minors. Many states have moved to ban the product outright. Others will have to confront the same question and, if policymakers decide palcohol is legal, they will also have to decide if, and how, to tax it.

The Impact of Alcohol Taxation on Health and Consumption

Alcohol consumption is linked with over 60 different health conditions (Room et al. 2005), and the Centers for Disease Control and Prevention estimates that excessive drinking is responsible for 1 in 10 deaths among adults. But are alcohol taxes an effective tool to reduce consumption and improve health outcomes? Findings here are less ambiguous than those on tobacco. Multiple studies suggest an inverse relationship between alcohol pricing and consumption; higher prices, either through minimum pricing policies or taxes, reduce consumption, especially over the long run (Elder et al. 2010; Xu and Chaloupka 2011). Taxes that raise the price of the cheapest alcoholic beverages reduce consumption (Vandenberg and Sharma 2016). One meta-analysis of 50 studies on the impact of alcohol prices (inclusive of taxes) suggested that doubling tax rates would reduce alcohol-related deaths from conditions like liver cirrhosis by an average of 35%, reduce traffic deaths by 11%, and lead to single-digit declines in sexually transmitted diseases, violence, and crime (Wagenaar et al. 2010). Although most studies suggest that consumers reduce consumption in response to price increases, elasticities are not consistent across different beverages. Relative to other alcoholic drinks, beer is more inelastic (Gallet 2007).

But as with tobacco, alcohol taxes can drive the market underground or compel consumers to seek out substitutes. In response to price increases, whether tax-driven or market-driven, consumers can easily substitute a cheaper brand for an expensive brand with the same alcohol content (Hobday et al. 2016). Alcohol taxes also shift purchasing to lower-tax jurisdictions. *Drinking in the Shadow Economy*, a report issued by the Institute for Economic Affairs, a British think tank, found that higher alcohol taxes do not reduce consumption but instead drive the market underground. The result is higher consumption of unregulated alcohol, greater smuggling, and lower tax revenue—not unlike the rum-running and moonshine production that occurred during prohibition.

This phenomenon is well-documented at the state level. Policymakers in Pennsylvania, where alcohol is tightly regulated and highly taxed, are well aware that residents cross the border to purchase alcohol in states like Delaware, where prices are lower. The practice occurs despite its illegality and the possibility, if caught, of a fine of $10 per can of beer and $25 per bottle of liquor.

Likewise, Illinois policymakers know that residents cross the border to Indiana to purchase alcohol, where taxes are lower. And in neighboring Michigan, officials estimate that smuggled alcohol costs the state $14 million per year in lost revenue.[16] Their report did not, however, recommend reducing the state's alcohol taxes.

If policymakers wish to reduce alcohol consumption, taxes may not be the best answer. Instead, limitations on advertising may be the ticket. Underage drinkers exhibit brand loyalty independent of cost (Albers et al. 2014), and reduced advertising depresses drinking levels, especially among heavy users (Saffer et al. 2016). Minimum price levels or content-based taxation, as opposed to value-based taxation, may also be more effective (Meier et al. 2016).

However, efforts to reduce consumption of alcohol may increase consumption of another vice: marijuana. Research suggests that these commodities are substitutes rather than complements (Crost and Rees 2012), and policies designed to reduce alcohol consumption increase marijuana use (Crost and Guerrero 2013). The legalization of marijuana for medical purposes was found to reduce traffic fatalities by between 8% and 11%, with a larger impact on fatalities also involving alcohol, meaning that wider availability of marijuana reduced alcohol consumption (Anderson et al. 2013).

Honey Without Bees: The Taxation of Sugar

History and Current Sugar Tax Landscape

Although taxes on sugar are much less prevalent than taxes on alcohol and tobacco, the history of taxes on sugar in the United States stretches back nearly as far. The Sugar Act, passed by British parliament in 1764, placed a duty on sugar and molasses imports. The Act was unpopular with colonists and many of the founders, including Samuel Adams, contributing to the American Revolution. The early federal government levied taxes on domestic sugar sparingly, enacting a temporary excise to fund the War of 1812 and later to fund the Civil War.

Taxes on sugar or sugar products returned twice in the twentieth century. The War Revenue Act of 1917 instituted multiple taxes, including a new excise of between five and 20 cents per gallon on additives (e.g., syrup) used to flavor soft drinks, which themselves were taxed one cent per gallon. The taxes were repealed in 1924. A sugar tax was brought back during the Great Depression. The Agricultural Adjustment Act of 1933, as amended, authorized the Secretary of Agriculture to levy a "processing tax" on agricultural commodities, including sugar. The proceeds were used to stabilize commodity prices, such as by paying farmers to reduce output. The Roosevelt-era redistribution scheme was ruled unconstitutional in 1936.[17] Although there are no longer federal excise taxes on sugar, duties are charged on sugar imports, just as they have been for most of the nation's history.

At the state and local levels, sugar is taxed, albeit indirectly, only if state and/or local retail sales taxes are applied to goods that contain sugar. Because most state and local governments do not charge their retail sales tax on groceries, sugar-containing beverages and food purchased at supermarkets or other outlets are not taxed. And whereas 14 states do levy a sales tax on groceries, only half charge the state's "full" tax rate.

Moreover, tax treatment of sugar-containing foods and beverages is contingent on the method of purchase. In most states, a consumer can purchase a can of soda or ice cream from a grocery store and not pay a sales tax, whereas consumption of the exact same soda or ice cream at a restaurant would be subject to taxation. State laws also differ on whether retail sales taxes apply to goods purchased through vending machines. Some charge excise taxes, but most do not.

Special Interest Groups and the Taxation of Sugar

In recent years, policymakers have shown a renewed interest in taxing sugar, especially sugar-sweetened beverages (SSBs), in response to rising obesity rates and the concomitant increase in health care costs. Not surprisingly, many of the voices lobbying in favor of new taxes on sugar are groups linked to public health. In 2016, the World Health Organization's Commission on Ending Childhood Obesity issued a report that recommended national governments implement taxes on SSBs and, perhaps, "other unhealthy foods." Countless other groups, including the Obesity Action Coalition, the American Medical Association, the American Heart Association, and the Prevention Institute, have also endorsed SSB taxes.

Another characteristic that is common to sugar tax advocates and tobacco tax advocates alike is their predilection for invoking children to win hearts and minds for their cause. The banner on the Berkeley Healthy Child Coalition's homepage (berkeleyvsbigsoda.com), a group formed in 2013 to advance that city's proposal for a tax on sugary beverages, depicts a cross-section of society—including three children—holding up signs that say either "Berkeley vs. Big Soda" or "Protect Our Children." As Philadelphia debated a similar tax in 2016, the city's Coalition Against Hunger published an editorial in the *Philadelphia Inquirer* that proclaimed the tax was "an investment in Philly's children." Maud Lyon, president of the Greater Philadelphia Cultural Alliance, wrote a commentary for local news site Newsworks.org titled "Soda Tax Presents Opportunity for Greater Access to the Arts." The accompanying picture shows a small group of minority children sitting around a table at a local art exhibit. Nearest to the camera, pieces of clay have been used to write out "I have a dream." Mayor Jim Kenney, a Democrat who proposed the tax, dodged a *New York Times* question about the tax's potential health benefits. Instead, Kenney invoked children: "There's really serious health benefits in pre-K." Philadelphia's city council ultimately authorized the tax.

The sugar industry itself has, thus far, remained noncommittal on SSB taxation. American Crystal Sugar Company, the largest sugar beet producer in the United

States, has no official position on a sugar tax but spent $2.5 million on lobbying in 2015, according to the Center for Responsive Politics. Since 1990, 60% of the company's campaign contributions have gone to Democrats. Two trade groups, the United States Beet Sugar Association and the American Sugar Alliance, also have not established positions on sugar taxes, but both spend money on lobbying and campaign contributions, which skew in favor of Democrats.

Opposition to sugar taxation is much stronger among interests that derive profits from the sale of products that contain sugar. Coca Cola and PepsiCo generally oppose the measures. During a quarterly earnings conference call in 2014, PepsiCo CEO Indra Nooyi opined that "discriminatory taxes on certain categories"—like the Berkeley measure—"are just wrong." Coca Cola spent roughly $8.7 million on lobbying in 2015, and the company's top issue area was taxes—predominantly corporate taxes, tax reform, and international tax issues, but also beverage taxation. PepsiCo, which spent about $4.5 million on lobbying the same year, had much less interest in beverage taxation, focusing instead on food labeling proposals and corporate tax reform.

Food and beverage industry trade groups also tend to oppose sugar taxes. The National Restaurant Association has opposed state-level efforts to tax beverages and other efforts to ban certain beverages outright, such as the unsuccessful attempt to ban soda servings over 20 ounces in New York City. Their efforts have been enhanced by forceful lobbying from the American Beverage Association, which also funded the now-defunct group Americans Against Food Taxes.

Case Studies in the Taxation of Sugar

The Mexican Experience

Among OECD nations, Mexico has the highest rate of overweight or obese adults and the highest rate of Type 2 diabetes. In January 2014, Mexico implemented a one-peso per liter excise tax on beverages with added sugar, which equated to about a 10% price increase.[18] The tax was levied on beverage producers and, by all indications, producers forward-shifted the tax to consumers. Policymakers assumed that higher prices would reduce consumption and reduce the substantial burden associated with well-above-average rates of obesity and diabetes.

Evaluations of the tax began almost immediately. One of the most frequently cited studies (Colchero et al. 2016) found that the volume of taxed beverages sold declined throughout 2014, and that the decline accelerated as the year progressed. By January 2016, American media sources hailed the tax's success. "Mexico's Soda Tax Is Working. The US Should Learn From It" opined an editorial in *Wired*. *Bloomberg* published an editorial titled "Mexico's Soda Tax Success."

Within months, the headlines—relatively few in number—changed. "Soda Sales in Mexico Rise Despite Tax" wrote the *Wall Street Journal* on May 3, 2016. Data from market research firms Canadean and Euromonitor indicated that beverage consumption rebounded following the tax's first year in effect. The non-diet, full-calorie versions of Coca Cola and Pepsi alone enjoyed a 59% market share. A report from the Beverage Marketing Corporation, an industry consulting firm, found that the tax reduced average calorie consumption by about 0.2%.

How could the media get it so wrong? The study they relied on so heavily was observational, not causal, and therefore could draw no clear link between the tax and reduced consumption, a point the authors but not the media were clear to make. The study was also funded in part by the Robert Wood Johnson Foundation and the Bloomberg Philanthropies, both of which had previously supported and funded campaigns and research favorable to soda taxes in the United States.[19] Bloomberg Philanthropies, in fact, donated $10 million in 2012 to El Poder del Consumidor ("Consumer Power"), which lobbied for the same tax this study now suggested had been effective. If, as research suggests, industry-funded studies arrive at conclusions favorable to their sponsor (Lesser et al. 2007), then a similar skepticism should apply when they are funded by interest groups with definite policy positions.

Berkeley, California

In 2014, voters in Berkeley, California, approved Measure D, making the city the first in the United States to levy a tax on sugary beverages (refer also to Chapter 2). The measure instituted a temporary one-cent per ounce tax on distributors of soft drinks, sports drinks, energy drinks, and certain other beverages with caloric sweeteners.[20] But the measure explicitly exempts beverages in which the main ingredient is milk (e.g., chocolate milk), infant formulas, and liquids sold as meal replacement products. Although it clearly fits the definition of an excise tax, the city's ordinance language plainly states that the tax "is not a sales, use, or other excise tax on the sale, consumption or use of Sugar-sweetened beverage products." Instead, the tax is for "the privilege of Distributing Sugar-sweetened beverage products" inside the city.

After the tax was implemented in March 2015, prices increased, indicating that distributors forward-shifted the burden to consumers. But early evidence suggests that distributors under-shifted the tax—i.e., prices have not increased by the same amount as the new tax (Cawley and Frisvold 2015). By November, observers were cautiously declaring the tax a success. Jennifer Falbe, Professor at the University of California-Berkeley School of Public Health, told the San Jose *Mercury News*, "I would say there is evidence that (the tax) is beginning to work, that it's going in the right direction." Dr. Lynn Silver, director of California Project LEAN and advisor to the Public Health Institute, in the same article hailed the tax for "successfully raising money for city programs for improving nutrition and health" (Lochner 2015).

Yet Measure D has already caused some unintended consequences. The price of Diet Coke, which contains no added sugar, increased despite not being subject to taxation (Falbe et al. 2015), suggesting producers and/or retailers were taking advantage of price increases for regular Coke to increase profit margins on similar, perhaps substitute, products. If distributors and/or retailers are absorbing some of the tax burden as some preliminary data suggested, it's more likely that larger rather than smaller outlets are able to do so. Tax competition is also alive and well. Consumers need not buy sugary beverages in Berkeley; they can easily travel to neighboring communities—perhaps on public transit—and purchase the same products without incurring the tax.

Public Policy Issues in Sugar Taxation

Policy Objective and Motive

Just as with taxing other vices, policymakers proceeding with taxes on sugar have largely done so without clarifying their objective. Is the goal of sugar taxes to simply reduce sugar consumption? Or do policymakers conceive sugar taxes as a way to reduce obesity? Or perhaps merely slow the rise in obesity? These goals overlap, but they are not one and the same, and even on paper SSB taxes do a poor job of achieving them. For instance, whether policymakers desire a reduction in sugar consumption regardless of obesity levels, or they in fact wish to reduce obesity, then they should tax all sugar-containing products. It is inconsistent and ultimately ineffective to tax sugary soft drinks while leaving baked goods, fruits, candy, and flavored coffees untaxed.

Fairness and Equity

A number of proposals to tax SSBs, or sugar more generally, are predicated on a strategy to allocate revenues to public education, museums, and cultural activities. But this begs the question of fairness; why, for instance, should the cost of those public goods fall disproportionately on sugar consumers?

The equity of sugar taxes depends both on the structure of the tax and the prevalence of consumption within different groups. Clearly, consumers that do not purchase sugar-sweetened beverages do not directly shoulder any burden from sugar taxes. Among those that do consume the beverages, a larger burden will fall on heavy users, similar to the incidence of tobacco and alcohol taxes. Etilé and Sharma (2015) found that elasticities decline at higher levels of consumption, indicating that heavy sugar users (again, as with the other vices) are less responsive to tax-driven price increases. Taxes may reduce the pool of casual, infrequent sugar consumers, leaving behind heavy consumers who are increasingly less likely to reduce their own consumption if governments levy or increase existing sugar taxes.

Research also indicates that sugar consumption differs across income grouping. Lower-income individuals tend to consume more calories from added sugars than higher-income individuals (Han and Powell 2013; Thompson et al. 2009). As a result, any tax on sugar will likely be regressive, and evidence suggests this is true in practice. Sharma et al. (2014) examined the impact of two types of taxes on low- and high-income households: a sales tax of 20% and a tax of 20 cents per liter. Both taxes had a disproportionate impact on low-income households, although for both groups, the burden of the sales tax was higher than the volume-based tax.

The Impact of Sugar Taxation on Consumption and Health

In theory, raising the price of sugary beverages reduces consumption and consequently reduces obesity and the incidence of related health conditions. Gortmaker et al. (2015) found that an excise tax was among the most cost-effective policies for reducing childhood obesity. A study of Australian adults estimated that a tax-driven 20% increase in the price of sugary beverages would reduce that country's health care expenditures, reduce new Type 2 diabetes cases by 800 per year and, after 25 years, an additional 1,600 people would be alive (Veerman et al. 2016). Long et al. (2015) estimate that a one-cent excise tax per ounce of beverage would reduce consumption by 20%, reduce average body mass index values by anywhere from 0.03 to 0.37, and increase life expectancy.

But research is far from conclusive that sugar taxes yield meaningful health benefits. Consider the Long et al. (2015) study. Since the average adult body mass index is about 28.6, the one-cent excise tax would reduce values by between 0.10% and 1.29%, hardly a significant change. Other studies have found that taxes reduce obesity and body mass index values, but not to a substantively meaningful degree (Fletcher et al. 2010). Others find that tax increases fail to reduce consumption of soft drinks at all (Colantuoni and Rojas 2015). Although sugar tax advocates often react to failed experiments by saying the tax was too low to have a concrete impact, research suggests otherwise (Fletcher et al. 2015).

Underperformance of taxes on sugar-sweetened beverages can be traced to two underlying problems. The first is the design of the tax itself, which is often based on volume (e.g., a certain excise per ounce or liter) or unit (e.g., a certain excise per bottle). The failure of those taxes is that they fail to incorporate differences in caloric density. Under per-bottle tax regimes, a 200-calorie beverage is taxed the same as a 600-calorie beverage. That, notably, is not the approach taken by federal or state governments when levying taxes on alcoholic beverages. Not surprisingly, per-calorie taxes have a more substantial impact on caloric consumption. Zhen et al. (2014a) estimate that an excise tax of 0.04 cents per calorie would reduce per-capita beverage consumption by 5,800 calories.[21] Sharma et al. (2014) found that a volume-based tax resulted in higher weight reduction and also had lower tax burdens on both low- and high-income households relative to a sales tax.

The second tax design problem is a failure to recognize market reality. Common sense dictates that targeting a tax on certain sugar-dense goods will be ineffective at reducing consumption as long as consumers have easy access to substitutes. Taxes may reduce soda consumption, but they do not necessarily reduce overall calorie intake (Fletcher et al. 2015). Soda taxes, for instance, may simply drive consumers toward fruit juices just as high, if not higher, in sugar content (Dharmasena and Capps 2012; Taber et al. 2015). They may also substitute sugar with other goods that contain higher levels of fat and sodium (Zhen et al. 2014b).

Policymakers have shown little evidence of recognizing such realities. Some sugar tax proposals explicitly exempt dairy, meaning that soda is taxed but chocolate milk is not, as is the case in Berkeley. Others target sodas but not coffee, meaning that Starbucks drinks, which can easily contain hundreds of calories from sugar, are untaxed. When the Institute for Fiscal Studies, a British economic research firm, released its 2016 "Green Budget" aimed at shaping federal budget debates, it said of excise taxes on sugary beverages:

> A sugary soft drinks tax is likely to lead consumers to switch away from taxed products, but the efficacy of the policy will depend on what products they switch to and how firms change their prices. Some consumers might switch to chocolate, for example, which is also high in sugar and contains saturated fat to boot. Some manufacturers and/or retailers might respond to the tax by increasing the prices of diet drinks, dampening the extent of any consumer switching to these products.[22]

The Future of Sugar Taxation

Ghosh and Hall (2015) found that, holding all else equal, Democratic states as measured by presidential popular vote and those with higher rates of adult obesity are more likely to tax sodas, but that in every state, the number of convenience stores per capita has a large, negative effect on the likelihood of taxation. Whereas the imposition of excise taxes on SSBs has had some local success, similar measures have been rejected elsewhere, including Richmond, Virginia; San Francisco, California; and Davis, California, sometimes by voters and sometimes by legislative bodies.

Some policymakers are proceeding, but with caution, waiting for more consistent research on the impact of sugar taxation. One area of attention is the need for additional data on the health impacts of lower-calorie sweeteners and fruit juices. As likely substitutes for sugar, those substances cannot be ignored in policy design if the objective is to improve public health (Popkin and Hawkes 2016). Sugar taxes have also grown more complicated as the issue has become entangled with public education and food access policy. Taber et al. (2014) found that students with access to in-school vending machines consumed less soda and fast food, particularly in states where those items were taxed at lower rates than food more generally. But, at the same time, many policymakers have moved to eliminate vending machines from public schools.

A Blunt Instrument: The Emerging Taxation of Marijuana

History and Legal Context

For a little over three decades during the mid-twentieth century, marijuana was legal in certain circumstances and taxable under United States federal law. The Marihuana Tax Act of 1937 stipulated that marijuana sellers and producers register with the federal government and pay a tax based on their status.[23] Importers and manufacturers were charged an annual tax of $24, equivalent to about $395 in 2016 dollars. Doctors prescribing marijuana as well as most users were ordered to pay an annual tax of $1, equivalent to about $17 in 2016 dollars.[24] Violators risked a fine of up to $2,000, the equivalent of about $32,900 in 2016 dollars, five years in prison, or both. However, a federal report issued in 1967 stated that marijuana taxes yielded very little revenue, in part because most market participants never registered with the government and hence never paid their tax liability.[25]

The Marihuana Tax Act was declared unconstitutional by the Supreme Court in 1969. The case, *Leary v. United States*, was brought by famed psychologist Timothy Leary. Leary had been convicted of violating the law after a customs agent in Texas found marijuana in Leary's vehicle. Leary argued that the only way for him to comply with federal law would be to register the marijuana in his possession, which at that time was illegal under Texas state law. Thus, adhering to federal law required that Leary incriminate himself under state law, a violation of his Fifth Amendment rights. The Court agreed. Congress responded in 1970 by enacting the Controlled Substances Act, which rendered marijuana an illegal drug.

Subsequent federal enforcement of marijuana prohibition has been inconsistent. The lack of enforcement opened the door for state and local governments to act in defiance of federal law. Several states have legalized marijuana for medicinal purposes, and a small but growing number have also legalized marijuana for recreational, or casual, purposes. Indeed, policymakers increasingly seem less interested with reducing marijuana consumption—perhaps because it is so commonplace despite federal prohibition and because of mixed evidence that the substance is as harmful as critics once contended—and more interested in bringing the marijuana market "out of the shadows" to reap tax revenues.

State Marijuana Tax Experimentation and Early Results

By mid-2016, four states had moved to legalize and tax recreational marijuana: Alaska, Colorado, Washington, and Oregon. As Table 6.5 illustrates, these states' marijuana tax regimes are highly idiosyncratic. Colorado, Washington, and Oregon levy an ad valorem sales tax, but Alaska charges a flat dollar amount per ounce.

TABLE 6.5 Marijuana Taxation in Select States

State	Medical Tax	Recreational Tax	Revenue Allocation
Alaska	No difference between medical and recreational use; $50 per ounce of flower or bud and $15 per ounce for remainder of plant		Unallocated
Colorado	2.9% state retail sales tax + local retail sales tax	2.9% state retail sales tax + 10% marijuana sales tax + 15% excise tax + local retail sales tax	State general fund and public school capital projects
Oregon	None	17%	Public education; drug rehabilitation programs; law enforcement
Washington	None, if tax exemption granted	37% state retail sales tax	Distributed to state, county, and city governments; also health and social services

Sources: Individual states' websites.

Alaska is the only state that taxes medical and recreational marijuana equally; Washington does in principle, but only if medical users apply for and receive a special tax exemption. Colorado's medical tax (2.9%) is significantly lower than the recreational tax (27.9%), and local option sales taxes may further increase both rates. Oregon does not tax medical marijuana, but recreational marijuana is taxed at 37%. In addition to sales tax revenue, most states also charge marijuana sellers various business license fees.

Tax and licensing revenue is generally earmarked for general government operations, public education, law enforcement, and social programs. By all accounts, policymakers in these states have welcomed the additional tax revenue. After Colorado decriminalized recreational marijuana in 2014, the state treasury recorded consistent monthly increases in marijuana tax revenue (See Figure 6.7). The first full year of legalization in Colorado yielded $76.1 million in tax revenue. Those revenues increased 77.5% in 2015 and another 43% in the first half of 2016.

However, the tax revenues are far from a major component of state budgets. Colorado's 2015 marijuana tax haul represented just over one-half of 1% of the state's total budget. Likewise, although Washington collected an estimated $70 million in marijuana tax revenue during 2014–2015, the proceeds represented less than 1% of the state's overall budget.

The Politics of Marijuana Legalization

Beyond using revenue as a selling point, supporters of marijuana legalization have changing public sentiment on their side. Public opinion on the subject has

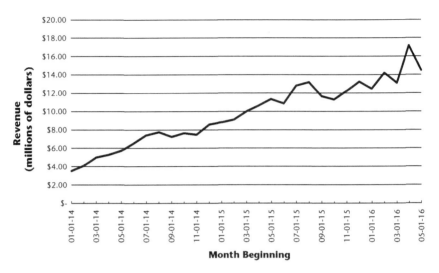

FIGURE 6.7 Monthly Marijuana Tax and Fee Revenue in Colorado, 2014—Mid 2016

Source: Colorado Department of Revenue, Taxation Division.

undergone a profound shift in the last half-century. An October 2015 Gallup poll found that 58% of American adults favored legalization, a marked increase from 1969, when just 12% agreed with the same position. The evolution in public opinion is largely generational. Whereas all age groups have grown more permissive of legalization, support is weakest among adults born prior to 1951 (Jones 2015). As a result, opposition to legalizing marijuana has lessened over time.

Perhaps bolstering the case for marijuana, legalization for medicinal purposes has not increased marijuana use among teenagers, as many critics feared (Anderson et al. 2015). In fact, juvenile marijuana consumption has declined. According to the 2015 Monitoring the Future Study, 9.3%, 17.1%, and 24.7% of 8th, 10th, and 12th grade students reported using marijuana within the past 30 days, levels mostly at or below recent historical trends. In fact, according to the study, reported use in all three groups was much higher in the mid-1990s (16.0%, 24.1%, and 26.9%, respectively, in 1997).[26]

Many interest groups have expressed support for legalizing and taxing marijuana. New voices have entered the fray, including the Marijuana Policy Project, the Marijuana Majority, the Campaign to Regulate Marijuana Like Alcohol, and the National Organization for the Reform of Marijuana Laws, but traditional groups have also offered support. The United States Conference of Mayors in 2013 passed a resolution urging the Obama Administration to let state governments establish their own marijuana policies free from federal interference.[27] A report the same year released by the liberal American Civil Liberties Union called for legalizing, regulating, and taxing marijuana for individuals age 21 and over, in part to remedy the stunning racial disparities in arrests and sentences under current federal law.[28] Although some think tanks have remained relatively quiet on the issue, including the Center for Budget and Policy Priorities, the Economic Policy Institute, the American Enterprise Institute, and the Heritage Foundation, libertarian organizations, including the Cato Institute and the Reason Foundation, have advocated legalizing and taxing marijuana.

Support from state and local officials is tempered by uncertainty regarding future federal policy on marijuana. Indeed, many state governments are reluctant to pursue legalization for fear of future shifts in federal enforcement. They must also contend with dozens of interest groups against legalization, including Citizens Against Legalizing Marijuana, Smart Approaches to Marijuana, the Drug Free America Foundation, Save Our Society from Drugs, Parents Opposed to Pot, and the Community Anti-Drug Coalitions of America. These groups invariably try to educate policymakers and the public about potential harm from legalization, such as impaired driving and the potential for addiction, and often point out the clear conflict between state legalization and current federal policy.

Some of the most powerful advocacy against marijuana legalization comes from organizations that have a vested interest in maintaining the status quo. Some groups view legal marijuana as competition. For example, the California Beer & Beverage Distributors provided funding to defeat California's Proposition 19 (2010), which would have made marijuana legal and taxable. Bentsen (2014) notes that other opposition comes from police unions and organizations, prison employee unions and companies, and even the pharmaceutical industry. Each group represents individuals and companies that have an economic interest in keeping marijuana illegal, so much so that they are willing to spend tens of millions of dollars to keep it that way.[29]

Challenges to Implementing a Tax on Marijuana

Uncertainty surrounding federal marijuana enforcement creates uncertainty in each state's marijuana marketplace, even in states that have legalized the substance. Policymakers considering further legalization efforts thus must contend with this reality. More specifically, Section 280E of the federal tax code also limits growers' and retailers' ability to deduct basic expenses, such as overhead and raw materials costs, from their revenue to determine taxable income, thus spiking their federal tax liability. Not surprisingly, these issues compel distributors and retailers to conduct transactions outside of public view, even in states that have fully legalized marijuana. Tax revenues are consequently lower than they would be otherwise.

Many financial institutions also refuse to open bank accounts and extend credit to growers and retailers. Because marijuana remains a largely cash-based market, states have had to confront a rather practical matter: how to actually collect tax revenues. Oregon, for example, allows for electronic fund transfers direct to the state treasury. But Alaska mandates that growers remit marijuana taxes monthly in cash—in part because many have no bank accounts—and that they travel to the state capitol in Anchorage to do so. The state's Tax Division concluded this arrangement was the most cost efficient, after considering alternatives such as armored courier services or secured cash drop boxes located around the state (Andrews 2016).

A final implementation issue is how to align the medical and recreational marijuana markets within the same state (Anderson et al. 2015; Pacula et al. 2015). When the tax on medical marijuana is lower than the tax on recreational marijuana—as it is in three of the first four states to legalize both—there is a strong incentive for users to seek medical cards and avoid paying the higher tax. This, in turn, lowers tax revenue below what it would be otherwise. Future state policy experimentation in this field will also have to disentangle the relationship between medical and recreational uses (Anderson et al. 2015; Pacula et al. 2015).

Conclusion: Vice Taxes and Paternalism

By their nature, public policies have always contained an element of paternalism—the notion that policymakers more than citizens know what is best for society and, perhaps, the individual. Although some paternalistic approaches are motivated by religious or moral beliefs, and progressive thought itself has always had a strong foundation in paternalism, the growing popularity of behavioral economics has sparked new, seemingly objective, rationales for policies that aim to reduce the incidence of activities that policymakers have deemed "wrong" for society. Taxes on tobacco, alcohol, sugar, and marijuana are only four of innumerable examples of the state's efforts to "nudge" citizens toward "better" choices (Thaler and Sunstein 2009).

But vice taxes illustrate the pitfalls and failures of that approach to public policy and to taxes in particular. One common trait of efforts to tax tobacco, alcohol, sugar, and marijuana is that policymakers generally failed to account for the likelihood of both avoidant behaviors and the use of substitute goods. When taxes on tobacco increase, smokers become more efficient users, purchase cigarettes in lower-tax jurisdictions, buy products on the black market, or reduce spending on other goods. In response to alcohol taxes, consumers produce their own, purchase in lower-tax jurisdictions, or switch to lower-cost brands with equivalent alcohol content. In response to taxes on SSBs, consumers substitute with other high-calorie but untaxed drinks or with food high in fat and carbohydrates. Efforts to legalize and tax marijuana with high excise taxes have had the effect of keeping the market underground. Making it harder to consume alcohol can increase marijuana consumption and perhaps vice versa.

Policymakers' response to these well-supported patterns is rarely to undo the taxes and other policies that caused them; instead, they tend to favor higher taxes and more regulations, which in turn create even more unintended consequences.

Ironically, the externalities policymakers seek to reduce are often the result of their own actions—i.e., other public policies (Browning 1999).

What all efforts to tax vices have in common, especially from the progressive movement to today, is the widespread inclination of policymakers consigning too much faith in their own ability and that of "experts" to improve civil society over and above what would have occurred in the absence of their interventions. Like any attempt to engage in social engineering, using the tax code to shape behavior betrays four critical mistakes.

First, there is no guarantee that policymakers and the experts on which they depend possess complete, accurate information from which to draw inferences about human behaviors, much less to model the underlying data completely and appropriately, and much less to draw implications for tax policy. Rizzo and Whitman (2009) argue that to make better policy, policymakers must have six different types of knowledge about consumer preferences at both the individual and population level, a requirement that is impossible to meet. Merely collecting more data does not necessarily generate knowledge, nor is it a useful approach. Underlying measurements may lack both accuracy and precision, and social scientific laboratory experiments and econometric modeling cannot hope to duplicate the complexity of the real world. It should thus come as no surprise that academic research on the efficacy of vice taxes is best described as noncommittal. Some studies suggest the taxes "work," others find the opposite, and others conclude that it depends. In short, so-called experts producing the associated research have covered all the possible outcome angles. It should also not come as a surprise that replication problems and a spike in retractions have recently plagued the social and physical sciences, which should—but likely will not—increase skepticism of their use in policymaking.[30]

Second, policymakers and experts are not immune from the very cognitive biases possessed by the ordinary citizens they imply are inferior. Common sense dictates that this simple fact should compel policymakers and experts to question their own abilities to direct tax policy toward socially optimal ends. But surprisingly, 96% of studies in top behavioral economics journals that recommend paternalistic policy interventions do not question policymakers' cognitive abilities or biases (Berggren 2012). This comes despite mounting evidence to the contrary. State policymakers in particular have a strong tendency to imitate actions taken in other states, the so-called bandwagon effect. Such decisions may be motivated by competitive concerns, but psychology also plays a role. Policymakers interpret the popularity of a policy in other jurisdictions as a proxy for success and seek to emulate that success, an overreaction that creates policy bubbles (Maor 2014). Policymakers also respond to emotional manipulation (Maor 2016). On the other side of the coin, theory and research suggest that policymakers have an intellectual reluctance to oppose policies they previously supported (de Leon 1978) and may support inefficient policies out of fear that changing positions will significantly harm their likelihood of reelection (Durr 2001).

Third, scholarly biases impose their own problems. Analyses of vice taxes frequently ignore substitution. Once substitution is factored in, researchers often find that the efficacy of vice taxes declines and that the taxes may actually do more harm than good (O'Donoghue and Rabin 2006). Still another analytical bias is that of ignoring the full costs and benefits of policy changes. Perhaps the best example is ignoring the "benefit" of having smokers die sooner, and hence saving health care and social security costs, or the "cost" of having a healthier population—i.e., health and entitlement costs are higher.

Fourth, policymakers and the experts on which they depend are economic creatures that respond to incentives, and the incentives they face are not tied to improved social welfare. Elected officials have one primary goal—reelection—and in a political system heavily influenced by money, reelection comes not by improving social welfare, but by creating the illusion that you have. Academic researchers are beholden to a hyper-competitive grant system; insufficient grant support could mean a loss of prestige or, worse, job loss. The incentive is to do whatever is necessary to win grants, and that often means tailoring research findings to the clients' desires. Competitive pressures also drive faster research and data collection, which can have the ripple effect of poor measurements and insufficient modeling of econometric data.

Given all of the above, why do vice taxes persist? Taxes on two of the four vices profiled in this chapter have historical momentum: tobacco and alcohol. Both taxes benefit from lingering moral sentiments against consumption and, having been on the books for over a century, the likelihood of their termination or reduction is low. Over that timeframe, taxes on both have become self-sustaining. The taxes support large bureaucracies tasked with collecting them, and the members of those bureaucracies, as economic creatures, generally resist proposals that may reduce their prestige or jeopardize their job security.

But vice taxes are entangled in countless other bureaucracies, where they provide the funding to maintain programs for favored constituencies. Perhaps the best example is the use of tobacco taxes to subsidize CHIP or other policies that mandate vice tax revenues be allocated toward public education. Because these programs have broad, emotionally favorable constituencies, and the burden is believed to fall on a much narrower segment of the population engaging in unfavorable behaviors, it is not surprising that vice taxes have lasted as long as they have. Consider the difficulty of trying to balance "the children" against "big tobacco," "big sugar," or "big alcohol."

Finally, vice taxes invite rent-seeking from multiple parties. Proposals to increase or expand vice taxes invite heightened lobbying activity, just as they do for any other consumption tax (Hoffer et al. 2014). Disparate parties may seek or lobby in favor of vice taxes not for any public health or moral reason, but because the taxes are a convenient source of revenue that avoids having to reduce budgets—and thereby reduce the state's role in individual affairs and civil society.

Notes

1 Sumptuary taxes were not always labeled as taxes. For example, colonial records indicate that a woman named Mary Stebbins was fined 10 shillings in 1667 after she was caught wearing silk clothing in violation of law. In 1674, a man named Nathaniel Ely was fined for not preparing beer according to legal requirements.

2 James' manifesto, now well within the public domain, is titled "A Counterblaste to Tobacco."

3 Sultan Murad IV made tobacco and alcohol consumption punishable by death. His successors preferred taxes to the sword.

4 The recommended tax was 10 cents per pound of snuff and eight cents per pound on other manufactured tobacco products.

5 A federal tax on snuff was briefly reintroduced in 1814.

6 For instance, the total weight of certain tobacco products imported from Europe cannot exceed 10,000 metric tons per year. Import caps range from a low of 2,750 metric tons (Chile) to 80,200 metric tons (Brazil).

7 The initiative publishes a "Technical Manual on Tobacco Tax Administration" for policymakers. Perhaps surprisingly, the manual's stated objective is not merely to improve public health but to help "governments . . . raise revenues."

8 For additional exploration of this dynamic, see Bagchi and Feigenbaum (2012).

9 See The Tax Foundation Fiscal Fact #450, "Cigarette Taxes and Cigarette Smuggling by State," 2013.

10 From 1995 to 2002, multiple federal, state, and local agencies ran Operation Smoke-screen, a smuggling operation in which members of a Hezbollah terror cell purchased cigarettes in low-tax states like North Carolina and resold them in high-tax states like Michigan, funneling the profits back to Hezbollah. In a separate case, Elmar Rakhami-mov was sentenced in 2016 to 18 months in prison for selling cigarettes in New York that had been purchased in Maryland, where the tax is lower, but without paying applicable excise taxes, a scheme that netted millions of dollars.

11 The move toward alcohol prohibition started well before the Constitution was ratified. As early as 1619, the Virginia colony outlawed drunkenness. By 1633, Massachusetts required a license to sell alcohol. Many colonies would later prohibit the sale of alcohol to Native Americans and ban outright the sale of hard liquor.

12 See National Wholesale Liquor Dealers Association of America, "The Anti-Prohibition Manual: A Summary of Facts and Figures Dealing with Prohibition," 1917.

13 See National Institute on Alcohol Abuse and Alcoholism, Division of Epidemiology and Prevention Research, "Apparent Per Capita Alcohol Consumption: National, State, and Regional Trends, 1977–2009," 2011.

14 See http://abc.nc.gov/Pricing/Breakdown.

15 Positions on this question vary by agency. In 2010, the Community Preventative Services Task Force, part of the Department of Health and Human Services, recommended higher alcohol taxes as a tool to reduce excessive consumption. But the National Institute on Alcohol Abuse and Alcoholism does not appear to have taken a firm position on alcohol taxes one way or the other.

16 See Michigan Liquor Control Commission, "Illegal Importation of Alcohol into Michigan: An Assessment of the Issue and Recommendations," 2008.

17 *United States v. Butler*, 297 U.S. 1 (1936).

18 In 2002, Mexico enacted a 20% tax on beverages not sweetened with domestic cane sugar—in effect, a tariff on foreign sweeteners, especially corn syrup from the United States. After involvement from the World Trade Organization, Mexico and the United States agreed to free trade of sweeteners to take effect in 2008.

19 The Robert Wood Johnson Foundation provided a $3.5 million grant in 2009 for "Save the Children," an interest group that used the funds to lobby in favor of state-level soda

taxes. In 2014, the foundation's website highlighted the soda tax in Berkeley, California, as one of 10 "signs we are building a culture of health."

20 As approved, Measure D is scheduled to sunset on December 31, 2026.

21 This study was also funded in part by the Robert Wood Johnson Foundation.

22 The full text of the budget is available at https://www.ifs.org.uk/publications/8158.

23 The common spelling at the time was "marihuana," but the term was not familiar to most observers, who more commonly knew marijuana as hemp or cannabis.

24 The American Medical Association opposed the Act because of the direct tax on physicians.

25 See "The Challenge of Crime in a Free Society: A Report by the President's Commission on Law Enforcement and the Administration of Justice," 1967.

26 The full text of the study is available at https://www.ifs.org.uk/publications/8158.

27 See The United States Conference of Mayors, "In Support of States Setting Their Own Marijuana Policies Without Federal Interference," 2013.

28 See The American Civil Liberties Union, "The War on Marijuana in Black and White," 2013.

29 Not all law enforcement organizations are aligned against legalization (e.g., Law Enforcement Against Prohibition).

30 In 2015, the Open Science Collaboration attempted to replicate 100 psychological studies that reported statistically significant positive results; on replication, 65% failed to show any significance, and the remaining replications suggested smaller effects. In another experiment, researchers submitted a paper with eight major errors to the *British Medical Journal*. It was reviewed by 221 scientists—none of whom caught all eight errors, and only 30% recommended the paper be rejected.

References

Adda, Jérôme, and Francesca Cornaglia. 2006. "Taxes, Cigarette Consumption, and Smoking Intensity." *American Economic Review* 96(4): 1013–1028.

Adda, Jérôme, and Francesca Cornaglia. 2010. "The Effect of Bans and Taxes on Passive Smoking." *American Economic Journal: Applied Economics* 2(1): 1–32.

Albers, Alison B., William DeJong, Timothy S. Naimi, Michael Siegel, and David H. Jernigan. 2014. "The Relationship Between Alcohol Price and Brand Choice Among Underage Drinkers: Are the Most Popular Alcoholic Brands Consumed by Youth the Cheapest?" *Substance Use & Misuse* 49(13): 1833–1843.

Anderson, D. Mark, Benjamin Hansen, and Daniel I. Rees. 2013. "Medical Marijuana Laws, Traffic Fatalities, and Alcohol Consumption." *Journal of Law & Economics* 56(2): 333–369.

Anderson, D. Mark, Benjamin Hansen, and Daniel I. Rees. 2015. "Medical Marijuana Laws and Teen Marijuana Use." *American Law and Economics Review* 17(2): 495–528.

Andrews, Laurel. 2016. "Alaska Pot Businesses Will Have to Pay Cash Taxes in Anchorage." *Alaska Dispatch News*, January 20.

Apollonio, Dorie E., and Lisa A. Bero. 2007. "The Creation of Industry Front Groups: The Tobacco Industry and 'Get the Government Off Our Back'." *American Journal of Public Health* 97(3): 419–427.

Bagchi, Shantanu, and James Feigenbaum. 2012. "Is Smoking a Fiscal Good?" *Review of Economic Dynamics* 17(1): 170–190.

Bentsen, Kendall. 2014. "Money, Not Morals, Drives Marijuana Prohibition Movement." Center for Responsive Politics.

Berggren, Niclas. 2012. "Time for a Behavioral Political Economy? An Analysis of Articles in Behavioral Economics." *The Review of Austrian Economics* 25(3): 199–221.

Browning, Edgar K. 1999. "The Myth of Fiscal Externalities." *Public Finance Review* 27(1): 3–18.

Callison, Kevin, and Robert Kaestner. 2014. "Do Higher Tobacco Taxes Reduce Adult Smoking? New Evidence of the Effect of Recent Cigarette Tax Increases on Adult Smoking." *Economic Inquiry* 52(1): 155–172.

Carpenter, Christopher S., and Michael T. Mathes. 2016. "New Evidence on the Price Effects of Cigarette Tax Competition." *Public Finance Review* 44(3): 291–310.

Cawley, John, and David Frisvold. 2015. "The Incidence of Taxes on Sugar-Sweetened Beverages: The Case of Berkeley, California." National Bureau of Economic Research Working Paper No. 21465.

Chaloupka, Frank J., Ayda Yurekil, and Geoffrey T. Fong. 2012. "Tobacco Taxes as a Tobacco Control Strategy." *Tobacco Control* 21(2): 172–180.

Cherrington, Ernest Hurst. 1920. *The Evolution of Prohibition in the United States of America.* Westerville, OH: American Issue Press.

Colantuoni, Francesca, and Christian Rojas. 2015. "The Impact of Soda Sales Taxes on Consumption: Evidence from Scanner Data." *Contemporary Economic Policy* 33(4): 714–734.

Colchero, M. Arantxa, Barry M. Popkin, Juan A. Rivera, and Shu Wen Ng. 2016. "Beverage Purchases from Stores in Mexico under the Excise Tax on Sugar Sweetened Beverages: Observational Study." *The BMJ* 2016(352). doi: http://dx.doi.org/10.1136/bmj.h6704

Crost, Benjamin, and Santiago Guerrero. 2013. "The Effect of Alcohol Availability on Marijuana Use: Evidence from the Minimum Legal Drinking Age." *Journal of Health Economics* 31(1): 112–121.

Crost, Benjamin, and Daniel I. Rees. 2012. "The Minimum Legal Drinking Age and Marijuana Use: New Estimates from the NLSY97." *Journal of Health Economics* 32(2): 474–476.

Daley, James I., Mandy Stahre, Frank J. Chaloupka, and Timothy S. Naimi. 2012. "The Impact of a 25-Cent-Per-Drink Alcohol Tax Increase." *American Journal of Preventative Medicine* 42(4): 382–389.

DeCicca, Phlip, Donald Kenkel, and Feng Liu. 2013. "Excise Tax Avoidance: The Case of State Cigarette Taxes." *Journal of Health Economics* 32(6): 1130–1141.

de Leon, Peter. 1978. "Public Policy Termination: An End and a Beginning." *Policy Analysis* 4(3): 369–392.

DePew, Chauncey M. 1895. *One Hundred Years of American Commerce.* New York: D. O. Haynes & Co.

Dharmasena, Senarath, and Oral Capps. 2012. "Intended and Unintended Consequences of a Proposed National Tax on Sugar-Sweetened Beverages to Combat the U.S. Obesity Problem." *Health Economics* 21(6): 669–694.

Durr, Robert. 2001. "Why Do Policy Makers Stick to Inefficient Decisions?" *Public Choice* 107(3/4): 221–234.

Elder, Randy W., Briana Lawrence, Aneeqah Ferguson, Timothy S. Naimi, Robert D. Brewer, Sajal K. Chattopadhyay, Traci L. Toomey, and Jonathan E. Fielding. 2010. "The Effectiveness of Tax Interventions for Reducing Excessive Alcohol Consumption and Related Harms." *American Journal of Preventative Medicine* 38(2): 217–229.

Etilé, Fabrice, and Anurag Sharma. 2015. "Do High Consumers of Sugar-Sweetened Beverages Respond Differently to Price Changes? A Finite Mixture IV-Tobit Approach." *Health Economics* 24(9): 1147–1163.

Evans, William N., and Matthew C. Farrelly. 1998. "The Compensating Behavior of Smokers: Taxes, Tar, and Nicotine." *The RAND Journal of Economics* 29(30): 578–595.

Falbe, Jennifer, Nadia Rojas, Anna H. Grummon, and Kristine A. Madsen. 2015. "Higher Retail Prices of Sugar-Sweetened Beverages 3 Months After Implementation of an Excise Tax in Berkeley, California." *American Journal of Public Health* 105(11): 2194–2201.

Farrelly, Matthew C., Jeremy W. Bray, Terry Pechacek, and Trevor Wollery. 2001. "Response by Adults to Increases in Cigarette Prices by Sociodemographic Characteristics." *Southern Economic Journal* 68(1): 156–165.

Farrelly, Matthew C., James M. Nonnemaker, and Kimberly A. Watson. 2012. "The Consequences of High Cigarette Excise Taxes for Low-Income Smokers." *PLoS ONE* 7(9): e43838.

Fletcher, Jason M., David E. Frisvold, and Nathan Tefft. 2010. "Can Soft Drink Taxes Reduce Population Weight?" *Contemporary Economic Policy* 28(1): 23–35.

Fletcher, Jason M., David E. Frisvold, and Nathan Tefft. 2015. "Non-Linear Effects of Soda Taxes on Consumption and Weight Outcomes." *Health Economics* 24(5): 566–582.

Franks, Peter, Anthony F. Jerant, J. Paul Leigh, Dennis Lee, Alan Chiem, Ilene Lewis, and Sandy Lee. 2007. "Cigarette Prices, Smoking, and the Poor: Implications of Recent Trends." *American Journal of Public Health* 97(10): 1873–1877.

Gallet, Craig A. 2007. "The Demand for Alcohol: A Meta-Analysis of Elasticities." *Australian Journal of Agricultural and Resource Economics* 51(2): 121–135.

Ghosh, Sriparna, and Joshua C. Hall. 2015. "The Political Economy of Soda Taxation." West Virginia University Department of Economics Working Paper Series, Paper #15–50.

Givel, Michael S., and Stanton A. Glantz. 2001. "Tobacco Lobby Political Influence on US State Legislatures in the 1990s." *Tobacco Control* 10(2): 124–134.

Gortmaker, Steven L., Y. Claire Wang, Michael W. Long, Catherine M. Giles, Zachary J. Ward, Jessica L. Barrett, Erica L. Kenney, Kendrin R. Sonneville, Amna Sadaf Afzal, Stephen C. Resch, and Angie L. Cradock. 2015. "Three Interventions That Reduce Childhood Obesity Are Projected to Save More Than They Cost to Implement." *Health Affairs* 34(1): 1932–1939.

Han, Euna, and Lisa M. Powell. 2013. "Consumption Patterns of Sugar Sweetened Beverages in the United States." *Journal of the Academy of Nutrition and Dietetics* 113(1): 43–53.

Hobday, Michelle, Elise Gordon, Eveline Lensvelt, Lynn Meuleners, Wenbin Liang, and Tanya Chikritzhs. 2016. "The Effect of Price Increases on Predicted Alcohol Purchasing Decisions and Choice to Substitute." *Addiction Research & Theory*. doi: http://dx.doi.org /10.3109/16066359.2016.1155563

Hodge, Frederick Webb. 1907. *Handbook of American Indians North of Mexico: Part I.* Washington, DC: Smithsonian Institution.

Hodgeland, William. 2015. *The Whiskey Rebellion: George Washington, Alexander Hamilton, and the Frontier Rebels Who Challenged America's Newfound Sovereignty.* New York: Simon & Schuster.

Hoffer, Adam J. 2016. "Special Interest Spillovers and Tobacco Taxation." *Contemporary Economic Policy* 34(1): 146–157.

Hoffer, Adam J., and Adam Pellillo. 2012. "The Political Economy of Tobacco Control Spending." *Applied Economic Letters* 19(2): 1793–1797.

Hoffer, Adam J., William F. Shughart II, and Michael D. Thomas. 2014. "Sin Taxes and Sindustry: Revenue, Paternalism, and Political Interest." *The Independent Review* 19(10): 47–64.

Hofmann, Annette, and Martin Nell. 2012. "Smoking Bans and the Secondhand Smoking Problem: An Economic Analysis." *European Journal of Health Economics* 13(3): 227–236.

Jones, Jeffrey M. 2015. "In U.S., 58% Back Legal Marijuana Use." *Gallup*. http://www.gallup.com/poll/186260/back-legal-marijuana.aspx

Lesser, Lenard I., Cara B. Ebbeling, Merrill Goozner, David Wypij, and David S. Ludwig. 2007. "Relationship between Funding Source and Conclusion among Nutrition-Related Scientific Articles." *PLoS Medicine* 4(1): 41–46.

Lochner, Tom. 2015. "Berkeley: First-in-Nation Soda Tax Begins to Show Results." *Mercury News*. http://www.mercurynews.com/2015/11/18/berkeley-first-in-nation-soda-tax-begins-to-show-results/

Long, Michael W., Steven L. Gortmaker, Zachary J. Ward, Stephen C. Resch, Marj L. Moodie, Gary Sacks, Boyd A. Swinburn, Rob C. Carter, PhD, and Y. Claire Wang. 2015. "Cost Effectiveness of a Sugar-Sweetened Beverage Excise Tax in the U.S." *American Journal of Preventative Medicine* 49(1): 112–123.

MacLean, Johanna Catherine, Asia Sikora Kessler, and Donald S. Kenkel. 2016. "Cigarette Taxes and Older Adult Smoking: Evidence from the Health and Retirement Study." *Health Economics* 25(4): 424–438.

Maor, Moshe. 2014. "Policy Bubbles: Policy Overreaction and Positive Feedback." *Governance* 27(3): 469–487.

Maor, Moshe. 2016. "Emotion-Driven Negative Policy Bubbles." *Policy Sciences* 49(2): 191–210.

Meier, Petra S., John Holmes, Colin Angus, Abdallah K. Ally, Yang Meng, and Alan Brennan. 2016. "Estimated Effects of Different Alcohol Taxation and Price Policies on Health Inequalities: A Mathematical Modeling Study." *PLoS Med* 13(2): e1001963.

Merriman, David. 2010. "The Micro-Geography of Tax Avoidance: Evidence from Littered Cigarette Packs in Chicago." *American Economic Journal: Economic Policy* 2(2): 61–84.

Naimi, Timothy S., James I. Daley, Ziming Xuan, Jason G. Blanchette, Frank J. Chaloupka, and David H. Jernigan. 2016. "Who Would Pay for State Alcohol Tax Increases in the United States?" *Preventing Chronic Disease*. doi: http://dx.doi.org/10.5888/pcd13.150450

O'Donoghue, Ted, and Matthew Rabin. 2006. "Optimal Sin Taxes." *Journal of Public Economics* 90(10–11): 1825–1849.

Okrent, Daniel. 2010. *Last Call: The Rise and Fall of Prohibition*. New York: Scribner.

Pacula, Rosalie L., David Powell, Paul Heaton, and Eric L. Sevigny. 2015. "Assessing the Effects of Medical Marijuana Laws on Marijuana Use: The Devil is in the Details." *Journal of Policy Analysis and Management* 34(1): 7–31.

Popkin, Barry M., and Corinna Hawkes. 2016. "Sweetening of the Global Diet, Particularly Beverages: Patterns, Trends, and Policy Responses." *The Lancent Diabetes & Endocrinology* 4(2): 147–186.

Remler, Dahlia K. 2004. "Poor Smokers, Poor Quitters, and Cigarette Tax Regressivity." *American Journal of Public Health* 94(2): 225–229.

Rizzo, Maril J., and Douglas Glen Whitman. 2009. "The Knowledge Problem of New Paternalism." *BYU Law Review* 2009(4): 905–968.

Room, Robin, Thomas Babor, and Jürgen Rehm. 2005. "Alcohol and Public Health." *Lancet* 365(9458): 519–530.

Sacks, Jeffrey J., Katherine R. Gonzales, Ellen E. Bouchery, and Laura E. Tomedi. 2015. "2010 National and State Costs of Excessive Alcohol Consumption." *American Journal of Preventative Medicine* 49(5): 73–79.

Saffer, Henry, Dhaval Dave, and Michael Grossman. 2016. "A Behavioral Economic Model of Alcohol Advertising and Price." *Health Economics* 25(7): 816–828.

Sharma, Anurag, Katharina Hauck, Bruce Hollingsworth, and Luigi Siciliani. 2014. "The Effects of Taxing Sugar-Sweetened Beverages across Different Income Groups." *Health Economics* 23(9): 1159–1184.

Shrestha, Vinish, and Sara Markowitz. 2016. "The Pass-through of Beer Taxes to Prices: Evidence from State and Federal Tax Changes." *Economic Inquiry* 54(4): 1946–1962.

Stehr, Mark. 2005. "Cigarette Tax Avoidance and Evasion." *Journal of Health Economics* 24(2): 277–297.

Taber, Daniel R., Jamie F. Chriqui, Renee Vuillaume, and Frank J. Chaloupka. 2014. "How State Taxes and Policies Targeting Soda Consumption Modify the Association between School Vending Machines and Student Dietary Behaviors: A Cross-Sectional Analysis." *PLoS ONE* 9(8): e98249.

Taber, Daniel R., Jamie F. Chriqui, Renee Vuillaume, Steven H. Kelder, and Frank J. Chaloupka. 2015. "The Association between State Bans on Soda Only and Adolescent Substitution with Other Sugar-Sweetened Beverages: A Cross-Sectional Study." *International Journal of Behavioral Nutrition and Physical Activity* 12(Suppl 1): S7.

Thaler, Richard H., and Cass R. Sunstein. 2009. *Nudge: Improving Decisions about Health, Wealth, and Happiness.* New York: Penguin.

Thompson, Frances E., Timothy S. McNeel, Emily C. Dowling, Douglas Midthune, Meredith Morrissette, and Christopher A. Zeruto. 2009. "Interrelationships of Added Sugars Intake, Socioeconomic Status, and Race/Ethnicity in Adults in the United States: National Health Interview Survey 2005." *Journal of the Academy of Nutrition and Dietetics* 109(8): 1376–1383.

van Baal, Pieter H. M., Johan J. Polder, G. Ardine de Wit, Rudolf T. Hoogenveen, Talitha L. Feenstra, Hendriek C. Boshuizen, Peter M. Engelfriet, and Werner B. F. Brouwer. 2008. "Lifetime Medical Costs of Obesity: Prevention No Cure for Increasing Health Expenditure." *PLOS Medicine* 5(2). doi: http://dx.doi.org/10.1371/journal.pmed.0050029

Vandenberg, Brian, and Anurag Sharma. 2016. "Are Alcohol Taxation and Pricing Policies Regressive? Product-Level Effects of a Specific Tax and a Minimum Unit Price for Alcohol." *Alcohol and Alcoholism* 51(4): 493–502.

Veerman, J. Lennert, Gary Sacks, Nicole Antonopoulos, and Jane Martin. 2016. "The Impact of a Tax on Sugar-Sweetened Beverages on Health and Health Care Costs: A Modelling Study." *PLoS ONE* 11(4): e0151460.

Vuolo, Mike, Brian C. Kelly, and Joy Kadowaki. 2016. "Independent and Interactive Effects of Smoking Bans and Tobacco Taxes on a Cohort of US Young Adults." *American Journal of Public Health* 106(2): 374–380.

Wagenaar, Alexander C., Amy L. Tobler, and Kelli A. Komro. 2010. "Effects of Alcohol Tax and Price Policies on Morbidity and Mortality: A Systematic Review." *American Journal of Public Health* 100(11): 2270–2278.

Xu, Xin, and Frank J. Chaloupka. 2011. "The Effects of Prices on Alcohol Use and Its Consequences." *Alcohol Research & Health* 34(2): 236–245.

Zhang, Bo, Joanna Cohen, Roberta Ferrence, and Jürgen Rehm. 2006. "The Impact of Tobacco Tax Cuts on Smoking Initiation among Canadian Young Adults." *Preventative Medicine* 30(6): 474–479.

Zhen, Chen, Ian F. Brissette, and Ryan Richard Ruff. 2014a. "By Ounce or by Calorie: The Differential Effects of Alternative Sugar-Sweetened Beverage Tax Strategies." *American Journal of Agricultural Economics* 96(4): 1070–1083.

Zhen, Chen, Eric A. Finkelstein, James M. Nonnemaker, Shawn A. Karns, and Jessica E. Todd. 2014b. "Predicting the Effects of Sugar-Sweetened Beverage Taxes on Food and Beverage Demand in a Large Demand System." *American Journal of Agricultural Economics* 96(1): 1–25.

PART IV

Taxes on Assets

7

TAXING LAND AND PROPERTY

Hitting You Where You Live

In contrast to levies based on transactions, such as income taxes on the exchange of labor for wages or consumption taxes on the exchange of currency for goods and services, asset taxes are levied on the value of an asset(s) at a certain point in time. There are two primary forms of asset taxation in the United States. The most common, and the subject of this chapter, are property taxes, including those based on the value of land, homes, real estate, and commercial structures. The second form of asset taxation, examined in the following chapter, are estate taxes, such as those charged against land and other assets when they are transferred from one party at death to one or more other parties. Although each tax base is linked with the value of taxable assets, there is one vital distinction: property taxes are perpetual and often assessed annually, but estate taxes are incurred once, typically after the owner has died.

While never widespread at the federal level, property taxes have been an important source of revenue for state and especially local governments. From 1922 through 2015, property tax revenues grew appreciably, both in the aggregate and in per-capita terms (see Figure 7.1 and Figure 7.2). Over the same timeframe, property taxation grew more prevalent across local jurisdictions relative to state governments. In 2015, state and local governments combined raised $517.7 billion in property taxes, but only $15.5 billion of that amount was levied by states. Fully 97% of revenue was collected by municipalities, such as counties, cities, townships, villages, and public school districts.

Property taxes are characterized by a unique collection of historical, political, and policy considerations. Indeed, one of the major sources of property tax contention is reflected in both Figure 7.1 and Figure 7.2: the consistent increase in revenue even as revenues from nearly every other tax exhibit at least some variability across economic cycles (refer to Figure 3.1, Figure 3.15, Figure 4.1,

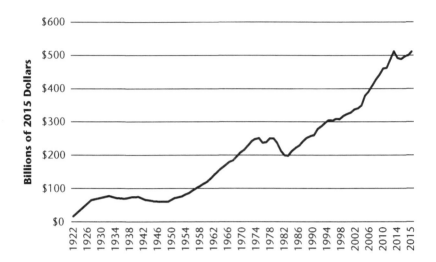

FIGURE 7.1 State and Local Property Tax Revenue, 1922–2015, in Constant Dollars

Sources: Author's analysis of data reported in the United States Census Bureau Quarterly Summary of State & Local Tax Revenue and the *Historical Statistics of the United States, Colonial Times to 1970.*

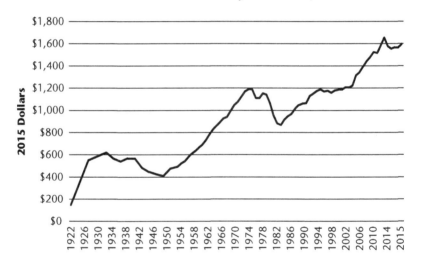

FIGURE 7.2 State and Local Property Tax Revenue per Capita, 1922–2015, in Constant Dollars

Sources: Author's analysis of data reported in the United States Census Bureau Quarterly Summary of State & Local Tax Revenue, the Current Population Survey, and the *Historical Statistics of the United States, Colonial Times to 1970.*

Figure 5.4, Figure 5.6, Figure 8.1, and Figure 8.2). An examination of Figure 7.1 and Figure 7.2 also reveals the unmistakable, although temporary, decline in property tax revenue during the late 1970s, itself the result of tax revolts prompted by complaints about rising tax burdens. Revenues have since more than rebounded, but the underlying tensions remain over fairness, equity, and the role of asset-based taxes in state and local governments' revenue frameworks. This chapter explores those issues.

History

Asset taxation traces its historical roots to ancient Athens, Egypt, and Rome. Property taxes were not consistently based on land value, however; residents were often taxed on the value of their harvest, which was then easier to monetize. Land taxation grew more pervasive in medieval Europe. For example, parts of modern-day England levied the Danegeld, a tax based on land value, from the ninth through the eleventh centuries and used the revenue to pay tributes to Danish forces.[1] Under feudal systems, monarchies also charged land-based duties to lords and nobles. During the Song dynasty, land and other property taxes were imposed in China.

Within what would become the United States, the first asset-based tax was enacted by the Massachusetts Bay Colony in 1638. The levy was a general property tax, meaning that it applied not only to land, but also to land improvements, machinery, livestock, and other assets. Outside Massachusetts, colonies and local governments instituted their own variants of property taxation, including levies based on land quantity (usually measured in acres) and value, the value of goods produced by land (e.g., a tithe of a landowner's grain harvest), and targeted taxes on other assets, such as livestock and housing (Ely 1888).

Early property tax revenues were used to finance local public goods. For instance, to fund local fire protection services, New Netherland in 1657 enacted a tax on each house so that the province could purchase between 100 and 150 leather buckets and ladders. To cover repair and maintenance costs, a separate tax was charged to building owners based on the number of chimneys contained on their property, similar to the hearth taxes employed in parts of Europe. Boston levied a property tax on all residents—collected by the sheriff—with some revenue used to support the city's budget and other revenue directed to local churches to provide education. The city held council meetings to resolve tax disputes and grant tax preferences to residents who had fallen on hard times (Trattner 1999).

By the time of the American Revolution, every colony had instituted some form of property taxation in order to pay its war debts. Property taxes were more common across northern communities; the disproportionate number of land estates and plantations worked against widespread property taxation in the south. The federal assumption of state debt through the Compromise of 1790 undermined property taxes' continued necessity, and states' reliance on property taxes declined gradually through the 1830s. States reversed course in the mid-1800s as they sought revenue to pay for new debts incurred during the canal and infrastructure building boom.

The unpopularity of property taxation across the south and constitutional direct-tax apportionment requirements constrained efforts to enact a federal property tax. Perhaps the most illustrious federal effort to tax property, the Federal Direct Tax of 1798, inspired Fries's Rebellion. That tax was repealed in 1802. Congress later enacted a property tax during the War of 1812. Assessment and collection responsibilities were delegated to the states which, for their troubles, were reimbursed 15% of revenues.[2] When that war ended, so did the tax. The last federal venture into property taxation occurred during the Civil War. That tax, too, ended with the war.

By the late nineteenth century, policymakers were growing aware of political and administrative difficulties wrought by general property taxation. Many of those challenges had existed from the earliest colonial property taxes. There were ever-present questions of fairness; for instance, should all types of property be taxed at the same rate? And there were also administrative questions, such as how to determine asset value, how often land and other assets should be reassessed, who should do the assessing, and how to obtain an accurate census of assets that could be hidden to avoid taxation (e.g., jewelry and livestock). Implementing general property taxes as legislated became an increasingly complicated, and expensive, endeavor. Some state and local governments responded by conferring tax preferences on certain assets, but that invariably compromised revenues and raised further questions about fairness.

Policymakers were also aware that national economic changes meant more individuals earned labor income but held little property, thereby avoiding property taxation altogether. As discussed in Chapter 3 and Chapter 4, this led farmers and other landowners to complain about unfair treatment. They were joined by prominent progressive leaders; economist E.R.A. Seligman (1890) derided property taxes as a "dismal failure" and "the worst tax known in the civilized world." The recommended solution was often a mix of new taxes on individual income, corporate income, and inheritances, and at the federal level, tariff reform.[3] The rationale was not to increase tax revenues per se, but to recalibrate the tax burden's distribution so that it did not fall disproportionately on landowners.

Declining property values during the Great Depression led to broad acceptance of two realities, particularly among state policymakers. First, a reliance on property taxes put state budgets at the mercy of land and real estate markets, which were largely out of state and local control. Second, diversified revenue streams were necessary to budget stability (Beito 1989, O'Sullivan 2000). States consequently began to pursue other sources of revenue, including gross receipts taxes.

The Great Depression also sparked new complaints from taxpayers. Although property assessments declined, they often did not do so in proportion to their drop in market value. Tax delinquencies and foreclosures skyrocketed. The federal Home Owner's Loan Corporation was formed in 1933 to provide mortgage and other financial assistance to homeowners, including allowing customers to borrow money to cover unpaid property taxes. The eventual result was the diffusion of state tax limitations as well as homestead exemptions intended to make property taxes less regressive.

Another round of property tax limitations swept across states starting in the 1970s, part of a broader movement for tax reform (Martin 2008). California's Proposition 13, approved by 63% of voters in 1978, rolled back property values, reduced property tax liabilities, and restricted annual tax increases. Massachusetts' Proposition 2 ½, approved by voters in 1980 by a nearly three-to-one margin, instituted caps on property tax revenues and annual increases. Other states that enacted tax rate caps or other limits during this period include Alabama, Alaska, Delaware, Kentucky, Louisiana, Michigan, and Rhode Island.

Although state governments moved away from property taxes, aided in part by the diffusion of tax limitations, municipal governments did not follow suit. Compared to states, local governments and school districts, then as now, have fewer revenue alternatives. In some states, city and county governments cannot raise their own income taxes without state legislative approval, if at all. Consumption tax options are similarly limited in scope; recall that not all states allow municipalities to implement a LOST (see Chapter 5). Whereas user fees have displaced some local reliance on property taxes, the tax continues to provide the bulk of funding for K–12 and K–16 public education systems across the United States.

How Do Property Taxes Work?

Over the course of American history, property taxes have been applied to one or both of two distinct types of property. "Real" property is the type of property most people are thinking of when discussing property taxes, which includes land, buildings, real estate, and related improvements. "Personal" property includes other assets of value but that are generally less fixed in location, such as equipment, vehicles, jewelry, furnishings, and investments. For a good deal of American history, state and local governments levied a general property tax on both real and personal property. Because of administrative problems inherent to taxing personal property—not to mention its unpopularity—jurisdictions have shifted toward taxes on real property.

In the simplest of terms, a taxpayer's property tax liability is the product of a tax rate multiplied by property value. But neither the tax rate nor the property value is as straightforward as this calculation implies. In any given jurisdiction, the rate may be uniform or based on a classified system in which a different rate is applied to different categories of real property, perhaps based on where the land or facility is located or how it is used. Tax rates may be quoted as a percentage or as a certain number of dollars per $100 of property value. Some communities quote tax rates as millage rates, which is the tax per $1,000 of property value. Furthermore, multiple jurisdictions may levy different tax rates on the same property. For instance, a homeowner may be liable for one county tax and an additional, but different, city, village, or township tax. Property value is most often based on what a local assessor believes is the market value of the property in question. In some jurisdictions, however, property taxes are based on the property value the last time it was bought or sold.

Local governments also have different property tax administration practices. Values may be reassessed every year, every other year, or over a longer interval. Taxes may be due quarterly, semiannually, or even annually. Unpaid property taxes are handled with a variety of approaches. Most jurisdictions immediately count unpaid taxes as a lien against the property in question, as opposed to taking legal action as a first step. All jurisdictions inevitably charge late penalties, just as the IRS charges penalties and interest on unpaid income taxes. Accumulated unpaid taxes may entangle mortgage lenders and, ultimately, lead to foreclosure proceedings.

Tax preferences alter property tax liabilities in jurisdictions that make them available. Most jurisdictions have instituted certain exemptions from a piece of property's assessed value that, in effect, renders only a portion of the value subject to taxation. Such exemptions may be fairly uniform (e.g., a 50% exemption on all principal residence property), or targeted (e.g., lower or higher exemptions based on property use or owner characteristics). Other governments institute tax preferences for environmentally-friendly projects (Shazim et al. 2016). Properties owned by government units and nonprofit organizations are often entirely exempt from taxation. State and local governments may also work to reduce property tax liabilities for businesses as part of economic development programs. Some jurisdictions make credits and other preferences available to low-income individuals in order to make the property tax system more progressive. Depending on their structure, some tax credits may favor rural over urban areas (Fisher and Rasche 1984).

Property tax limitations also modify tax liabilities. Depending on the jurisdiction, there may be one or more limits in place. Among the most common are rate caps, which place a limit on property tax rates, and assessment caps, which limit the amount a property owner's tax liability will increase from one year to the next. Some jurisdictions also have a limit in place that caps the total amount of revenue they may raise through property taxes.

The sum total of wide-ranging state and local property tax rates, values, preferences, and limitations is a spectrum of effective rates and burdens (see Table 7.1).[4] New Jersey, Illinois, and New Hampshire were home to the highest average

TABLE 7.1 Effective Personal Property Tax Rate and Burden by State, 2015

State	Rate	Rank	Burden	Rank
Alabama	0.43%	49	$708	48
Alaska	1.18%	20	$3,404	9
Arizona	0.80%	35	$1,033	42
Arkansas	0.62%	42	$886	46
California	0.81%	34	$1,311	37
Colorado	0.61%	43	$852	47
Connecticut	1.98%	4	$2,228	17

State	Rate	Rank	Burden	Rank
Delaware	0.55%	47	$1,464	31
Florida	1.06%	25	$1,468	30
Georgia	0.95%	27	$1,271	38
Hawaii	0.28%	50	$563	49
Idaho	0.75%	38	$1,241	40
Illinois	2.32%	2	$5,904	3
Indiana	0.86%	28	$1,652	28
Iowa	1.49%	14	$1,852	23
Kansas	1.39%	15	$1,850	24
Kentucky	0.85%	32	$2,372	16
Louisiana	0.51%	48	$530	50
Maine	1.28%	17	$1,585	29
Maryland	1.10%	22	$1,383	33
Massachusetts	1.21%	18	$1,738	27
Michigan	1.78%	8	$4,103	6
Minnesota	1.19%	19	$2,080	18
Mississippi	0.80%	36	$958	45
Missouri	1.02%	26	$2,007	21
Montana	0.86%	29	$2,033	20
Nebraska	1.84%	7	$4,916	4
Nevada	0.86%	30	$2,694	12
New Hampshire	2.15%	3	$3,799	7
New Jersey	2.38%	1	$2,989	10
New Mexico	0.73%	40	$1,022	43
New York	1.64%	11	$8,659	1
North Carolina	0.85%	33	$1,318	36
North Dakota	1.11%	21	$3,762	8
Ohio	1.55%	12	$2,562	14
Oklahoma	0.86%	31	$1,362	34
Oregon	1.09%	23	$2,052	19
Pennsylvania	1.54%	13	$2,647	13
Rhode Island	1.67%	10	$2,470	15
South Carolina	0.57%	46	$1,412	32
South Dakota	1.32%	16	$1,744	26
Tennessee	0.75%	39	$1,770	25
Texas	1.90%	6	$4,849	5
Utah	0.68%	41	$968	44
Vermont	1.71%	9	$2,782	11
Virginia	0.78%	37	$1,870	22
Washington	1.09%	24	$1,134	41
West Virginia	0.59%	45	$1,266	39
Wisconsin	1.96%	5	$8,089	2
Wyoming	0.61%	44	$1,362	35

Sources: Author's analysis of data collected by the Tax Foundation and reported in the United States Census Bureau American Community Survey.

property tax rates in 2015. But since average home and land values also vary nationally, states with the highest tax rates do not necessarily also have the highest tax burden. New York was home to the highest average tax burden in 2015, even though that state's average tax rate ranks eleventh. Washington's average tax rate ranks 24th, but due to relatively low home and land values, the state's property tax burden in dollars ranks 41st.

Within any given region, tax rates and burdens vary across local jurisdictions, sometimes significantly.[5] For instance, the average property tax levy in Marin County, California, in 2013 was $9,283; but in neighboring Sonoma County, the average was less than half that figure, $4,502. In Shelby County, Tennessee, the average was $3,767; in nearby Fayette County, the average was $1,597. In Cook County, Illinois, the average levy was $6,551, but across the state border, the average burden in Lake County, Indiana, was $2,879.

Property Taxes: Good or Bad, Fair or Unfair?

Seligman may have called property taxes "the worst tax known in the civilized world," but his description overstates their downsides. As a taxpayer-passive levy, costs of administration are indeed higher than other forms of taxation. Policymakers should be mindful of the important relationship between the quality of property assessments and revenue volatility (Carroll and Goodman 2011) as well as the differences in performance between elected and appointed assessors (Ross 2013). They also have to work to emphasize on-time payments, as delinquent property taxes have a spillover effect that negatively impacts the values of surrounding property (Alm et al. 2016). Given the explosion in property tax burdens over the past nine decades, taxpayers have every reason to express concern about continued growth and its implications for homeownership, especially given that government-assessed property values do not fall in proportion to their market values (Lutz et al. 2011).

Still, by many accounts, property taxes have many desirable characteristics relative to other forms of taxation. As opposed to income taxes, property tax revenues are primarily spent in the same jurisdictions from which the taxes are collected. Local property tax policymaking and administration facilitates a national marketplace in which taxpayers can, in the long run, locate and reside in jurisdictions in which the cost of property taxes matches their desired level of public services. Local jurisdictions can likewise calibrate taxes and public service provisions to those desires—the Tiebout sorting process discussed in Chapter 3, named for economist Charles Tiebout (1956). Youngman (2016) summarizes just some of the more general advantages of property taxation:

> The unsung benefits of the property tax begin with its generally visible and transparent nature. A tax computed as a percentage of value can be clear and understandable—a dramatic contrast to the enormous complexity of

the federal income tax or to the relative invisibility of a sales tax collected over thousands of transactions annually but never totaled for the taxpayer, so that its cumulative impact is unknown. The property tax imposes no filing burden, and taxpayers need not employ experts simply to determine the amount they owe. Because property tax bills send a visible signal concerning the cost of local public services, they provide vital information to the electorate.

Like any other, property taxes are subjected to issues of equity and fairness. The classic defense of property taxation lies in the benefit principle—in particular, that property value and hence tax burdens are proportional public service consumption. Hypothetically, a large section of land with a higher market value should incur a large tax burden because, as a result of its size, value, and perhaps location, that piece of land requires a higher level of public services (e.g., roads, utilities, and waste management). The benefit principle rationale is acutely effective when offered in relation to corporate-owned property and structures, where the ability to pay principle may also serve as a justification for property taxes.

On the other hand, many classical liberal theorists argue that property taxation is a poor basis for distributing individuals' financial obligation to the state, regardless of local, state, or federal level, because many individuals do not pay property taxes, at least not directly. Unless land and other real estate value is equally distributed, the associated tax burden will fall disproportionately on landowners, thereby exempting from state contribution nonowners, who nevertheless benefit from public services (Hale 1985). Non-property owners, of course, pay other taxes, such as those on income and consumption, but so do property owners. Other inequities result from basing property taxation on selling price rather than market value (Sexton et al. 1999).

The common practice of allocating property tax revenue toward public education raises additional questions of fairness. Why should public education funding be tied to the value of land in a surrounding jurisdiction? This system has facilitated decades of plainly unequal, and arguably unfair, funding disparities between urban, suburban, and rural school districts. Furthermore, it goes without saying that the cost of providing an education, from instructional salaries to overhead to supplies, is not in any way correlated to the value of the surrounding land, nor does it ebb and flow with the rise and fall of housing and real estate markets.

Whereas state and local governments have approached property tax revenue and public school funding disparities with a variety of policy prescriptions (e.g., hold harmless provisions and equalization payments), the more important question often goes unaddressed: why does the cost of funding public education fall disproportionately on property owners? Is it fair that property owners with no children enrolled in public schools are coerced by the state to subsidize other individuals' children that are enrolled? What about property-owning parents that elect to send their children to non-public schools? Setting those questions aside, does the owner of a $500,000 property enjoy five times the benefits of public education as the owner of a $100,000 property?

Charges of unfairness are often heightened when local officials grant tax preferences to corporate entities. Common economic development tools that leverage property taxes, including tax increment financing, enterprise zones, and tax abatement programs, lower some business tax burdens relative to other businesses as well as individuals. That tends to generate complaints from long-time businesses and residents, who have arguably done more to sustain local economies than a new entrant to the community. This normative charge is emboldened by empirical research on such tax incentives, which generally finds they are ineffective at creating and sustaining broad-based economic growth (Elvery 2009; Lynch and Zax 2010; Neumark and Kolko 2010; Reese 2014; Wilder and Rubin 1996) but can increase commercial property valuations (Kang et al. 2016). These findings should not come as a surprise; like any tax preference, property tax incentives encourage rent-seeking and a misallocation of scarce public resources (Coyne and Moberg 2015).

The exemption of property owned by the public and nonprofit sectors from taxation raises a similar question of unfairness. If property taxes are predicated on the benefit principle, then the cost of public services should, in theory, apply equally to all property owners. Indeed, a property owner's tax status does not render their consumption of public services somehow less impactful to local jurisdictions; street lighting and waste treatment costs are incurred by nonprofit properties (e.g., schools, universities, hospitals, and government offices) just as they are for residential or commercial properties, yet the former are exempt from property taxation. That inequity is compounded by the fact that tax exemptions for nonprofit organizations confer larger benefits on those with valuable property assets (e.g., a public university) than those with less-valuable property (e.g., a soup kitchen).

To balance the inequities and compensate for the revenue forgone by the occupation of property by non-tax-paying entities, many state and local governments pursue a "payment in lieu of taxes" (PILOT) arrangement. PILOTs are voluntary—tax-exempt property owners are under no legal obligation to agree, although many do—but have grown more common in the past decade (Kenyon and Langley 2010). A handful of state governments and dozens of municipalities currently make use of PILOT arrangements; in fact, they are especially common in Massachusetts. PILOT structures vary by jurisdiction, but often include fees or other charges intended to compensate local governments for public services consumed by nonprofit entities that do not otherwise pay local property taxes. However, PILOT revenues often fail to cover the entire cost of property tax exemptions.

One of the largest nonprofit owners of land in the United States is actually the federal government, and the Department of the Interior began making payments in 1976 to jurisdictions impacted by the tax-exempt status of federally owned land.[6] This includes land controlled by the National Park System, the National Forest System, the Bureau of Land Management, the National Wildlife Refuge System, the Army Corps of Engineers, and the Department of Agriculture, but not the Fish and Wildlife Service. In 2016, $451.6 million in federal PILOT payments were made to about 1,900 local governments.

Federal payments do not fully compensate affected jurisdictions for forgone property tax revenues. Compensation authorized by law is instead calculated by a formula that incorporates acreage, population, and participation in other federal reimbursement programs, but congressional appropriations have not always been sufficient to cover what the formula dictates.[7] This has led local government interest groups, such as the National Association of Counties, and states with large proportions of federally owned land (especially in the west) to lobby Congress for full funding.

The Effects of Property Taxes and Property Tax Limits

In all their varied forms, property tax limitations affect state–local fiscal interdependence. Simply put, state-level property tax regulations constrain local budget decision-making. For instance, even if voters in a local jurisdiction desire to raise their own property taxes, they may be prevented from doing so by a state tax limitation. Those constraints have pushed some local governments to grow more reliant on state fiscal assistance, thereby losing a degree of local autonomy (Hayes 2015; Shires 1999). That shift is exacerbated in states where local governments have other limits in place that constrain their own revenue options (Carroll and Johnson 2010). Where more local flexibility does exist, jurisdictions usually compensate for "missing" property tax revenue by reducing spending and/or increasing other taxes and fees that are not limited by statutory or constitutional limitations (Fulton 1997; Hoene 2004; Seljan and McCubbins 2015; Sun 2014).

Property taxes add one other layer of fiscal interdependence and complexity to the tax system, that between local jurisdictions and the federal government, which has made available a property tax deduction for individual property taxpayers. According to the Joint Committee on Taxation, the federal tax expenditure for individual property tax deductions amounted to $34.7 billion in 2016 and, combined with the deductibility of other state and local taxes, about two-thirds of the benefits go to individuals with incomes in excess of $200,000.[8] In effect, the federal deduction subsidizes local property taxes, but it also introduces another inequity. Recall from Chapter 3 that, holding all else equal, an individual who pays for local services through property taxes has a lower federal income tax burden than one who pays for the same services through user charges. Thus, despite being predominantly local in orientation, property taxes have very real fiscal, and political, national consequences.

Beyond the impact of property taxes and property tax limitations on intergovernmental fiscal relationships, debate over their merits tends to focus on three questions. The first and most general is whether limits are "good" or "bad." Some research finds that the net impact of limits on overall welfare is generally positive (McGuire 1999), but that all other findings are conditioned on one's view of the proper role of the state in society. A number of studies have found that property tax limitations force state and local governments to reduce spending (Bradbury et al. 2001; Brooks et al. 2016; Chapman and Gorina 2012; Dove 2016; Dye and McGuire 1997) and serve to control public sector salaries (Poterba and Reuben 1995). But other studies find just the opposite—that property tax limits lead to higher taxes and spending (Springer et al. 2009).

The second question centers on the relationship between property taxation and the quality of public services. This particular link has been the subject of decades of academic research, especially with respect to the impact of property taxes on public schools. While studies abound, their findings on the matter are not consistent. Residents in jurisdictions that experience lower taxes as a result of a property tax limit are more likely to report that the quality of public safety and public education has declined (Taylor 2015). Low property taxes have also been linked with reduced education outcomes, including increased student/teacher ratios and instructional spending declines (Figlio 1997; Nguyen-Hoang 2012; Sirmans and Sirmans (2012). Conversely, other studies call the negative impact hypothesis into question (Eom et al. 2014; Shadbegian 2002), and still others find that the alleged negative effect of property tax limits is the result of poor government planning, not tax policy (Davis et al. 2016).

The third and most debated question is whether property tax limitations actually restrict revenue. Even though limits have diffused across state and local governments over the past century, property tax revenues have surged (refer to Figure 7.1 and Figure 7.2). After adjusting for inflation, total state and local property tax revenue increased 3,106% between 1922 and 2015. On an inflation-adjusted per-capita basis, revenue increased 994% over the same period.

Those jaw-dropping figures are possible because, on one hand, some tax limitations are not immutable; they are designed such that if certain conditions are met, the limit can be revised or waived entirely. For example, local voters in Massachusetts have elected to override the state's property tax limit literally thousands of times (Hawley and Rork 2015), sometimes in response to decreases in state fiscal assistance (Wu 2009).

Even when limitations are strict, property tax revenues will increase along with land and real estate values. Consider the pre- and post-Proposition 13 property tax revenue in Los Angeles County, California's most populous (see Figure 7.3). Revenue plunged after the limit was enacted in 1978, reaching its lowest point in 1980. But in spite of Proposition 13, the county's property tax revenue grew 167% from that low through 1992 alone, after adjusting for inflation. Note also that by 1992, revenues had returned to their pre-Proposition 13 level. They have only moved higher since.

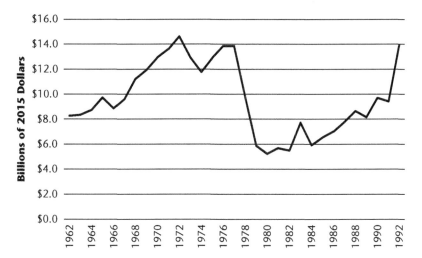

FIGURE 7.3 Property Tax Revenue in Los Angeles County, 1962–1992, in Constant Dollars

Source: Author's analysis of data reported in the United States Census Bureau Quarterly Summary of State & Local Tax Revenue.

Conclusion

Contrasted against other taxes, property taxes attract less partisan bickering. That's largely a result of their widespread use by local governments, where political polarization is less extreme than that at the state and federal levels. The decentralized nature of property taxation also means that the levies attract less centralized interest from nationally oriented interest groups. Prominent think tanks also have less well-defined views on property taxes. Neither the conservative American Enterprise Institute nor the libertarian Cato Institute has a strong position on property taxes, and whereas the progressive Center on Budget and Policy Priorities has published several related analyses and commentaries, most are moderate in tone, urging policymakers to proceed with caution when making changes to property taxes—a very nonpartisan instruction.

Notes

1 The Middle/Old English translation of Danegeld is "Dane tribute."
2 The administrative structure was praised for its efficiency. By delegating assessment and collection duties to the states, the federal government avoided the time and expense of creating a redundant bureaucracy. Using state and local officials also avoided one of the issues that contributed to Fries's Rebellion: that distant federal officials were riding into town and meddling in local affairs.
3 Progressives were not uniformly opposed to property taxation. Well before the income tax was made permanent, economist Henry George (1884) called for an overhaul of

the federal tax system through the institution of a so-called single tax on land, defined as "all natural materials, forces, and opportunities."

4 For a more complete discussion of states' varied methods of determining effective property tax rates, see Bell and Kirschner (2009).

5 See Alan Cole, "How Do Property Taxes Vary Across The Country?" The Tax Foundation, 2015.

6 The federal program uses a different abbreviation: PILT.

7 See M. Lynne Corn, "PILT (Payments in Lieu of Taxes): Somewhat Simplified," Congressional Research Service, 2015.

8 See Joint Committee on Taxation, "Estimates of Federal Tax Expenditures for Fiscal Years 2015–2019," Report Number JCX-141R-15.

References

Alm, James, Zackary Hawley, Jin Man Lee, and Joshua J. Miller. 2016. "Property Tax Delinquency and Its Spillover Effects on Nearby Properties." *Regional Science and Urban Economics* 58: 71–77.

Beito, David T. 1989. *Taxpayers in Revolt: Tax Resistance during the Great Depression*. Chapel Hill: University of North Carolina Press.

Bell, Michael E., and Charlotte Kirschner. 2009. "A Reconnaissance of Alternative Measures of Effective Property Tax Rates." *Public Budgeting & Finance* 29(2): 111–136.

Bradbury, Katharine L., Christopher J. Mayer, and Karl E. Case. 2001. "Property Tax Limits, Local Fiscal Behavior, and Property Values: Evidence from Massachusetts under Proposition 2 ½." *Journal of Public Economics* 80(2): 287–311.

Brooks, Leah, Yosh Halberstam, and Justin Phillips. 2016. "Spending within Limits: Evidence from Municipal Fiscal Restraints." *National Tax Journal* 69(2): 315–351.

Carroll, Deborah A., and Christopher B. Goodman. 2011. "The Effects of Assessment Quality on Revenue Volatility." *Public Budgeting & Finance* 31(1): 76–94.

Carroll, Deborah A., and Terri Johnson. 2010. "Examining Small Town Revenues: To What Extent Are They Diversified?" *Public Administration Review* 70(2): 223–235.

Chapman, Jeffrey, and Evgenia Gorina. 2012. "Effects of the Form of Government and Property Tax Limits on Local Finance in the Context of Revenue and Expenditure Simultaneity." *Public Budgeting & Finance* 32(4): 19–45.

Coyne, Christopher J., and Lotta Moberg. 2015. "The Political Economy of State-Provided Targeted Benefits." *The Review of Austrian Economics* 28(3): 337–356.

Davis, Matthew, Andrea Vedder, and Joe Stone. 2016. "Local Tax Limits, Student Achievement, and School-Finance Equalization." *Journal of Education Finance* 41(3): 289–301.

Dove, John A. 2016. "Property Tax Limits, Balanced Budget Rules, and Line-Item Vetoes: A Long-Run View." *Eastern Economic Journal*. doi: 10.1057/s41302-016-0001-1

Dye, Richard F., and Therese J. McGuire. 1997. "The Effect of Property Tax Limitation Measures on Local Government Fiscal Behavior." *Journal of Public Economics* 66(3): 469–487.

Elvery, Joel A. 2009. "The Impact of Enterprise Zones on Resident Employment: An Evaluation of the Enterprise Zone Programs of California and New York." *Economic Development Quarterly* 23(1): 44–59.

Ely, Richard T. 1888. *Taxation in American States and Cities*. New York: Thomas Y. Crowell & Company.

Eom, Tae Ho, William Duncombe, Phuong Nguyen-Hoang, and John Yinger. 2014. "The Unintended Consequences of Property Tax Relief: New York's STAR Program." *Education Finance and Policy* 9(4): 446–480.

Figlio, David N. 1997. "Did the 'Tax Revolt' Reduce School Performance?" *Journal of Public Economics* 65(3): 245–269.

Fisher, Ronald C., and Robert H. Rasche. 1984. "The Incidence and Incentive Effects of Property Tax Credits: Evidence from Michigan." *Public Finance Review* 12(3): 291–319.

Fulton, William. 1997. *The Reluctant Metropolis: The Politics of Urban Growth in Los Angeles.* Point Arena, CA: Solano Press.

George, Henry. 1884. *Progress & Poverty: An Inquiry into the Cause of Industrial Depressions and Increase of Want with Increase of Wealth.* London: William Reeves.

Hale, Dennis. 1985. "The Evolution of the Property Tax: A Study of the Relation between Public Finance and Political Theory." *Journal of Politics* 47(2): 382–404.

Hawley, Zackary, and Jonathan C. Rork. 2015. "Competition and Property Tax Limit Overrides: Revisiting Massachusetts' Proposition 2 ½." *Regional Science and Urban Economics* 52: 93–107.

Hayes, Michael S. 2015. "The Differential Effect of the No Child Left Behind Act (NCLB) on States' Contributions to Education Funding in States with Binding School District Tax and Expenditure Limitations." *Public Budgeting & Finance* 35(1): 49–72.

Hoene, Christopher. 2004. "Fiscal Structure and the Post-Proposition 13 Fiscal Regime in California's Cities." *Public Budgeting & Finance* 24(4): 51–72.

Kang, Sung Hoon, Laura Reese, and Mark Skidmore. 2016. "Do Industrial Tax Abatements Spur Property Value Growth?" *Journal of Policy Analysis and Management* 35(2): 388–414.

Kenyon, Daphne A., and Adam H. Langley. 2010. "Payments in Lieu of Taxes: Balancing Municipal and Nonprofit Interests." Lincoln Institute of Land Policy Report.

Lutz, Byron, Raven Malloy, and Hui Shan. 2011. "The Housing Crisis and State and Local Government Tax Revenue: Five Channels." *Regional Science and Urban Economics* 41(4): 306–319.

Lynch, Devon, and Jeffrey S. Zax. 2010. "Incidence and Substitution in Enterprise Zone Programs: The Case of Colorado." *Public Finance Review* 39(2): 226–255.

Martin, Isaac. 2008. *The Permanent Tax Revolt: How the Property Tax Transformed American Politics.* Palo Alto, CA: Stanford University Press.

McGuire, Therese J. 1999. "Proposition 13 and Its Offspring: For Good or for Evil?" *National Tax Journal* 52(1): 129–138.

Neumark, David, and Jed Kolko. 2010. "Do Enterprise Zones Creat Jobs? Evidence from California's Enterprise Zone Program." *Journal of Urban Economics* 68(1): 1–19.

Nguyen-Hoang, P. 2012. "Fiscal Effects of Budget Referendums: Evidence from New York School Districts." *Public Choice* 150(1): 77–95.

O'Sullivan, Arthur. 2000. "Limitations on Local Property Taxation: The U.S. Experience." *State Tax Notes* (May 15): 1697–1713.

Poterba, James M., and Kim S. Reuben. 1995. "The Effect of Property-Tax Limits on Wages and Employment in the Local Public Sector." *American Economic Review* 85(2): 384–389.

Reese, Laura A. 2014. "If All You Have Is a Hammer: Finding Economic Development Policies That Matter." *American Review of Public Administration* 44(6): 627–655.

Ross, Justin M. 2013. "A Socioeconomic Analysis of Property Tax Assessment Uniformity: Empirical Evidence on the Role of Policy." *Public Budgeting & Finance* 33(1): 49–75.

Seligman, Edwin R.A. 1890. "The General Property Tax." *Political Science Quarterly* 5(1): 24–64.

Seljan, Ellen, and Colin McCubbins. 2015. "Fee for Service: Proposition 13 and Municipal Revenue Substitution." *California Journal of Politics and Policy* 7(2): 1–20.

Sexton, Terri A., Steven M. Sheffrin, and Arthur O'Sullivan. 1999. "Proposition 13: Unintended Effects and Feasible Reforms." *National Tax Journal* 51(1): 99–112.

Shadbegian, Ronald J. 2002. "Did the Property Tax Revolt Affect Local Public Education? Evidence from Panel Data." *Public Finance Review* 31(1): 91–121.

Shazim, S.A.A., I. Sipan, and M. Sapri. 2016. "Property Tax Assessment Incentives for Green Building: A Review." *Renewable and Sustainable Energy Reviews* 60: 536–548.

Shires, Michael A. 1999. "Patterns in California Government Revenues since Proposition 13." Public Policy Institute of California.

Sirmans, G. Stacy, and C. Stace Sirmans. 2012. "Property Tax Initiatives in the United States." *Journal of Housing Research* 21(1): 1–13.

Springer, Job D., Aaron K. Lusby, John C. Leatherman, and Allen M. Featherstone. 2009. "An Evaluation of Alternative Tax and Expenditure Limitation Policies on Kansas Local Governments." *Public Budgeting & Finance* 29(2): 48–70.

Sun, Rui. 2014. "Reevaluating the Effect of Tax and Expenditure Limitations: An Instrumental Variable Approach." *Public Finance Review* 42(1): 92–116.

Taylor, Charles D. 2015. "Property Tax Caps and Citizen Perceptions of Local Government Service Quality: Evidence from the Hoosier Survey." *American Review of Public Administration* 45(5): 525–541.

Tiebout, Charles. 1956. "A Pure Theory of Local Expenditures." *Journal of Political Economy* 64(5): 416–424.

Trattner, Walter I. 1999. *From Poor Law to Welfare State: A History of Social Welfare in America.* New York: Free Press.

Wilder, Margaret G., and Barry M. Rubin. 1996. "Rhetoric versus Reality: A Review of Studies on State Enterprise Zone Programs." *Journal of the American Planning Association* 62(4): 473–491.

Wu, Yonghong. 2009. "How Municipal Property Tax Responded to State Aid Cuts: The Case of Massachusetts Municipalities in the Post-2001 Fiscal Crisis." *Public Budgeting & Finance* 29(4): 74–89.

Youngman, Joan. 2016. *A Good Tax: Legal and Policy Issues for the Property Tax in the United States.* Cambridge, MA: Lincoln Institute of Land Policy.

8

TAXING GIFTS, ESTATES, AND INHERITANCES

Death and Taxes

"In this world nothing can be said to be certain, except death and taxes." So wrote Benjamin Franklin in 1789.[1] Only one tax has the dubious honor of having a nickname that connects life's certainties together, the so-called death tax. But that label is misleading. The tax in question is not a tax on death—the state does not charge individuals a fee for expiration, at least not yet—but rather a tax against the assets an individual leaves behind. Those assets are referred to as the individual's "estate," and therefore the death tax is more accurately identified as the estate tax.

The tax on estates is one example from a larger category of taxation known as transfer taxes. Generally speaking, a transfer tax is applied against the value of a one-way asset transfer between parties.[2] Transferrable assets include cash, investments, land, real estate, and some intangible resources, such as intellectual property. Transfers are classified—and tax liabilities are determined—based on when the transfer occurs. A transfer between living individuals, known as an *inter vivos* transfer, is normally considered a gift.[3] The donor may be subject to a gift tax based both on the value of the gift and their relationship to the recipient. Postmortem transfers are taxed in one of two ways. If a tax is charged against the assets before they are transferred to beneficiaries, then the levy is an estate tax. Note that an estate tax essentially functions as a tax on wealth. If nothing is charged against the assets and each beneficiary is instead taxed on their share of the proceeds, then the levy is an inheritance tax.

The United States has often relied on transfer taxes for supplemental revenue, almost always as a temporary war-funding measure. The federal government since 1934 has collected at least $1 billion in transfer taxes each year, but annual revenues reflect some volatility (see Figure 8.1). Between the end of World War II and 1973, tax collections quadrupled, but the surge did not persist. After collapsing during the 1970s and 1980s, revenues increased again from the late 1980s

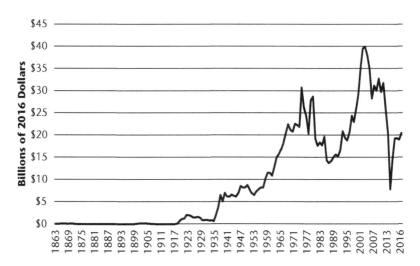

FIGURE 8.1 Federal Transfer Tax Revenue, 1863–2016, in Constant Dollars

Sources: Author's analysis of data reported in the *Historical Statistics of the United States, Colonial Times to 1970, Part 2*, and by the Office of Management and Budget.

FIGURE 8.2 State Transfer Tax Revenue, 1942–2014, in Constant Dollars

Source: United States Census Bureau Annual Survey of State Government Finances

through 2000 only to plummet again. In 2016, transfer taxes amounted to about $20 billion, representing less than 1% of total federal revenue.

Eighteen state governments charge an additional tax on transfers. Over time, state revenues have been less precarious than federal revenues. In the aggregate, transfer tax collections amounted to an estimated $5 billion in 2016, approximately 5% of state own-source revenues (see Figure 8.2).

Transfer taxes raise imperative questions about asset ownership, and they bring to mind the conflict between private property rights and coercive taxation. For instance, to what extent, if at all, do an individual's natural property rights endure past the end of their natural life? Since transfer taxes normally entangle only the wealthy, the tax raises additional questions of ability to pay, fairness, and distributive justice. This chapter explores these and other facets of transfer taxation.

History

Taxes on asset transfers have existed for thousands of years.[4] Historical evidence indicates that some form of inheritance taxation was implemented in ancient Egypt. One papyrus depicts a man being charged a heavy penalty for failing to pay the appropriate tax upon inheriting his father's home. Another papyrus depicts a man selling property to his sons at a discounted price in order to minimize or evade some form of estate tax. Under Emperor Augustus, Rome instituted a formal estate tax (*vicesima hereditatium*) in 6 AD to raise funds for military pensions. Assorted forms of transfer tax were also imposed throughout Europe during the middle ages (West 1908).

The first federal transfer tax in the United States was enacted as part of the Stamp Act of 1797. The tax imposed a graduated "legacy duty" on inheritances valued at over $50. Estates valued between $50 and $100 were taxed 25 cents, the equivalent of about $1,000, $2,000, and $5 in 2016 dollars, respectively. Estates valued between $100 and $500 were taxed 50 cents, the equivalent of about $2,000, $10,000, and $10 in 2016 dollars, respectively. Each additional $500 in estate value was taxed $1. Congress instituted one important tax preference: widows, children, and grandchildren were exempt. This iteration of the inheritance tax was repealed in 1802.

Transfer taxes returned under the Revenue Act of 1862, one of several Civil War funding measures. Rates were graduated and based on the donor-recipient relationship. Asset transfers to immediate relatives or siblings were taxed at 0.75%, but transfers to descendants of siblings were taxed at 1.5%. The highest tax rate of 5% applied to transfers to distant relatives and strangers. Spouses and all estates valued at less than $1,000, the equivalent of about $25,000 in 2016 dollars, were exempt. Rates were increased in 1864, but compliance was low, and the federal government collected relatively little revenue (refer to Figure 8.1). Congress added penalties for nonpayment but repealed the tax outright in 1870. Four years later, the Supreme Court ruled that the transfer tax was not a direct tax but an excise tax on the privilege of transferring assets, and therefore constitutional.[5]

The late-nineteenth-century progressive movement lobbied heavily for a return of transfer taxes, and the estate tax in particular, contending that federal action was essential to preventing the concentration of wealth in a small proportion of the population. Individual income tax provisions included in the

Wilson–Gorman Tariff Act of 1894 also applied to inheritances, but the Act and all taxes inclusive were overturned by the Supreme Court in 1895. Congress enacted another estate tax in 1898 that contained graduated marginal tax rates (MTRs) from a low of 0.74% to a high of 15%. The applicable rate was contingent on the value of the estate and the nature of the donor-recipient relationship. This version of the federal estate tax was challenged, but again upheld by the Supreme Court.[6] But Congress repealed it in 1902.

During World War I, the Great Depression, and World War II, Congress turned to transfer taxes as a substitute for declining tariffs and to cover war costs. A new estate tax was instituted in 1916. Although challenged, the tax was again upheld by the Supreme Court in 1921.[7] MTRs were increased in 1924 to as high as 40% on estates valued at over $10 million, the equivalent of about $150 million in 2016 dollars. Congress also added a new levy, a distinct tax on gifts. The gift tax and some estate taxes were repealed in 1926 but received—yes, again—approval after the fact from the Supreme Court in 1929.[8] Estate taxes were raised, and the gift tax reintroduced, in 1932. Subsequent increases in 1941 pushed the highest MTR to 77% on estates valued at over $50 million, the equivalent of $810 million in 2016 dollars. Postwar changes were incremental, and the 77% rate remained in effect for decades. In short, war mobilization was a driving force behind imposition of the estate tax (Scheve and Stasavage 2012).

The next major transfer tax reform did not occur until 1976, when Congress unified the estate and gift taxes and added a new generation-skipping transfer (GST) tax in response to a perceived "loophole" in the transfer tax system. As the tax was originally designed by policymakers, assets transferred from an individual to their children would incur an estate tax at the individual's death. When those assets transferred again from those children to their own children—i.e., the first individual's grandchildren—the assets would incur a second round of taxation. The transfer-and-tax, transfer-and-tax process would theoretically continue into perpetuity. Some individuals and families responded by structuring assets such that an individual or married couple could transfer a large sum as a gift directly to their grandchildren, therefore allowing the asset transfer to skip a generation and avoid one round of federal transfer taxes. The GST tax provision did not ban this arrangement, but made it more difficult for related transfers to escape federal taxation.

Transfer taxes were changed incrementally throughout the 1980s, often as part of broader reform legislation, and the next extensive changes were enacted in 2001. Passage of the Economic Growth and Tax Relief Reconciliation Act implemented a phased-in repeal of the estate and GST taxes and lowered gift tax rates. The repeal was scheduled for full implementation in 2010, but the Act contained a sunset provision that reinstated all transfer tax reductions at the beginning of 2011. Congress did not move to keep the reductions in place, and transfer tax rates reverted upward. In 2016, the estate, gift, and GST tax rate stood at a flat 40%

applied to lifetime transfers valued in excess of $5.45 million for individuals, or $10.9 million for married couples.

Figure 8.3 and Figure 8.4 illustrate the historical evolution of the highest-transfer MTR and the transfer tax exemption, respectively. The rate was relatively low from the Civil War to the Great Depression—in most years, the rate was actually zero—but increases during World War II remained a matter of law until the

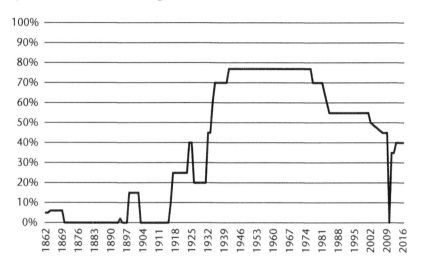

FIGURE 8.3 Top Federal Transfer Tax Rate, 1862–2016

Source: Internal Revenue Service.

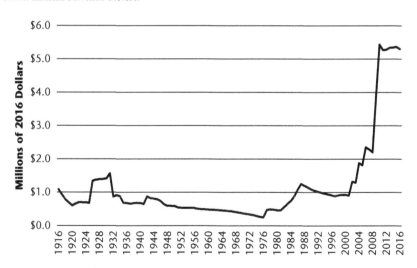

FIGURE 8.4 Federal Transfer Tax Exemption, 1916–2016, in Constant Dollars

Sources: West (1908), The Tax Foundation, and the Internal Revenue Service.

1976 reforms. The current transfer tax rate is among the highest ever levied outside of a war period, but the current exemption is the highest in United States history. Whereas in the 1950s the tax may have applied to transfers worth as little as the 2016 equivalent of $500,000, a transfer of identical size today would be mostly exempt from taxation. Relatively high exemption amounts render the existing transfer tax system one that applies to a narrow base but of high progressivity.

Transfer taxes have a long history of use across state governments. The first state to enact a transfer tax was Pennsylvania (1826). Several other states followed suit, including Louisiana (1828), Virginia (1843), Maryland (1845), North Carolina (1847), and Wisconsin (1868). State transfer taxes were diverse in form; some instituted graduated rates, whereas others applied a flat rate. Exemption amounts, the definition of what constituted an estate, inheritance, or gift, and how the tax interacted with varying types of familial relationships also differed.

Less than half of state governments today levy a transfer tax. In 2016, 12 states charged an estate tax, four charged an inheritance tax, and two charged both (see Table 8.1). Since 2010, four states (Indiana, Ohio, North Carolina, and most recently, Tennessee) repealed their transfer taxes.

TABLE 8.1 State Transfer Taxes, 2016

State	Tax Type	Exemption	MTR Range
Connecticut	Estate	$2.0 million	7.2–12%
Delaware	Estate	$5.4 million	0.8–16%
Hawaii	Estate	$5.4 million	0.8–16%
Illinois	Estate	$4.0 million	0.8–16%
Iowa	Inheritance	Varies	0–15%
Kentucky	Inheritance	Varies	0–16%
Maine	Estate	$2.0 million	8–12%
Maryland	Estate	$1.5 million	16%
	Inheritance	Varies	0–10%
Massachusetts	Estate	$1.0 million	0.8–16%
Minnesota	Estate	$1.4 million	9–16%
Nebraska	Inheritance	Varies	1–18%
New Jersey	Estate	$675,000	0.8–16%
	Inheritance	Varies	0–16%
New York	Estate	$2.1 million	3.06–16%
Oregon	Estate	$1.0 million	0.8–16%
Pennsylvania	Inheritance	Varies	0–15%
Rhode Island	Estate	$1.5 million	0.8–16%
Vermont	Estate	$2.8 million	0.8–16%
Washington	Estate	$2.1 million	10–20%

Note: The Nebraska inheritance tax is levied at the county level.

Sources: The Tax Foundation and individual states' websites.

How Do Transfer Taxes Work?

Federal transfer taxes (estate, gift, and GST) have been tied together as a matter of policy since 1976. Congress limits the value of assets that an individual or married couple is allowed to transfer over their lifetimes without incurring a tax. In 2016, the lifetime maximum amount an individual or married couple was allowed to transfer was $5.45 million and $10.9 million, respectively. These exemptions are a tax preference; all transfers below the relevant threshold are not subject to the 40% tax rate.

The unification of transfer taxes institutionalized a tradeoff between *inter vivos* transfers and the value of the estate an individual can bequeath without incurring a tax liability. The greater the value of gifts made during life, the smaller the value of the estate tax exemption at death. For example, if an individual that died in 2016 had made lifetime taxable gifts of $1 million, then their estate tax exemption would have been $4.45 million. If their lifetime taxable gifts had totaled $2 million, then the estate tax exemption would have been $3.45 million, and so on.

Not all gifts count against the lifetime exemption. The following are usually excluded from being counted against the exemption and do not incur other tax liabilities:

* Gifts to a spouse, regardless of amount, providing the spouse is a United States citizen
* Gifts to a political organization
* Gifts in the form of tuition directly paid on someone else's behalf
* Gifts in the form of medical expenses paid on someone else's behalf
* Most other gifts that do not exceed a different annual exemption amount established by the IRS, set at $14,000 in 2016

To determine an estate's taxability, it must be valued, but the taxable value is not simply the sum total of the estate's assets. At the owner's death, executors must determine the estate's worth based on the assets' fair market values. The IRS allows several deductions from that gross value, such as for the outstanding debts, charitable contributions, spousal transfers, and administration costs. The remaining net estate value is then subject to taxation. Anything above the lifetime exemption is taxed at a flat rate of 40%. Gifts made above the exemption are likewise taxed at a flat rate of 40%. Transfer taxes are paid by the donor, not the recipient, but if the donor fails to pay the appropriate liability, the IRS may attempt to collect the unpaid tax from the recipient.

As an illustration, consider an individual who died in 2016 and left an estate with a net value of $10 million. Assume that individual made no taxable gifts during their lifetime. The taxable portion of that individual's estate is thus most likely $4.45 million—i.e., the estate's net value less the lifetime transfer exemption—and

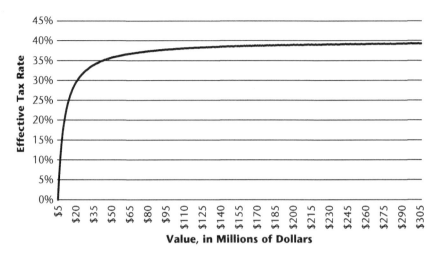

FIGURE 8.5   Effective Transfer Tax Rate, by Value of Transfer, 2016

Source: Author's analysis based on existing transfer tax rates and exemptions.

the federal estate tax due is consequently $1.78 million, which is equal to 40% of the taxable portion. Although the effective tax rate on this particular estate would be only 17.8%, the effective rate increases with estate value (see Figure 8.5). In practice, transfer taxes are highly progressive.

Once federal taxes have been paid, the remainder of the estate is divided as directed by legal documents or probate rules. Depending on the donor and recipient(s) domicile and state of residence, additional foreign and/or state transfer taxes may apply. Exemptions against the federal transfer tax may be allowed for taxes due to other governments.

One last tax may be triggered on certain transfers, the GST tax. The GST tax applies to transfers to recipients more than one generation younger than the donor (e.g., gifts from grandparents to their grandchildren) that otherwise escape estate and gift taxes. The rate is a flat 40% on transfers above the exemption amount established by the IRS.

Transfer Taxes, Private Property Rights, and Inequality

Like many other developed nations, the United States approaches transfer taxes with a broad but limited recognition of a natural, individual right to private property disposition (Beckert 2008). By law, individuals are allowed to transfer assets in life and direct that transfers occur after their death, but only within state-established boundaries. The value of transfers outside those boundaries is in jeopardy of being reduced, perhaps substantially, by federal and state levies.

Transfer taxes call to mind the same divergence that undergirds tax politics more generally: the classical liberal belief in private property rights that are antithetical to most coercive taxes versus progressives' disavowal of absolute private property rights and high salience attached to inequality. If one believes that a right of property disposition is natural and binding on all individuals, then they cannot, with any intellectual consistency, call for punitive state treatment on some individuals. Natural rights are contingent on an individual's material well-being; that an individual may die with $10 million in assets does not mean they relinquish any measure of their property rights compared to an individual that dies with $10 in assets.

Progressives avoid justifying transfer taxes by discussing the limits of property rights and instead appeal to other normative concepts (Duff 1993; Graetz and Shapiro 2005). A key progressive basis for transfer taxation is distributive justice. Subsumed within that basis is the idea that the tax's virtue should be judged not from the point of view of an individual but from civil society as a whole (Halliday 2013). Recall the words of progressive leader Walter Weyl (1913) discussed in Chapter 1:

> By progressive taxes on property, income, or inheritances . . . the state can do much towards preventing too insensate an accumulation of individual wealth.

Rawls (1971) supported estate taxes as a route to prevent concentrations of wealth, which he argued were "detrimental" to "equality of opportunity." The Rawlsian premise was that more opportunity is present in a civil society in which the state confiscates a portion of certain wealthy individuals' estates compared to one in which that confiscation does not occur. Other progressive academics tend to agree, often with research that suggests estate taxes reduce inequality (e.g., Aaron and Munnell 1992; Piketty and Saez 2013; Stiglitz 1978). Some scholars argue that more radical policies, including outright bans on large transfers and total confiscation of wealth by the state, would be more effective (Haslett 1986).

Progressive support of transfer taxes is also rooted in a deeply held conviction that wealth cannot be accumulated independent of the state. Recall the comments from Senator Elizabeth Warren and President Barack Obama discussed in Chapter 2, the gist of which was a belief that since public goods facilitate wealth, whoever achieves wealth has a duty to repay the state for their success. This line of thought traces back over a century. Consider this excerpt from progressive President Theodore Roosevelt's 1906 State of the Union speech:

> the National Government should impose a graduated inheritance tax, and, if possible, a graduated income tax. The man of great wealth owes a peculiar obligation to the State, because he derives special advantages from the mere existence of government. Not only should he recognize this obligation in the way he leads his daily life and in the way he earns and spends his money, but it should also be recognized by the way in which he pays for the protection the State gives him.

Following up on those remarks, Roosevelt said in 1907:

> The government has the absolute right to decide as to the terms upon which a man shall receive a bequest or devise from another, and this point in the devolution of property is especially appropriate for the imposition of a tax.

Contemporary progressivism continues to emphasize the relationship of transfer taxation to economic fairness and justice with allusions to the ability to pay and benefit principles. For example, the progressive Center on Budget and Priorities calls the estate tax "an economically efficient way to raise revenue that supports public services and lowers deficits" and says that "it is appropriate that people who have prospered the most in this society help to preserve it for future generations through tax revenues that derive from their estates." Moreover:

> the very wealthy benefit from public investments in areas such as defense, education, health care, scientific research, environmental protection, and infrastructure. And they rely even more than others on the government's protection of individual property rights, since they have so much more to protect.[9]

Ideological differences on property rights and transfer taxes are reflected in party positions on the issue.[10] Estate taxes are an indelible feature of tax proposals from Democrats. As a candidate and as president, Barack Obama supported direct increases to the estate tax (e.g., through lower exemptions and/or higher tax rates) as well as indirect increases (e.g., by changing the integration of capital gains taxes with estates). As a candidate in the 2016 presidential primary, Bernie Sanders, citing Theodore Roosevelt's defense of transfer taxes, proposed lowering the estate tax exemption to $3.5 million and instituting a new system of graduated MTRs. Sanders suggested a 45% rate on estates valued at between $3.5 million and $10 million, 50% on estates valued between $10 million and $50 million, and 55% on estates valued higher than $50 million, with an additional 10% surtax on "billionaires." Sanders' opponent and Democrats' eventual nominee, Hillary Clinton, proposed the same $3.5 million exemption and a higher, but flat, tax rate of 45%.

Republican candidates eschew the estate tax. What is unique about the partisan cleavage over transfer taxes is that the split isn't over policy specifics (e.g., what rate should apply to what level of income or assets), but whether the policy should exist at all. Indeed, most Republicans and other conservatives do not accept the premise that transfer taxes are necessary and fair. The reduction and later elimination of the estate tax was one of many changes included in Republican President George W. Bush's 2001 tax reform bill. Republican candidate Mitt Romney in 2012 and all major Republican candidates in 2016 proposed repealing the estate tax outright.[11]

Transfer Taxes and Fairness

Beyond disagreements over the bounds of private property rights and inequality, opponents of transfer taxes often raise the issue of fairness. Regardless of an individual's asset accumulation at the point of death, their assets were most likely accrued over time with post-tax dollars. An individual's estate is what remains after that individual paid a lifetime of federal taxes on labor, capital, and other sources of income in addition to consumption taxes, property taxes, and other fees. If, after all of those levies, an individual elects to transfer assets to another, it is arguably unfair to tax those assets again, regardless of their value, although a case can be made for an inheritance tax charged to the recipient.

A different perspective on fairness emerges if one compares two hypothetical individuals, A and B, for whom all characteristics are equal, including their ability to pay, but they differ in how their earnings are used. Individual A spends nearly all of their income in life and, at death, leaves a small estate. Individual B saves nearly all of their income and, at death, leaves a substantial estate. Over their respective lifetimes, Individual A will pay more in consumption taxes and Individual B will pay more in estate taxes. Since consumption tax rates are lower—much lower—than estate tax rates, Individual B's overall tax burden will be significantly higher than Individual A's, and this despite their equal ability to pay. Not only does this scenario illustrate the lack of horizontal equity that can result when evaluating the broader tax system instead of one levy at a time, it also demonstrations how estate taxes disincentivize savings.

Transfer taxes may also appear unfair when the United States is compared to other nations. The current federal transfer tax is the fourth-highest in the world, and the United States is home to the highest estate tax, not including potential state-level taxes (see Table 8.2 and also refer to Table 8.1). By comparison, most other nations tax inheritances rather than estates.

TABLE 8.2 Highest Transfer Tax Rates Worldwide, 2015

Nation	Type	Rate
Japan	Inheritance	55%
South Korea	Inheritance	50%
France	Inheritance	45%
United Kingdom	Inheritance	40%
United States	Estate	40%
Ecuador	Inheritance	35%
Spain	Estate	34%
Ireland	Inheritance	33%
Belgium	Inheritance	30%
Germany	Inheritance	30%

Note: The U.S. rate does not include possible state estate/inheritance taxes.

Sources: The Tax Foundation and the OECD.

Critics of transfer taxes are sometimes uncomfortable with the levy for its role in delegating to policymakers the task of determining which ancestral relationships are worthy and unworthy of tax exemptions, and the unfairness and discrimination that may result. Before the legalization of same-sex marriage, same-sex couples faced different estate tax treatment than opposite-sex couples. One discrimination lawsuit filed by a female couple went all the way to the Supreme Court in 2013 and eventually led to a partial strike down of the federal Defense of Marriage Act, opening the door to subsequent legalization of same-sex marriage.[12] Yet the spousal exemptions included in federal and state transfer taxes retain an inherent bias against unmarried individuals of any sexual orientation. Why, for instance, should a married woman be allowed to bequeath a large estate to her husband free of estate taxation whereas an unmarried woman cannot bequeath an estate of the same size to an unrelated caretaker without incurring federal and perhaps state taxes?

A Minor Tax with Major Interest Group Attention

Partisans on either side of the aisle have interest groups supporting their respective efforts. The progressive United for a Fair Economy has lobbied for continuation of the estate tax. In 2005, when estate tax changes were under consideration, the group paid for newspaper advertisements that read:

> Should we fire 1,000 more teachers? Cut health care? Slash Social Security? And give the money to a few millionaires? Better idea: Keep the estate tax. And keep funding these vital human services. A trillion dollars is at stake.

United's efforts have been complemented by those from other groups, like Americans for a Fair Estate Tax, a coalition of labor unions, women's groups, and other progressive causes, as well as the Center for American Progress. United has more recently lobbied for a reduced estate tax exemption and the imposition of graduated tax rates, similar to Bernie Sanders' 2016 proposal.

Industries that benefit from transfer taxes have also lobbied to keep current policy in effect. The Association for Advanced Life Underwriting, whose members sell estate-planning services, has pushed for a continuation of the estate tax, even as it also lobbies to keep life insurance benefits tax-free. The American Council of Life Insurers (ACLI) has likewise fought to keep the estate tax in place. In fact, one of ACLI's chief lobbyists during the mid-2000s debate over estate taxes, Kimberly Dorgan, was married to a sitting senator, Democrat Byron Dorgan, an ardent supporter of the estate tax. During the temporary 2010 estate tax repeal, Dorgan announced from the Senate floor that it was "embarrassing that we have a zero estate tax for the wealthiest Americans."

In the other corner, all manner of tax reform and business groups support eliminating estate taxes, including Club for Growth, Americans for Tax Reform, and the National Federation of Independent Businesses. One of the largest advocates for eliminating estate and inheritance taxes is the Family Business Coalition. The coalition argues that many family-owned businesses are harmed by federal and state transfer taxes, especially those in which a majority of the assets are held in land, real estate, and/or inventory. When the owner of such a business dies, their estate may have to liquidate those assets in whole or in part to pay the applicable federal and state transfer taxes, which can irreparably harm the business.

The Congressional Budget Office has noted that few, but not all, family-owned businesses and other estates have sufficient assets to incur federal estate tax liabilities.[13] For example, in 2005, the estates of 1,137 farmers and 8,291 small business owners had sufficient assets to file an estate tax return. Earlier estimates suggested that a small proportion of all such estates, less than 10%, lacked liquidity to pay their tax liability.[14] In those situations, the Congressional Budget Office has noted that estates can "pay the tax in installments over 15 years at low interest rates."[15]

Conclusion

Transfer taxes are a negligible contributor to the federal treasury, but that hasn't stopped them from rousing robust political conflicts that are just as impassioned as those centered on more far-reaching taxes. In spite of that divisiveness, public opinion on transfer taxes is consistently unfavorable. As far back as 1935, a Roper poll conducted for *Fortune* magazine asked respondents how much money they believed an individual should be allowed to inherit. A majority of adults said that there should be no limit, a view shared by 47% of the poor.

More recent national polls suggest that a majority of the public supports the elimination of transfer taxes. For instance, a 2005 CBS News/*New York Times* survey found that 76% of respondents were opposed to the estate tax. When prompted for their opinion within the context of a hypothetical scenario in which the estate tax was levied only on estates valued at more than $1.5 million, 46% remained opposed and just 27% were in favor. A 2016 Gallup poll revealed similar findings; 54% of respondents supported the elimination of the estate tax and 19% were opposed. Nearly three-quarters of adults in a 2015 Fox News poll agreed that inheritance taxes were unfair. Whereas self-identified Democrats are more likely than Republicans and independents to support keeping the estate tax, their collective support is tepid. A 2014 poll of California residents found only 29% of that state's Democrats supported raising the tax from 40% to 50%, compared to 11% of Republicans and 14% of independents (Ahler et al. 2015).

It is curious that so many individuals oppose a tax that affects so few.[16] What explains opposition to the estate tax—opposition that *The Atlantic* describes as "un-American" (Martin 2016)? The "death tax" label certainly doesn't help. A not-insignificant number of people believe their work ethic and upward mobility over time will lead to the accumulation of significant assets, and they recoil at the idea of being robbed of some of those assets by the government. And many individuals are also aware that a body of research indicates that transfer taxes do not improve economic outcomes. The taxes have been shown to constrain human capital accumulation (Alonso-Carrera et al. 2012), which is key for economic growth, and reduce the number of firms (Yakovlev and Davies 2014), which lessens competition.

But disagreement with the estate and other transfer taxes is perhaps fundamentally conditioned on how an individual incorporates the tax with their attitudes toward fairness and the broader tax system (Birney et al. 2006; Prabhakar 2015). All things considered, individuals from diverse political and economic backgrounds share a common belief that perhaps after a lifetime of paying taxes, no matter how much an individual is or isn't worth when they die, that individual should be allowed to dispose of their assets—all of their assets—as they see fit, free from state interference.

Notes

1   Letter to Jean-Baptiste Leroy, November 13, 1789.
2   Quid pro quo exchanges are not subject to any transfer taxes.
3   The Latin translation of *inter vivos* is "between the living."
4   This section highlights major developments in the federal estate tax; for a more comprehensive investigation, see Graetz and Shapiro (2005) and West (1908).
5   *Scholey v. Rew*, 90 U.S. (23 Wall. 331) (1874).
6   *Knowlton v. Moore*, 178 U.S. 41 (1900).
7   *New York Trust Co. v. Eisner*, 256 U.S. 345 (1921).
8   *Bromley v. McCaughn*, 280 U.S. 124 (1929).
9   See http://www.cbpp.org/research/federal-tax/eliminating-estate-tax-on-inherited-wealth-would-increase-deficits-and.
10 Not surprisingly, think tanks aligned with the political right position themselves against transfer taxes and the estate tax in particular. The libertarian Cato Institute and the conservative Heritage Foundation and American Enterprise Institute have argued in favor of repealing the federal estate tax, although Heritage has suggested replacing it with an inheritance tax. The center-left Brookings Institute has recommended keeping the estate tax in place, but with reforms to make the tax even more progressive than it already is. Progressive think tanks, including the Economic Policy Institute and the Center on Budget and Policy Priorities, contend the estate tax should be increased.
11 In 2008, John McCain proposed raising the estate tax exemption and lowering the rate to 15%, making him the only recent exception to the rule of Republican candidates' embrace of estate tax elimination.
12 *United States v. Windsor*, 570 U.S. (2013).
13 See Congressional Budget Office, "Small Firms, Employment, and Federal Policy," 2012.
14 See Congressional Budget Office, "Effects of the Federal Estate Tax on Farms and Small Businesses," 2005.
15 See Congressional Budget Office, "Federal Estate and Gift Taxes," 2009.
16 This is a common refrain, especially among progressives who puzzle at repeated surveys that find pluralities of adults oppose the estate tax. The motivation behind the query would seem to be an assumption of selfishness, i.e., that individuals have no problem with a tax as long as they personally are exempt.

References

Aaron, Henry J., and Alicia H. Munnell. 1992. "Reassessing the Role for Wealth Transfer Taxes." *National Tax Journal* 45(2): 119–143.

Ahler, Douglas J., Beckett Kelly, Gabriel Lenz, Ethan Rarick, and Laura Stoker. 2015. "Californian's Beliefs about Income Inequality." *California Journal of Public Policy* 7(4): 1–12.

Alonso-Carrera, Jaime, Jordi Caballé, and Xavier Raurich. 2012. "Fiscal Policy, Composition of Intergenerational Transfers, and Income Distribution." *Journal of Economic Behavior & Organization* 84(1): 62–84.

Beckert, Jens. 2008. *Inherited Wealth*. Princeton: Princeton University Press.

Birney, Mayling, Michael J. Graetz, and Ian Shapiro. 2006. "Public Opinion and the Push to Repeal the Estate Tax." *National Tax Journal* 59(3): 439–461.

Duff, David G. 1993. "Taxing Inherited Wealth: A Philosophical Argument." *Canadian Journal of Law and Jurisprudence* 6(1): 3–62.

Graetz, Michael J., and Ian Shapiro. 2005. *Death by a Thousand Cuts: The Fight over Taxing Inherited Wealth*. Princeton: Princeton University Press.

Halliday, Daniel. 2013. "Is Inheritance Morally Distinctive?" *Law and Philosophy* 32(5): 619–644.

Haslett, D.W. 1986. "Is Inheritance Justified?" *Philosophy & Public Affairs* 15(2): 122–155.

Martin, Stephen. 2016. "America's Un-American Resistance to the Estate Tax." *The Atlantic*, February 23.

Piketty, Thomas, and Emmanuel Saez. 2013. "A Theory of Optimal Inheritance Taxation." *Econometrica* 81(5): 1851–1886.

Prabhakar, Rajiv. 2015. "Why Do the Public Oppose Inheritance Taxes?" *Philosophical Explorations of Justice and Taxation* 40: 151–166.

Rawls, John. 1971. *A Theory of Justice*. Cambridge, MA: Harvard University Press.

Scheve, Kenneth, and David Stasavage. 2012. "Democracy, War, and Wealth: Lessons from Two Centuries of Inheritance Taxation." *American Political Science Review* 106(1): 81–102.

Stiglitz, Joseph E. 1978. "Notes on Estate Taxes, Redistribution, and the Concept of Balanced Growth Path Incidence." *Journal of Political Economy* 86(2): 137–150.

West, Max. 1908. *The Inheritance Tax*. New York: Columbia University Press.

Weyl, Walter E. 1913. *The New Democracy: An Essay on Certain Political and Economic Tendencies in the United States*. New York: Macmillan.

Yakovlev, Pavel A., and Antony Davies. 2014. "How Does the Estate Tax Affect the Number of Firms?" *Journal of Entrepreneurship and Public Policy* 3(1): 96–117.

PART V

The Way Forward

9

TAX REFORM

Ideas Without Action

Tax reform proposals aren't a dime a dozen—they're a dime a gross.

That's partly because the phrase "tax reform" is imprecise. "Tax" might refer to any one of the array of taxes levied in the United States—income taxes, consumption taxes, property taxes, and so on. "Reform" could mean increasing or decreasing rates, changing the tax base, altering tax preferences, or simply changing how the tax is administered. Depending on the tax in question, reform could be a local, state, or federal matter. Because everyone has a unique interaction with taxes and government services, opinions on how to improve the system are, not surprisingly, rather diverse.

Tax reform deliberations are nearly always about the federal taxes on individuals' income—a $2.5 trillion elephant in the room.[1] Since that tax was made permanent in 1913, reform has occurred through incremental adjustments to the ballooning tax code. Since the last major reform was enacted in 1986, discussions have continued about how to "fix" the tax system. The debate often traces familiar paths, with varied opinions on the competing utilities of simplicity (e.g., by reducing the number of marginal tax rates), efficiency (e.g., by eliminating tax preferences and broadening the tax base), and both vertical and horizontal equity. But a larger issue has gained salience over the years, that concerning whether the federal government should maintain its reliance on taxing income with graduated tax rates or if it should pursue more significant reforms.

Because trillions of dollars are at stake, tax reform is a persistent interest of both policymakers and taxpayers. So important are tax reforms that simply announcing them can have an immediate economic impact (Ahmad and Xiao 2013). This chapter examines some of the most promising ideas for reforming the federal tax system and explores why reform is so hard to accomplish. Although the emphasis here is on federal reform, many of the proposals have applicability at the state level.

Modernizing the Status Quo

We're Here to Help: Progress and Challenges to Making the IRS Taxpayer-Friendly

As tax forms have followed the tax code's growth in scope and density, Congress has enacted reforms that attempt to make the process of paying federal income taxes easier and reduce taxpayers' fear of the IRS. The Office of the Taxpayer Advocate, established in 1996, and its director, the National Taxpayer Advocate, are positioned as taxpayers' "voice" within the IRS, identifying and fixing problems and unfair treatment. The Taxpayer Advocate works under the Commissioner of Internal Revenue and must submit annual reports to the House Ways and Means Committee and the Senate Finance Committee on the agency's progress.

Much of the IRS' effort to improve the taxpaying process is shaped by a 10-point Taxpayer Bill of Rights, a list of 10 rights articulated by the agency in accordance with a Congressional mandate in 1988. The document stipulates that every taxpayer should expect basic due process protections when dealing with the IRS (e.g., a right to challenge their tax situation, a right to representation, and a right to appeal decisions). Yet it also promises some rights that one would hope do not need explicit confirmation (e.g., that individuals don't have to pay more in taxes than they legally owe).

The National Taxpayer Advocate administers two noteworthy taxpayer assistance programs, which are important to sustaining compliance (Alm et al. 2010). The Low Income Tax Clinics program provides grants to organizations, such as law schools and social service groups, that operate clinics focused on assisting low-income individuals and non-native English speakers in completing their tax returns. The Taxpayer Advocate Service (TAS) provides resources to assist taxpayers in resolving difficult tax situations, especially those with severe financial consequences. Whereas there is only one national TAS office, each state has at least one "local taxpayer advocate" that provides more immediate support.

Of course, using the TAS requires paperwork, including the humorously numbered Form 911. Any individual using that form to report a frivolous claim risks a fine of $5,000. The IRS has even published a separate document (Publication 2105, titled "Why Do I Have to Pay Taxes?") with examples of claims taxpayers should avoid making.[2]

Despite these reforms, the IRS faces continued challenges related to information technology and privacy. Through its Taxpayer Protection Program, the IRS in 2015 halted processing of over four million tax returns suspected of involving identity theft. The program has a high rate of false positives; about one of every three returns flagged for potential identity theft is, in fact, a legitimate return. Resolving flagged returns is not a simple process. During peak periods in 2015, less than one in 10 impacted taxpayers was able to connect with a live IRS employee to discuss their situation, and the average wait times ranged from

20 minutes to an hour. Whereas the IRS has worked to protect taxpayers from identity theft, the agency has been criticized for failing to protect its own data. A 2016 General Accountability Office investigation found that the IRS failed to fully implement basic data integrity practices, including data encryption and server access restrictions.[3]

The IRS has also come under fire for its treatment of conservative political groups. For decades, organizations focused on promoting "social welfare" have been exempt from federal taxation. The IRS has generally interpreted this to include civic organizations, including those engaged in political activities.

But beginning in early 2010, officials at multiple IRS offices subjected applications for tax-exempt status coming from apparently conservative groups to added scrutiny. In most cases the agency "sat" on the applications, neither approving nor denying them for months. The practice gained notoriety when some conservative groups noticed that their applications had been ignored while those from progressive causes were approved, including groups that supported Obama Administration priorities, and one group in particular that sought "to build a more progressive Florida." The controversy gained momentum after the IRS in 2012 leaked the National Organization for Marriage's tax return to the Human Rights Campaign, an election year mistake—and violation of federal law—for which the agency later admitted wrongdoing and paid a small settlement.

Subsequent investigation by the Treasury Inspector General for Tax Administration found that the IRS had indeed unfairly targeted conservative groups.[4] IRS employees specifically targeted applications from groups with names including "Tea Party" or "patriot" and those that sought to educate people on the Constitution. Groups that referenced medical marijuana, Israel, opposing the Affordable Care Act, and even "occupy" were also targeted. Republicans were outraged, especially after the Department of Justice, under Obama-appointee Eric Holder, announced that no criminal charges would be filed.[5]

Unfortunately, anyone interested in finding out how the targeting started can't get very far. The Treasury Inspector General's official report redacted the contents of 14 separate IRS emails, including the first email that seemingly kicked off the practice. But based on the dates of those emails, which were not redacted, it appears that targeting started around February 2010, before the impact of the Supreme Court's *Citizens United* decision, which opened the floodgates for all sorts of political organizations to apply for tax-exempt status, was felt.

Truth in Taxation: Increasing the Transparency of Income Tax Burdens

In a perfect world, each individual would have precise knowledge of their total tax burden. But the overlapping tax systems under which we live in the United States, with a range of federal, state, and local taxes, makes acquiring that knowledge impossible. But progress could be made toward reducing the imperfect information associated with federal income tax burdens, which represent the largest portion of most individuals' overall tax burden and that provide 80% of all federal revenue.

Little about the current process of paying income taxes is transparent. Annual tax returns and supporting documents are complicated, confusing, time-consuming, and costly to prepare. Figures are entered on tax forms in dollar terms rather than percentages, removing any real impetus for a taxpayer to calculate their taxes as a proportion of their income. Many individuals don't even prepare their own forms. Regular tax withholding only adds to the confusion. Pay stubs report the dollar value of tax withholdings, but they rarely report the associated tax rates. The waters are further muddied by the receipt of a tax refund, which alters the tax burden that would be calculated based simply on tax withholding, and that is often interpreted as some kind of windfall from the government.

At no point does any federal agency communicate to each taxpayer their overall, net income tax burden—and that's ironic, given that Congress habitually intervenes to reduce information asymmetries between consumers and businesses. Airlines must separate for customers the cost of base airfare from the cost of federal excise taxes. The Truth in Lending Act mandates that financial institutions involved in consumer loans use a standardized formula for calculating annual percentage rates and clearly disclose other borrowing costs. The Truth in Savings Act mandates similar transparency requirements on institutions that provide bank accounts. And the Nutrition Labeling and Education Act requires that foods regulated by the Food and Drug Administration carry a label that lists caloric and nutrient content.

Policymakers could greatly improve income tax transparency by sending each individual an annual "truth-in-taxation" statement.[6] They could go one step further and use the statement to illustrate how each individual's taxes were allocated across government agencies based on that year's enacted appropriations bills. Congress would likely find it difficult to coerce each state with an income tax into following their lead on a federally-initiated reform, but simple enactment at the federal level would increase local political pressure for states to follow suit. Congress could also threaten to withhold certain federal funds from state governments unless they meet other tax transparency requirements, similar to the tactic used to raise the national drinking age to 21.[7]

Is it likely that policymakers will move toward truth-in-taxation statements anytime soon? Unfortunately, no. One reasonable objection would be that the task is too complex and costly; memories of the disastrous and embarrassing roll-out of healthcare.gov undoubtedly linger. But technology continues to advance, and significant amounts of income and tax data are already reported to federal and state governments. The administrative burden of consolidating that information into a single annual estimate of each individual's tax burden is in decline. It is also worth noting that the federal government already has a similar arrangement in place. The Social Security Administration tracks individuals' wages and payroll taxes paid, and it will furnish, upon request, a statement listing annual figures and an estimate of future benefits.

More significantly, any proposal to introduce greater tax transparency will face stiff political headwinds. Such a reform would convey to taxpayers in a much clearer fashion the proportion of their income that they must, by law, remit to the government. That alone will enhance taxpayer attentiveness to how those tax dollars are spent, an outcome more than a few policymakers and interest groups will not look upon favorably. The reform would also show millions of individuals that their tax burden is nowhere near what they—mistakenly—assume; recall the misperceptions discussed in Chapter 3. That would alter the perpetual "fair share" debate—another outcome certain vested interests are not likely to embrace—and change public perceptions about the merits of more substantial tax reform ideas.

We'll Do It for You: A Return-Free System

A more sweeping proposal to change how individuals pay income taxes, a "return-free" system, has gained notice in Congress, thanks to the efforts of Senator Elizabeth Warren.[8] Under a return-free system, the IRS would send a pre-filled return to each individual based on data already reported to the federal government. The IRS would use that data to calculate the individual's taxes due or their tax refund; note, incidentally, the compatibility between a truth-in-taxation reform and a return-free system. For millions of taxpayers, this tax-filing process would eliminate much of the confusion, anxiety, and costs currently associated with tax preparation. It would also benefit the IRS by reducing errors, and the federal treasury by reducing the tax gap.

Unlike almost every other aspect of tax policy, the return-free concept has long had support from policymakers in both political parties. The bipartisan IRS Restructuring and Reform Act, enacted in 1998, mandated that the IRS develop a return-free system by 2008. But nearly 10 years after that deadline, the agency has yet to comply. A 2003 report from the Treasury Department identified several hurdles to implementing a return-free system in the United States.[9] The report concluded that the federal tax code is too complicated to convert to a return-free system, especially because it relies so heavily on life events—e.g., marriage, childbirth, health care expenses, charitable contributions—that the federal government does not track. Whereas some European nations have implemented return-free systems, the report noted that those nations have far simpler tax laws and significantly smaller populations.

Although the federal government has not moved forward with a return-free system, some state governments have experimented with their own versions. In 2004, California launched ReadyReturn, a pilot program in which about 50,000 resident taxpayers received pre-filled returns from the state's Franchise Tax Board.[10] Surprisingly, 77% of the targeted taxpayers chose not to participate and decided to complete their own returns.[11] Among taxpayers that did participate, satisfaction was high and error rates were low.[12]

Notwithstanding bipartisan support and a consumer-friendly orientation, return-free proposals have a powerful interest working against them: the tax preparation industry. Led by Intuit, owner of the popular TurboTax software, the industry opposes return-free tax filing. Disclosures filed by Intuit in 2012 showed that the company spent $60,000 to retain two lobbyists to urge both the House of Representatives and the Senate to maintain the federal FreeFile program, from which the industry benefits, and to oppose any legislation that would allow the IRS to pre-fill tax returns. Intuit's Form 10-K, filed with the Securities and Exchange Commission in 2012, admits that the firm "faces significant competition from the public sector, where we face the risk of federal and state taxing authorities developing software or other systems to facilitate tax return preparation and electronic filing at no charge to taxpayers." In 2016, an Intuit representative told ProPublica that the firm remained "a staunch opponent to government prepared tax returns" (Day 2013).

Reshaping Policy: Select Federal Tax Reform Proposals

In contrast to making the existing federal income tax more convenient, a number of stakeholders have advanced proposals for game-changing tax systems. Some proposals rely on a similar tax base—e.g., they would still tax income, but with a different method—but others call on the United States to shift from taxing income to taxing consumption. Some recommend a combination of the two.

The Flat Income Tax

Flat-tax proposals invariably recommend eliminating the current system of graduated income tax rates on individuals and corporations in favor of a single, flat tax rate. Most proposals further recommend the drastic simplification or outright elimination of other complicating elements of the tax code, including tax preferences. Tens of millions of Americans are already familiar with the concept of a flat tax because they pay a flat tax to their state and/or local governments (refer to Table 3.4).

Multiple variants of the flat tax have been proposed, generally differing in terms of their recommended tax rate, definition of income, and income exemptions. The Hall and Rabushka (1983, 2007) proposal calls for a flat tax of 19% on both individuals and corporations. Individuals would be taxed on both labor income and retirement plan income, such as pensions, but be allowed deductions based on marital status and family size.[13] Otherwise, the proposal includes no individual tax preferences—i.e., no above-the-line adjustments, deductions, or credits. Corporations would pay the same 19% rate on net income, straightforwardly defined as revenue less the sum of expenses and employee retirement contributions. Individuals would not pay taxes on their share of any corporate income, because a tax is already paid at the corporate level. Thus, the Hall–Rabushka flat tax eliminates the double taxation of corporate income.

Under a plan developed by former Republican presidential candidate Steve Forbes (2005), individuals would be subject to a flat rate of 17% on labor earnings. All capital and miscellaneous income would be exempt from the tax, thereby eliminating double taxation. The plan includes simple income exemptions for individuals, couples, and families, and retains the Earned Income Tax Credit. The effective tax rate paid by low-income individuals would be negative, and many moderate-income families would have an effective rate of less than 5%. Corporate entities would be subject to a flat rate of 17% on net domestic income, calculated as the simple difference between revenue and wages, raw materials, and equipment. All corporate tax preferences would be eliminated. Pass-through entities would be subject to the flat tax, but their owners would not.

The flat income tax has mass appeal. Over two decades of opinion surveys generally but not consistently show that the public is supportive of the concept, although sizable proportions are either unsure or lack sufficient knowledge to render a judgment (see Table 9.1). Support or opposition to a flat income tax is also conditioned on how the proposal would alter the existing tax code. Many people support a flat tax in theory, but when told about the prospect of losing certain tax preferences, change their minds.

The flat tax has its share of opponents. Bartlett (2012) notes three common criticisms. First, some individuals may have larger tax liabilities under a flat tax, particularly those in the lowest MTRs, depending on the tax rate, income

TABLE 9.1 Sample of Public Opinion Toward a Flat Income Tax

Year	Survey Sponsor(s)	Supportive (%)	Unsupportive (%)	Neither (%)
1992	NBC News/*Wall Street Journal*	49	44	7
1995	CBS News/*New York Times*	26	38	35
1995	*Newsweek*	59	29	12
1995	CNN/*Time*	62	28	10
1995	*Los Angeles Times*	40	48	12
1996	CBS News/*New York Times*	27	33	38
1996	*Newsweek*	50	32	18
1996	CNN/*Time*	41	48	11
1997	Fox News	57	27	16
1999	Harris Interactive	60	35	5
2004	CBS News/*New York Times*	26	34	37
2011	CBS News	32	36	28
2011	Rasmussen Reports	55	26	19
2012	Rasmussen Reports	58	31	11
2014	Reason Foundation	62	33	5
2016	Gallup	45	28	26

Note: Findings reported are not an exhaustive list of all surveys on a flat income tax. To maintain consistency, surveys with question wording that mentioned the possible retention or loss of specific tax deductions, and those that asked respondents to select a preferred tax system or rank-order different systems, are not included.

Sources: Individual sponsors' websites and Bowman et al. (2016).

exclusions, and the impact of lost tax preferences. Second, policymakers are not prevented from creating new tax preferences once a plan like the Hall–Rabushka or Forbes proposals is enacted. Third, some industries may bear disproportionate harm or benefit based on how they are impacted by flat tax proposals' elimination of corporate tax preferences and alteration to the definition of corporate income. Some studies have found that a flat tax would increase wealth concentration (e.g., Ventura 1999).

Flat-tax advocates argue that the reform has many redeeming qualities. Simplicity is chief among them, along with the economic and political benefits of eliminating scores of distortive, inefficient tax preferences and all of the lobbying they attract. Several studies have also found evidence that flat-tax systems confer broad economic benefits. Heer and Trede (2003) found a flat tax would have little effect on income distribution and facilitate higher savings and employment as well as overall welfare gains. Other studies have found similarly positive benefits for income growth (e.g., Cassou and Lansing 2007).

In sum, the impact of a flat tax is contingent upon the tax rate, the tax base, and integration with existing welfare programs. Like many policy reforms, the flat tax represents a tradeoff between equity and efficiency (Paulus and Peichl 2009). We may never know what the best tax system is, but Epstein (2002) reasoned that the flat tax is "a robust second-best choice for public finance, which counts as first-best in an imperfect world."

The FairTax

FairTax legislation would abolish the IRS and replace all existing federal taxes (personal and corporate income taxes as well as payroll and estate taxes) with a national retail sales tax of 23% embedded in the cost of all goods and services (Boortz and Linder 2005; Hoagland 2010). The tax rate approximates what some analysts estimate is required for the FairTax to operate as a revenue-neutral alternative to the status quo (Bachman et al. 2006). State governments would be delegated responsibility for collecting the tax and remitting proceeds to the federal government, and would be compensated with 0.25% of the collections. This partnership recalls state-federal cooperation during the War of 1812, when states were charged with collecting the federal property tax. To diminish the tax's regressivity, the FairTax proposal includes a tax rebate, called a "prebate," to each citizen based on their marital status and number of dependents. The prebate amount would be 23% of the federal poverty level for the individual's family. In effect, the prebate renders all consumption below the applicable poverty level tax-free. The FairTax would greatly increase take-home pay and corporate net income.

Legislation instituting the FairTax was first submitted to the House of Representatives in 1999 and has been introduced every year since. The concept was developed by Americans for Fair Taxation, an advocacy group formed in 1994 after three business owners—Bob McNair, Jack Trotter, and Leo Linbeck Jr.—each pledged $1.5 million to develop a proposal for replacing the existing federal income tax system. The result was the FairTax. Americans for Fair Taxation and similar interest groups, including Fair Tax Nation, continue to lobby for the Fair-Tax. They often receive support from conservative and libertarian groups. Indeed, support for the actual legislation is nearly entirely Republican in character, with heavy Democratic and even some Republican opposition.

Critics of the FairTax are quick to point out that the widely publicized 23% tax rate is disingenuous. Because the tax is embedded in the purchase price of goods and services, the prices paid by consumers are tax inclusive, not tax exclusive, and the effective tax rate is higher than 23%. For example, an item purchased for $100 under the FairTax system would, in fact, be a $77 good with a $23 sales tax added on top. Likewise, an item purchased for $200 would, in fact, be a $154 good with a $46 sales tax added on top. The effective tax rate is thus not 23%, but a significantly higher 29.9%. Regardless of whether the rate is 23% or nearly 30%, some analysts have argued that it is far from sufficient to remain revenue-neutral and, if enacted, would drastically lower federal revenues (Gale 2005). Others have said that a national retail sales tax rate should be lower, perhaps only 15% (Burton and Mastromarco 1997).

The FairTax has sustained several other criticisms. Many have argued that the tax is regressive (Kuang et al. 2011). Other opponents, including some conservatives, contend that the prebate is insufficient and that implementing the tax would carry enormous transition costs while harming entitlement programs like Social Security and Medicare (Adler and Hewitt 2009). The effect on homeownership, charitable contributions, and state and local government purchasing decisions is uncertain. Moreover, the high rate may encourage tax evasion by driving elements of the retail economy underground. If the tax were levied at multiple points of production, it would lead to tax cascading and tax pyramiding.

Supporters offer several rebuttals and often argue that FairTax benefits far outweigh the drawbacks.

Regardless of the debate over the "true" tax rate, the FairTax is markedly more straightforward and comprehensible than the existing income tax system. It does not require the average 15-hour, $270 annual ritual of completing Form 1040. It also carries much higher degrees of visibility. Under the FairTax, all consumers have a much better, and more accurate, sense of their tax burden—and, with it, a greater incentive to hold policymakers accountable for how those funds are spent. By eliminating tax preferences and establishing a uniform tax rate, the Fair-Tax largely removes Congress from the federal tax policy equation, thereby also undermining the rent-seeking tax lobby industry. The abolition of graduated tax rates on individual and corporate income and estate taxes eliminates the distortionary effects those taxes carry, eliminates the double taxation on C corporation income, and eliminates the incentive for corporate entities to transfer income to low-tax jurisdictions. Supporters also note that the FairTax is no more regressive, except in magnitude, than existing state retail sales taxes, and would come with the benefit of eliminating regressive federal payroll taxes (refer to Figure 3.14).

Both critics and supporters have expressed concern about two elements of the FairTax. The first is how to navigate the transition from the existing system to the FairTax, as individuals reorient their economic decisions—labor, savings, leisure—toward a radically different tax paradigm. Research suggests that despite what could be a bumpy transition period, the FairTax would eventually increase capital investment and overall economic growth compared to leaving the existing income tax framework in place (Bhattarai et al. 2016; Kotlikoff 1993).

The second and more important concern to the broader issue of federal tax reform is that the FairTax proposal does not and cannot repeal the Sixteenth Amendment, which can only be accomplished with a constitutional amendment. Absent a new amendment, the FairTax would abolish income taxes through legislation only, leaving the door open to Congress to reassert its authority and reinstitute an income tax at a later date, perhaps in addition to the FairTax.

The Negative Income Tax

The negative income tax (NIT) is unique in its focus on how to alter the relationship between low-income individuals, the tax code, and social welfare programs. Although it is not clear where the concept of a NIT originated, its most prominent advocate in the United States was economist Milton Friedman. The NIT has received attention in the academic literature, often in relation to its theoretical impact on poverty reduction (e.g., Lampman 1965; Moffitt 2003; Tobin et al. 1967; Zeckhauser 1971).

In essence, a "pure" NIT system requires that the federal government establish two parameters: an income threshold for different tax-filing statuses, and a negative income tax rate. Any individual or married couple with earnings below the threshold would receive a refund based on the difference between their earnings and that threshold. This refund would replace existing benefits provided by federal welfare programs (e.g., Temporary Assistance for Needy Families, the Earned Income Tax Credit, the Child Tax Credit, the Supplemental Nutrition Assistance Program, and so on). Earnings above the threshold could be taxed according to any framework (e.g., graduated rates or a flat tax.)

For a better idea of how the NIT works, consider this illustration. Assume Congress sets an earnings threshold of $50,000 for a married couple and a negative tax rate of 50%. If a married couple earns $0, they would receive a refund of $25,000 (i.e., the product of $50,000 and the 50% negative tax rate). If they earn exactly $50,000, they would receive no refund. If earnings fell between $0 and $50,000, the refund would fall between $25,000 and $0 (see Figure 9.1).

Critics attack the NIT for its negative impact on labor effort. By instituting what amounts to a guaranteed minimum, or basic income, the incentive to enter the workforce to earn less than the minimum is greatly reduced. From a different perspective, the NIT may incentivize underreporting of income; that way, an individual can receive a maximum refund and still work, without penalty. Skeptics

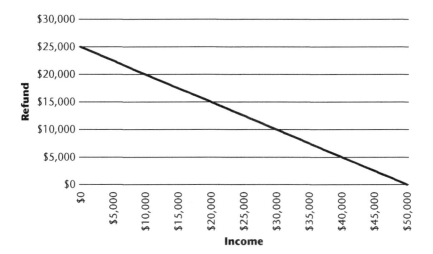

FIGURE 9.1 Negative Income Tax Refund Illustration

Source: Author's calculations based on assumptions outlined in the text.

also note that the transition to a NIT would be difficult, especially for individuals and families that have grown accustomed to welfare receipt.

Supporters say their approach to redistribution has many advantages over the existing system of means-tested tax preferences and welfare programs. The NIT retains the progressive nature of the status quo; effective rates increase with income, although the degree to which that continues above the income threshold depends. By granting cash refunds, the NIT eliminates the paternalism, distortions, and redundancies that characterize existing welfare programs and the billions spent on administering those programs. It also eliminates the stigma attached to using welfare benefits in public (e.g., redeeming Supplemental Nutrition Assistance Program or Women, Infants, and Children benefits at a grocery store). Because the NIT serves as a guaranteed income, it undercuts the need for a minimum wage, thereby expanding the labor market and lowering the cost of some goods and services. Research also suggests that the NIT's economic impact is superior to the flat tax (Lopez-Daneri 2016).

Other Reform Ideas

Over the years, many other proposals have been developed for some type of national consumption tax or a system of consumption and income taxes combined. As with any consumption tax, those proposals are rooted both in economic theory (e.g., that consumption taxes are preferable to income and capital taxation) and normative judgments (e.g., that an individual's ability to pay taxes is best measured in what they consume, not what they earn).

Many tax policy analysts as well as conservative and progressive policymakers have argued that the United States should implement a national value-added tax (VAT) like those common throughout Europe and currently in place in Australia and Canada. Others have suggested a graduated consumption tax that would, in various ways, require that the federal government measure consumption instead of, or in addition to, income, and then levy higher marginal tax rates on higher levels of consumption (Goldberg 2013; Seidman 1997). The Competitive Tax Plan, for instance, would impose a 12.9% VAT; individual income tax rates of 14%, 27%, and 31% with income below $50,000 exempt; and a flat corporate tax rate of 15% (Graetz 2008).[14]

A variation on the Hall–Rabushka flat tax, the X Tax, calls for flatter rates on certain types of income (Bradford 2004;Viard and Carroll 2012). X Tax proposals usually consist of two familiar tiers: a tax on individuals and a tax on corporations. The Bradford (2004) variation would apply graduated tax rates to individuals' wage income only, thereby exempting taxes on all other forms of income, and apply a flat tax rate to corporate cash flow, eliminating for both most of the existing system's tax preferences. The highest individual rate would be equal to the corporate rate. The corporate tax would apply to all corporate entities, eliminating the pass-through entity phenomenon. X Tax proposals often leave the door open to some redistributive tax preferences, such as the Earned Income Tax Credit.

Principles for a More Efficient System: Optimal Taxation

The design of any tax system cannot avoid confronting the fundamental tradeoff between efficiency and equity. In many areas of public policy, that tradeoff is imagined as a social lever system; if policy efficiency moves higher, then equity moves lower, and if equity moves higher, then efficiency moves lower. The objective behind tax reform—or any policy, for that matter—thus becomes a metaphorical balancing act, one that must also incorporate revenue demands.

That task is made all the more complicated by the fact that equity and efficiency are vague terms. If "efficiency" means Pareto efficiency, then it implies a tax framework in which no individual can be made better off without making another individual worse off. But if "efficiency" means Kaldor–Hicks efficiency, then it implies a tax framework in which the gains accrued to those made better off compensate for the losses accrued to those made worse off, which can ultimately lead to a Pareto efficiency. And as illustrated throughout the preceding chapters, "equity" has been ascribed vastly different and often incompatible meanings by policymakers, interest groups, taxpayers, and other citizens.

Consequently, translating those concepts into tax policy is not an objective task. Furthermore, the style in which policymakers craft policy is shaped not only by their definitions of efficiency and equity, but also by their beliefs about the relationship between the individual and the state, not to mention existing constitutional, statutory, and intergovernmental mandates. Tax reform proposals thus suffer significant path dependency; they are almost always developed as a way to modulate the status quo while leaving most of the framework in place.

But what if, instead, policymakers took a "blank page" approach to designing a federal tax system? One of the more recent frameworks that should serve as a guide is the theory of optimal taxation, which holds that the most desirable tax system is one that maximizes social welfare while minimizing the efficiency costs inherent to taxation (Boadway 2012; Slemrod 1990). Much of the theoretical work on optimal taxation views social welfare through a utilitarian lens, setting as an overarching policy objective the maximization of overall welfare (Ramsey 1927).

Maximizing efficiency requires maximum information about taxpayers' ability to pay. Although policymakers know that individuals in civil society populate a wide spectrum of ability, true ability is unmeasurable. Only blunt proxies are available (e.g., reporting income to the IRS), but those proxies are fraught with inaccuracies and time distortions. Work in optimal tax theory has attempted to overcome this imperfect information. The Mirrless (1971) solution recommends a tax system that minimizes the disincentives for individuals to produce at a level that matches, or comes close to, their true ability—i.e., a system that does not prevent individuals from realizing their full income-earning capacity. The Mirrless optimal tax approach can be distilled into lessons for policymakers (Mankiw et al. 2009), four of which are most salient.

First, marginal tax rates on individual income should not increase at higher income levels; tax rates should instead be flatter. In fact, Mirrless' theory suggests that tax rates should decline at higher income levels and eventually reach 0%. Several studies have supported the wisdom of declining rates (e.g., Boadway and Jacquet 2008; Dahan and Strawczynski 2000; Simula and Trannoy 2012). Although the proposal was and is of limited political feasibility, especially among progressives, the rate structure makes intuitive sense. After all, if the overarching tax policy objective is to encourage individuals to maximize their income-earning capacities, then each additional dollar of income should be taxed at lower rates to encourage labor market participation (Gorry and Oberfield 2012; Tuomala 1990). Graduated rates do the exact opposite—the more one earns, the less one is allowed to keep.

Second, a system of flat or flatter tax rates coupled with lump-sum redistributive transfers approaches optimality, similar to the flat tax and NIT proposals (Jacquet et al. 2013). What that flat tax rate should be, however, is not clear. The optimal rate depends on assumptions about the distribution of ability and the elasticity of income to tax changes. Generally speaking, the larger the assumed concentration of high-income earners, the higher the optimal flat tax rate (Saez 2001). But again, the tax rate should remain flat to avoid discouraging high earning ability. The resultant economic growth, in turn, yields revenues to fund lump-sum transfers. Some inequality will remain, such as wage and income inequality, but the lump-sum transfers reduce other types of inequality, such as consumption inequality, just as they do under the status quo (Auerbach et al. 2016).

Third, in the interest of efficiency, consumption taxes should apply a flat tax rate to final goods except those that generate negative externalities (Atkinson and Stiglitz 1976). Consumption taxes should not be levied on intermediate goods because doing so distorts their allocation, which creates inefficiency and may have unequal effects across different industries (Diamond and Mirrless 1971). Diamond and Mirrless argue that, because it is technically an input, machinery used in the production of final goods should be untaxed. By not taxing intermediates, the market—not the state—shapes the allocation of goods.

Fourth, capital should be excluded from the tax base. Indeed, taxes on capital create inefficiencies and, of course, raise questions about fairness. Taxes on dividends disincentivize savings, investment, and risk-taking; recall the Chapter 4 discussion regarding the double taxation of corporate profits. Taxes on capital gains can, in fact, be a tax on inflation. When computing short- and long-term capital gains, taxpayers are not allowed to factor in changes in the value of currency over the period the investment was held. Furthermore, when domestic taxes on capital exceed those in other jurisdictions, as they currently do in the United States, they serve as a competitive disadvantage.

Like any set of policy principles, optimal taxation has critics both normative (e.g., Sugin 2010) and empirical that recommend very different changes to the tax system. Diamond and Saez (2011) advocate more of the same: graduated rates on higher income levels and taxes on capital, paired with subsidies for low-income wage earners. Others critics find that the optimal tax system is one that features a flat tax on income but a higher tax rate on capital (Conesa et al. 2009).[15] Piketty (2014) famously suggested new, global wealth taxes.

Still others point out that placing an emphasis on an individual's ability to pay taxes requires that policymakers integrate more complicated, and controversial, facets of ability in the tax system. This includes factoring in an individual's prior earnings, a fairly old idea that never gained policy traction (Vickery 1939), and perhaps their future earnings potential. It also includes "tagging" certain characteristics that are linked to income-earning potential and hence ability to pay taxes, e.g., age, ability, height, skillset, gender, marital status, and location, and incorporating those traits into tax policy (Akerlof 1978; Alesina et al. 2011; Cremer et al. 2010; Guner et al. 2012; Mankiw and Weinzierl 2010; Weinzierl 2011). That approach, while consistent with optimal tax theory, is a political nonstarter, and the discrimination that would result is at odds with nondiscrimination laws. The tradeoff involved with optimal tax theory, and all other tax reform proposals, is perhaps not between efficiency and equity, but between what economics suggests and what political conditions allow.

Conclusion: Constraints on Reform

Ideas on tax reform abound, but few have any strong likelihood of becoming law in the immediate future. Quite simply, the deck is stacked against tax reform. A number of political and economic constraints hold back progress, but five are most significant.

The first is the sheer entrenchment of the existing tax system, which is far from only federal in character. We often discuss tax reform as if changes made at the federal level would not radiate across state and local governments, but they certainly would. Few are willing to attempt to design a reform that incorporates the potential implications it would have for 50 unique state tax systems and thousands of local tax systems. Moreover, because of our intergovernmental amalgam, the economic benefits of federal reform may be diluted by incompatible tax policies at the state and local level. The same is true from the bottom up. Subnational tax reforms can only accomplish so much if federal taxes remain unchanged.

Second, it goes without saying that the current tax system has countless beneficiaries that have little economic motivation to support reforms that may impact them negatively. Since 1998, the number of clients lobbying over aspects of federal tax policy has increased an astounding 58% (see Figure 9.2). The largest one-year gain—over 13%—occurred in 2007, following the Democrats' regaining control of the House of Representatives and the Senate during the latter portion of the Bush Administration. Broad-based tax reform cannot occur when thousands of interest groups and corporate entities deploy lobbyists to guard tiny fractions of the tax code. That's true in principle at the state and local level as much as it is at the federal level.

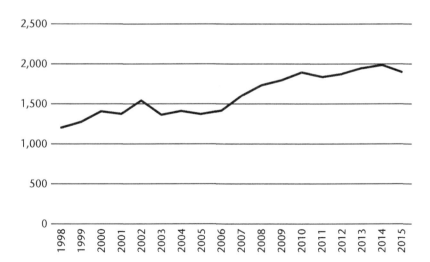

FIGURE 9.2 Number of Clients Lobbying on Taxes per Year, 1998–2015

Source: Center for Responsive Politics.

Third, reform proposals often fail because inadequate attention is paid to how the recommended tax changes will impact the overall budget. The "simple" tactic is to approach reform with a revenue-neutral lens. In that case, most attention is paid to how to alter the tax code with the end goal of raising the same amount of revenue as the status quo. The more complicated approach, commonly adopted by elected officials, is to propose revenue increases and program expansions or, conversely, revenue cuts and program eliminations. In each case, the discussion about tax policy—complicated enough in its own right—is homogenized with debates about adding or subtracting programs, which thus brings an entirely different army of interest groups and stakeholders into the mix. Many would-be tax reformers simply give up. The cognitive burden is too great, the politics too maddening.

Fourth, political polarization undermines policy compromise. The right- and left-ward movement of Republicans and Democrats in Congress, respectively, is indicative of deeper polarization in American politics and, with it, a declining probability of cooperation. Bartlett (2012) argues that fundamental reform won't occur without the blessing of conservative, small government interest groups like Americans for Tax Reform. Support from the Tea Party is almost certainly another prerequisite. The Republican preference for tax cuts, often without matching, actual spending reductions, is not sustainable. No government or political party can have the former without the latter and maintain any semblance of fiscal discipline. Not that Democrats are any better on this question. Incremental changes to the existing system (e.g., increases on high-income earners, estates, and corporate entities) coupled with new federal programs, Democrats' preferred approach, leaves much to be desired. Moderate Democrats are often outweighed by their party's progressive wing—which, ironically, expresses little willingness to progress beyond the graduated income tax, a relic of the last century. Apparently only some ideas are cast aside for being old-fashioned; natural rights must go, but taxes are here to stay.

The fifth and final constraint is the acrid tone of most public conversations about taxes. Without a doubt, tax debates throughout history have been characterized by sharp opinions, but too many recent protests have not involved a robust exchange of competing ideas grounded in any sense of objectivity. Instead, perhaps the most important issue in civil society—the intersection of the individual, the state, and taxation—has devolved into a gaudy spectacle of name-calling and seemingly involuntary recitation of partisan talking points. Flashing protest signs with slogans that pre-date the discovery of penicillin and blaming economic problems on thin caricatures of Gilded Age villains does little to improve tax policy in the twenty-first century.

The tone is hardly better among elected officials. Mention a tax increase or eliminating corporate tax preferences, and conservatives howl about the disastrous consequences for "job creators." One imagines running for shelter in empty factories as chunks of giant GDP line graphs fall from the sky. Mention tax or spending cuts, and progressives screech about "working families" with tales of impending woe that paint the United States as a contemporary version of Dickensian London. And when all else fails, we can expect to hear about "the children."

All things considered, our present political environment is incompatible with major tax reform. American history shows that major tax policy changes occur as a result of extraordinary events, either domestic (e.g., the Civil War) or global (e.g., the World War I and World War II). To blunt the current system's inertia, it will once again take a profound event, one with enough force to overcome a vastly larger and more complex tax code than was in place during all the wars. One shudders to think what that event might be, but chances are that a little partisan give-and-take would be a lot easier.

Notes

1 Because the Supreme Court has ruled that payroll taxpayers have no vested property right in their Social Security contributions, it is only fair to consider the payroll tax an "income tax" in the traditional sense. See *Flemming v. Nestor*, 363 U.S. 603 (1960) and *Helvering v. Davis*, 301 U.S. 619 (1937), and refer to Chapter 10.

2 Frivolous claims include but are not limited to: paying taxes is optional; filing a tax return violates the First, Fourth, Fifth, and Thirteenth Amendments (by violating religious beliefs, privacy, and protections against self-incrimination and involuntary servitude); or that certain minority groups are allowed to claim a tax credit for reparations.

3 See General Accountability Office, "IRS Needs to Further Improve Controls over Financial and Taxpayer Data," 2016.

4 See Treasury Inspector General for Tax Administration, "Inappropriate Criteria Were Used to Identify Tax-Exempt Applications for Review," 2013.

5 Worse but too late to make a difference, Judicial Watch discovered in August 2016 that one of the lawyers working on the Department of Justice investigation—spending more than 1,500 hours on the matter—was a 12-time donor to Obama for America. That lawyer's contributions to Obama and the Democratic National Committee totaled $6,750.

6 This idea is distinct from truth-in-taxation requirements in states (e.g., Illinois, Minnesota, and Texas, among others), which outline standards for communicating property tax burdens.

7 The National Minimum Drinking Age Act of 1984 punished states that did not raise the drinking age to 21 with a loss of federal highway funding.

8 See "Tax Maze: How the Tax Prep Industry Blocks Government from Making Tax Day Easier," a report prepared by the staff of Senator Elizabeth Warren, 2016.

9 See Department of the Treasury, "Report to The Congress on Return-Free Tax Systems: Tax Simplification Is a Prerequisite," 2003.

10 ReadyReturn has since been combined with CalFile, another tax preparation and filing program.

11 The state's report spun low participation in what should have been a convenient program as a positive: "taxpayers did not feel pressured to use ReadyReturn."

12 See State of California Franchise Tax Board, "ReadyReturn Pilot: Tax Year 2004 Study Results," 2006.

13 Due to the inclusion of income exemptions, the Hall–Rabushka and Forbes flat-tax proposals are not pure "flat" taxes, but rather have embedded some degree of progressivity.

14 An update for the Graetz Competitive Tax Plan is available from the Tax Policy Center at http://www.taxpolicycenter.org/briefing-book/graetz-competitive-tax-plan-update-2015.
15 Optimal capital tax simulations are highly conditioned on model assumptions; see Peterman (2013).

References

Adler, Hank, and Hugh Hewitt. 2009. *The FairTax Fantasy: An Honest Look at a Very, Very Bad Idea.* Washington DC: Townhall Press.

Ahmad, Nazneen, and Wei Xiao. 2013. "End of Double Taxation: Is the Policy Better When Announced?" *Journal of Policy Modeling* 35(6): 928–942.

Akerlof, George A. 1978. "The Economics of 'Tagging' as Applied to the Optimal Income Tax, Welfare Programs, and Manpower Planning." *American Economic Review* 68(1): 8–19.

Alesina, Alberto, Andrea Ichino, and Loukas Karabarbounis. 2011. "Gender-Based Taxation and the Division of Family Chores." *American Economic Journal: Economic Policy* 3(2): 1–40.

Alm, James, Todd Cherry, Michael Jones, and Michael McKee. 2010. "Taxpayer Information Assistance Services and Tax Compliance Behavior." *Journal of Economic Psychology* 31(4): 577–586.

Atkinson, Anthony, and Joseph E. Stiglitz. 1976. "The Design of Tax Structure: Direct versus Indirect Taxation." *Journal of Public Economics* 6(1–2): 55–75.

Auerbach, Alan J., Laurence J. Kotlikoff, and Darryl R. Koehler. 2016. "U.S. Inequality, Fiscal Progressivity, and Work Disincentives: An Intragenerational Accounting." National Bureau of Economic Research Working Paper #22032.

Bachman, Paul, Jonathan Haughton, Laurence J. Kotlikoff, Alfonso Sanchez-Penalver, and David G. Tuerck. 2006. "Taxing Sales under the FairTax: What Rate Works?" *Tax Notes* (November 13): 663–682.

Bartlett, Bruce. 2012. *The Benefit and the Burden: Tax Reform-Why We Need It and What It Will Take.* New York: Simon & Schuster.

Bhattarai, Keshab, Jonathan Haughton, and David G. Tuerck. 2016. "The Economic Effects of the Fair Tax: Analysis of Results of a Dynamic CGE Model of the US Economy." *International Economics and Economic Policy* 13(3): 451–466.

Boadway, Robin. 2012. *From Optimal Tax Theory to Tax Policy: Retrospective and Prospective Views.* Cambridge, MA: MIT Press.

Boadway, Robin, and Laurence Jacquet. 2008. "Optimal Marginal and Average Income Taxation under Maximin." *Journal of Economic Theory* 143(1): 425–441.

Boortz, Neal, and John Linder. 2005. *The FairTax Book: Saying Goodbye to the Income Tax and the IRS.* New York: HarperCollins.

Bowman, Karlyn, Heather Sims, and Eleanor O'Neil. 2016. "Public Opinion on Taxes: 1937 to Today." American Enterprise Institute, Public Opinion Studies.

Bradford, David F. 2004. *The X Tax in the World Economy: Going Global with a Simple, Progressive Tax.* Washington, DC: AEI Press.

Burton, David R., and Dan R. Mastromarco. 1997. "Emancipating America from the Income Tax: How a National Sales Tax Would Work." Cato Institute Policy Analysis No. 272.

Cassou, Steven P., and Kevin J. Lansing. 2007. "Growth Effects of Shifting from a Graduated-Rate Tax System to a Flat Tax." *Economic Inquiry* 42(2): 194–213.

Conesa, Juan Carlos, Sagiri Kitao, and Dirk Krueger. 2009. "Taxing Capital? Not a Bad Idea after All!" *American Economic Review* 99(1): 25–48.

Cremer, Helmuth, Firouz Gahvari, and Jean-Marie Lozachmeur. 2010. "Tagging and Income Taxation: Theory and an Application." *American Economic Journal: Economic Policy* 2(1): 31–50.

Dahan, Momi, and Michel Strawczynski. 2000. "Optimal Income Taxation: An Example with a U-Shaped Pattern of Optimal Marginal Tax Rates: Comment." *American Economic Review* 90(3): 681–686.

Day, Liz. 2013. "How the Maker of TurboTax Fought Free, Simple Tax Filing." *ProPublica*, March 26.

Diamond, Peter A., and James A. Mirrless. 1971. "Optimal Taxation and Public Production I: Production Efficiency." *American Economic Review* 61(1): 8–27.

Diamond, Peter, A., and Emmanuel Saez. 2011. "The Case for a Progressive Tax: From Basic Research to Policy Recommendations." *Journal of Economic Perspectives* 25(4): 165–190.

Epstein, Richard A. 2002. "Can Anyone Beat the Flat Tax?" *Social Philosophy and Policy* 19(1): 140–171.

Forbes, Steve. 2005. *Flat Tax Revolution: Using a Postcard to Abolish the IRS.* Washington, DC: Regenery.

Gale, William G. 2005. "The National Retail Sales Tax: What Would the Rate Have to Be?" *Tax Notes* (May 16): 889–911.

Goldberg, Daniel S. 2013. *The Death of the Income Tax: A Progressive Consumption Tax and the Path to Fiscal Reform.* New York: Oxford University Press.

Gorry, Aspen, and Ezra Oberfield. 2012. "Optimal Taxation over the Life Cycle." *Review of Economic Dynamics* 15(4): 551–572.

Graetz, Michael J. 2008. *100 Million Unnecessary Returns: A Simple, Fair, and Competitive Tax Plan for the United States.* New Haven, CT: Yale University Press.

Guner, Nezih, Remzi Kaygusuz, and Gustavo Ventura. 2012. "Taxing Women: A Macroeconomic Analysis." *Journal of Monetary Economics* 59(1): 111–128.

Hall, Robert E., and Alvin Rabushka. 1983. *Low Tax, Simple Tax, Flat Tax.* New York: McGraw Hill.

Hall, Robert E., and Alvin Rabushka. 2007. *The Flat Tax.* Stanford: Hoover Institution Press.

Heer, Burkhard, and Mark Trede. 2003. "Efficiency and Distribution Effects of a Revenue-Neutral Income Tax Reform." *Journal of Macroeconomics* 25(1): 87–107.

Hoagland, Ken. 2010. *The FairTax Solution: Financial Justice for All Americans.* New York: Sentinel/Penguin.

Jacquet, Laurence, Etienne Lehmann, and Bruno Van der Linden. 2013. "Optimal Redistributive Taxation with both Extensive and Intensive Responses." *Journal of Economic Theory* 148(5): 1770–1805.

Kotlikoff, Laurence J. 1993. "The Economic Impact of Replacing Federal Income Taxes with a Sales Tax." Cato Institute Policy Analysis No. 193.

Kuang, Yingxu, Ted Englebrecht, and Otis W. Gilley. 2011. "A Distributional Analysis of the FairTax Plan: Annual and Lifetime Income Considerations." *Southern Economic Journal* 78(2): 358–381.

Lampman, Robert J. 1965. "Approaches to the Reduction of Poverty." *American Economic Review* 55(1/2): 521–529.

Lopez-Daneri, Martin. 2016. "NIT Picking: The Macroeconomic Effects of a Negative Income Tax." *Journal of Economic Dynamics and Control* 68: 1–16.

Mankiw, N. Gregory, and Matthew Weinzierl. 2010. "The Optimal Taxation of Height: A Case Study of Utilitarian Income Redistribution." *American Economic Journal: Economic Policy* 2(1): 155–176.

Mankiw, N. Gregory, Matthew Weinzierl, and Danny Yagan. 2009. "Optimal Taxation in Theory and Practice." *Journal of Economic Perspectives* 23(4): 147–174.

Mirless, James A. 1971. "An Exploration in the Theory of Optimal Income Taxation." *Review of Economic Studies* 38(114): 175–208.

Moffitt, Robert A. 2003. "The Negative Income Tax and the Evolution of U.S. Welfare Policy." *Journal of Economic Perspectives* 17(3): 119–140.

Paulus, Alari, and Andreas Peichl. 2009. "Effects of Flat Tax Reforms in Western Europe." *Journal of Policy Modeling* 31(5): 620–636.

Peterman, William B. 2013. "Determining the Motives for a Positive Optimal Tax on Capital." *Journal of Economic Dynamics and Control* 37(1): 265–295.

Piketty, Thomas. 2014. *Capital in the Twenty-First Century*. Cambridge, MA: Belknap Press.

Ramsey, F.P. 1927. "A Contribution to the Theory of Taxation." *The Economic Journal* 37(145): 47–61.

Saez, Emmanuel. 2001. "Using Elasticities to Derive Optimal Income Tax Rates." *Review of Economic Studies* 68(1): 205–229.

Seidman, Laurence. 1997. *The USA Tax: A Progressive Consumption Tax*. Cambridge, MA: MIT Press.

Simula, Laurent, and Alain Trannoy. 2012. "Shall We Keep the Highly Skilled at Home? The Optimal Income Tax Perspective." *Social Choice and Welfare* 39(4): 751–782.

Slemrod, Joel. 1990. "Optimal Taxation and Optimal Tax Systems." *Journal of Economic Perspectives* 4(1): 157–178.

Sugin, Linda. 2010. "A Philosophical Objection to the Optimal Tax Model." *Tax Law Review* 64: 229–281.

Tobin, James, Joseph A. Pechman, and Peter M. Mieszkowski. 1967. "Is a Negative Income Tax Practical?" *Yale Law Journal* 77(1): 1–27.

Tuomala, Matti. 1990. *Optimal Income Tax and Redistribution*. Oxford: Clarendon Press.

Ventura, Gustavo. 1999. "Flat Tax Reform: A Quantitative Exploration." *Journal of Economic Dynamics and Control* 23(9–10): 1425–1458.

Viard, Alan D., and Robert Carroll. 2012. *Progressive Consumption Taxation: The X-Tax Revisited*. Washington, DC: AEI Press.

Vickery, William. 1939. "Averaging of Income for Income-Tax Purposes." *Journal of Political Economy* 47(3): 379–397.

Weinzierl, Matthew. 2011. "The Surprising Power of Age-Dependent Taxes." *Review of Economic Studies* 78(4): 1490–1518.

Zeckhauser, Richard J. 1971. "Optimal Mechanisms for Income Transfer." *American Economic Review* 61(3): 324–334.

10
REFLECTIONS

Although the United States is the indisputable product of tax resistance, if one implication may be drawn from the preceding chapters, it's that those days appear to be long gone. The tax system has transformed from a series of inconsequential levies to one that no individual can truly avoid. The average American now pays literally thousands of dollars per year in taxes to federal, state, and local governments. At the same time, the state has progressed from a minimal institution to one of considerable influence in private matters and civil society as a whole. The consequences of this evolution are many and the implications are great, but three points are worth reflection in conclusion.

First, the expansion of the state and concomitant dispersion of public goods provision across multiple levels of government reduces citizen knowledge of what public goods cost, an outcome that has consequences for tax policy and politics. Today, one can scarcely identify a public good or service that is entirely provided and funded by only one level of government. Local waste collection and treatment may seem like an obvious exception, but even that may entail compliance with federal environmental regulations, and perhaps federal grant dollars to subsidize that compliance. As overlap among federal, state, and local governments increases and the mix of funding streams changes, actual spending on public goods is obscured from the very people paying for them.

Education is perhaps the best example of this phenomenon and its broader implications. No elected official can expect to remain in office for long if they support school funding cuts, and even those who support nominal funding increases may be criticized for not going far enough. That's partly because polls consistently show that the public believes schools are underfunded. But those surveys assume that the public has accurate knowledge about public education spending.

Other polls suggest that's not the case. The 2015 Education Next poll, administered by Stanford University, gathered data on attitudes toward and knowledge about school funding in the United States. When asked to guess the amount spent per child enrolled in a public school, the average estimate offered across all respondents was $7,056, over 40% lower than the actual number, which was $12,010. Interestingly, average estimates varied by demographic group. African Americans gave the highest average estimate ($8,836, off just 25%), whereas self-identified Democrats gave the lowest ($6,400, off 47%).

But who can blame anyone for not having a good sense about the status of education spending? With funding contributed to public education by three different levels of government and certain interest groups claiming, without end, that funding is insufficient, it is no wonder that public perception is so different from reality. Still, this ignorance has important consequences. When citizens lack accurate information about government spending, it undermines efforts to hold policymakers accountable for how tax revenues are spent. And when citizens have complete information, opinions about that spending often change. Indeed, when respondents to the Education Next poll were given actual public school spending figures from their local district, support for education spending increases dropped among all demographic groups.

Second, with the exception of payroll taxes, the federal government collects very little revenue from taxes that Congress is required to direct toward specified purposes. In fact, the sole exceptions are some of the excise taxes discussed in Chapter 5. There are no formulas or mandates that dictate how individual or corporate income tax collections must be spent; indeed, for all of their rhetorical links to inequality, those taxes, as well as transfer taxes, are not directly reallocated to low-income individuals. Nor are there any real limits on congressional spending discretion. Nearly any project or program could be rationalized as serving the "general welfare," and moreover, the federal government does not come anywhere near operating within a balanced-budget framework.

More alarmingly, Congress has access to tax revenues ostensibly directed to specific programs perceived as immune to such political meddling. It is common to assume that an individual who contributes to Social Security and Medicare via payroll taxes is, at some point in the future, entitled to receive benefits from those programs. Such entitlement benefits are frequently described as an "earned right" granted by the federal government.

But nothing could be further from the truth, and Americans have the Supreme Court to thank for it. Ephram Nestor, an immigrant from Bulgaria, paid payroll taxes from 1936 until his retirement in 1955. Nestor was deported in 1956 for holding membership in the Communist Party from 1933 to 1939, and because federal law stipulated that communist deportees forfeit their Social Security benefits, his monthly payments were canceled. Believing that decades of payroll taxes granted him and his wife a right to those benefits, Nestor sued the federal government. His point of dispute was a little-known section of the Social Security

Act in which Congress granted itself the sole power to "alter, amend, or repeal any provision" of the law, such as by canceling benefits for individuals that had contributed to the system.

In a 5–4 decision, the Court ruled against Nestor.[1] The majority held that remunerating payroll taxes did not establish a right to Social Security. To assume otherwise would deprive the program "of the flexibility and boldness in adjustment to ever-changing conditions which it demands and which Congress probably had in mind when it reserved the right to alter, amend or repeal any provision of the Act." In other words, the assumption that payroll taxes purchase an earned right to future entitlement program benefits is false. Congress can alter those benefits at its discretion. It can—and has—borrowed against Social Security surpluses to support other government functions, incredibly calling the IOUs a "trust fund." Only future taxes can pay those monies back.

Third, the very tax policies that now reallocate trillions of dollars from the private sector to the public sector have, at least at the federal level, never been approved by a direct vote of the people. The Sixteenth Amendment was ratified in 1913 by state legislatures, in accordance with the Constitution, not state-by-state referenda or even a national referendum. The United States has, quite literally, never held a direct vote on the income tax or any other form of taxation. Never. The same is less often true at the state level. Instead, our system of government delegates the authority to tax to the same representatives who then also get to decide how the revenues are spent. Question that authority, and you may be called unpatriotic, ignorant, or uncaring.

All things considered, that misdirection might be what ails our tax system. Our focus becomes trained on the status quo and acceptance of the premise that state institutions need trillions of dollars, that policymakers and experts know best how to spend those dollars, and that our lives and civil society are better for it. If that's not the case, then tax reform alone is too limiting. What the United States needs instead is government reform, but not the sort that is so insignificant as to remain invisible to the naked eye. No, the American people deserve the kind of reform achieved by reexamining our philosophical roots, integrating our economic realities, and redrawing the boundary between the individual and the state—and then developing a tax framework to match. That may take a very different kind of resistance.

Note

1 See *Flemming v. Nestor*, 363 U.S. 603 (1960); see also *Helvering v. Davis*, 301 U.S. 619 (1937).

INDEX

Jackson, James 164
Jefferson, Thomas 8, 12, 156, 165
job creators 246
Jobs and Growth Tax Relief
  Reconciliation Act (2003) 54–5
Johnson, Lyndon 54
Johnstown Flood Tax 168
Joint Committee on Taxation (JCT) 43–4,
  45, 80, 207
Judicial Watch 247n5

Kaldor–Hicks efficiency 242
Kennedy, John F. 53
Kenney, Jim 176
Krugman, Paul 82

Labor Reform Party 22
land, taxation of 197; *see also* property taxes
landowners 199, 200, 205
law of conservation 6
law of gravity 6, 7
Leary, Timothy 182
Leary v. United States (1969) 182
Le Bon, Gustave 25–6
Leviathan (Hobbes) 12, 123
Lew, Jack 111
Linbeck, Leo, Jr. 238
lobbying: tax reform 245–6
local option sales taxes (LOST) 140–3
Locke, John 6, 7, 11, 27n14
Looking Backward: 2000–1887
  (Bellamy) 15
loopholes 117
Los Angeles: operating subsidies for public
  transit systems 110
Los Angeles County: property tax revenue
  208–9
Low Income Tax Clinics 232

McCain, John 65, 226n11
McDermott Incorporated 111
McNair, Bob 238
Madison, James 11, 27n12, 156
marginal income tax rates: highest and
  lowest (1862–2016) 55; number of
  (1862–2016) 56; by state 76–7; top
  corporate, by nation 106
marginal tax rates (MTRs) 51; corporate
  income 94; corporate income and
  number by state 101–2; federal
  corporate income 100; federal individual
  income 62; graduated 81–3; highest and

lowest federal income 95; number of
  federal corporate income 95
Marihuana Tax Act (1937) 182
marijuana taxation: challenges to
  implementing 185–6; experimentation
  by states 182–3; history of 182; interest
  groups 184–5; legal context of 182;
  monthly revenue in Colorado 184;
  politics of legalization 183–5
marketplace: shifting, of alcoholic
  beverages 173–4
Marketplace Fairness Act 148
Marx Karl 15, 18, 28n29
Mason, George 7
Massachusetts Proposition 2½ (1980)
  4, 201
measles, mumps, and rubella (MMR):
  vaccine 128
Medicaid 83, 116
Medicare 38, 43, 72, 83, 116, 239, 252
Mellon, Andrew 52, 53
Mencken, H. L. 29n37
Merriam, Charles 16
Mexico: sugar taxation case study 177–8,
  189n18
Mileage-Based User Fee Alliance 140
mileage-based user fees (MBUF) 138–9
Mineta Transport Institute 138
Mirrles optimal tax approach 243–4
Monardes, Nicolás 155
Montesquieu 5
Mortgage Bankers Association 69
mortgage interest: deductions 67, 68–9,
  86n16
Mothers Against Drunk Driving 171
motor fuels: excise taxes 132–5; federal
  excise tax by gallon 133; gasoline and
  diesel excise taxes by state 134–5;
  gasoline excise tax revenue 134

National Academy of Sciences 139
National Association of Counties 207
National Association of Home Builders 69
National Association of Realtors 69
National Commission on Fiscal
  Responsibility and Reform 68
National Credit Union Association 108
National Federation of Independent
  Businesses 225
National Forest System 207
National Low Income Housing
  Coalition 69